On the Road: Buying a Home

Sheryl Garrett, CFP®
Series Editor

Adapted and compiled by
Ellen Schneid Coleman

Dearborn™
Trade Publishing
A **Kaplan Professional** Company

President, Dearborn Publishing: Roy Lipner
Vice President and Publisher: Cynthia A. Zigmund
Senior Acquisitions Editor: Mary B. Good
Cover Design: Design Solutions

© 2006 by Dearborn Financial Publishing, Inc.

Published by Dearborn Trade Publishing
A Kaplan Professional Company

A Stonesong Press Book

Project Manager: Ellen Schneid Coleman
Interior Design: Brad Walrod/High Text Graphics, Inc.

Printed in the United States of America

06 07 08   10 9 8 7 6 5 4 3 2 1

Library of Congress Cataloging-in-Publication Data
Buying a home/edited by Sheryl Garrett; adapted and compiled by Ellen Schneid Coleman.
    p.   cm.—(On the road)
  Includes index.
  ISBN 1-4195-0046-5 (5 × 7.375 pbk.)
    1. House buying—United States.   2. Residential real estate—Purchasing—United States.   3. Mortgage loans—United States.   I. Garrett, Sheryl.
II. Coleman, Ellen Schneid.   III. On the road (Chicago, Ill.)
HD259.B893 2005
643'.12'0973—dc22   2005015091

Contents

Introduction

On the Road: Buying a Home is part of a new series of books from Dearborn Trade Publishing intended to help you deal with the financial issues, problems, and decisions concerning specific life events. The decisions you face when you're about to buy your first home are obviously very different from the decision to buy a car, for example. In fact, they are very different from just about any other purchase you might make. They are even somewhat different from the decision to buy your next home or a vacation home, although some of what you discover now can be applied to whatever property you may buy in the future.

Think of buying a home, particularly your first one, as an adventure, like a trip to a foreign country. First off, there's the language problem—the natives use words like *easement, margin,* and *amortization* so fast you can't follow them. And they have strange customs as well. Is it polite to ask questions? Should you tip the driver?

Financial planning shouldn't be intimidating. That's why we've created these books to take away the terror. *On the Road* books are like travel guides, which will help you make the best financial decisions at each stage of your life—in this case, when you are ready to buy your very first home. In this book we'll address the questions that concern you *now* as you are about to embark down the road toward buying a home:

1. How do I start to buy a house?
2. How much house can I afford?
3. Should I wait to save up more down payment?
4. Which mortgage plan is best?
5. Where can I find a good agent?
6. Do I need a lawyer?
7. Will I get a good price?
8. What about the neighborhood and the neighbors?
9. Can I afford the payments?
10. How do I deal with agents and sellers?
11. What if I end up with a house I don't like?

These financial decisions are part of your life's journey, so we've made them easy to navigate, with lots of helpful "Roadmaps" (charts and tables of financial information to help you with each issue or decision that comes up) and "Tollbooths" that help you calculate your expenses or savings, as well as "Hazard" signs that caution you on money pitfalls to watch out for. We even tell you "What to Pack" so you'll know what forms or other information you need to get a mortgage, for example. We've made sure you'll know what we're talking about, by providing "Learn the Language" definitions of unfamiliar or technical terms particular to each financial topic. And we've included "Postcards" that tell helpful stories of how other people have made successful financial journeys.

Finally, we've included an "Itinerary," a recap of all the key actions you should take—all of which are covered in detail in the seven chapters of this book. You can use these as a reminder at each stage of your journey toward home ownership. At the end we have included a list of other books and resources you could turn to if you want more in-depth information on any aspect of buying a home.

We hope you find this "travel" guide helpful as you map your route to financial success and peace of mind. Life is an adventure, and money paves the way. So let's get started on the road: The light is green, put your pedal to the metal, and go!

Plan Your Trip

The Realities of Real Estate

▶ Getting Started: Reasons to Buy

Like all long journeys, buying a home, especially your first home, can be an exciting but a somewhat daunting prospect. But if you decide to take it, it's a journey you would love. Owning a home can result in several emotional and lifestyle as well as financial benefits. In this book, we will explore the financial considerations to start you off on the right foot.

Today, more American families than ever—about 70 percent in recent surveys—own their own homes. Nearly two-thirds of them are married, but more and more unmarried people are buying homes. They are ready to invest even before they tie the knot. These unmarried couples, with or without dependents, now form a measurable segment of the homebuying population. At the same time, older homebuyers make up an increasing share of the market as well; they leave behind larger homes, thus creating trickle-down opportunities for younger homebuyers.

Most people who are ready to invest in a home have spent between two and five years saving for a down payment. Many first-timers will be helped out by parents or relatives. Most will buy a single-family home, with the remainder buying townhouses, condos, or co-ops. These homebuyers are as diverse as the ethnic and cultural variety of this country. And the homes they choose will include co-ops in New York, ranch-style houses in California, prairie models in Minnesota, condos in Florida, and everything you can imagine in between. However, what they all have in common with you is that the home-purchasing experience is a new one.

The reasons to buy a home are as varied as the buyers themselves: A desire to retreat from the pressures of an increasingly crowded society, inflation, tax savings, the need for self-expression, and the ever-increasing desire to "have it now"—all contribute to the decision of buying a home. Some might have other reasons: When you own your own home you can play the stereo at midnight (unless you're in a condo or co-op), have a menagerie of pets, plant a garden, drive nails into the wall wherever you want, sleep on a waterbed, paint the rooms chartreuse, and have your very own washer and dryer.

Adding to the excitement of this voyage, there's the potential for profit at the end of the road. Of late, most homes are going up in value. If you rent a home, the rent money goes down the drain; you can use the same money to make mortgage payments that are mostly deductible. What's more, the portion of your monthly mortgage payment that goes to reduce the principal acts as automatic forced savings.

Besides, planning the trip—house hunting—can be fun. There are literally hundreds of agents out there just dying to escort you to homes for sale. Then there are the eager builders who are ready to show you their new models. Once you get started, you won't have time to wonder what to do on a weekend. You'll be participating in the great American house hunt!

Chances are that you will be thrust into the world of real estate investing (after all, a home is the biggest single investment most people ever make), home financing, and deal making for the first time. And it's very easy to quickly feel overwhelmed by all that is happening around you. Don't get caught in the flurry; take a deep breath and your first step forward.

▶ Before You Go: What You Need to Know about Buying a Home

When that real estate agent starts asking if you want "fixed rate" or an "ARM with no negative," or whether you prefer a "fixer-upper" or a house with "curb appeal," it's easy to get frustrated. Or when you're asked to come up with a deposit check of $1,000 or more and to sign a contract that's five or more pages long and filled with legalese no one can understand, it's enough to make you want to throw in the towel and go back to the simple life of renting, where you can call the management when the toilet's stopped up!

Rest assured, like the majority of first-time homebuyers, you'll quickly pick up the new vocabulary and the techniques needed to successfully deal with agents and sellers. You'll also become adept at home inspections and even at handling the paperwork. But it helps to have a bit of guidance along the way, and that's where this book comes in. By the end of this trip, you will have learned how to

► determine exactly how much you can afford
► compare the different costs of condos, co-ops, and townhouses versus single-family residences
► understand the different types of financing available
► make an offer on any property
► understand the sales agreement
► negotiate terms and conditions like a pro
► be prepared for the closing and how to keep from being cheated
► save on your taxes

► Where Are You Now; Can You Afford to Buy?

Before taking the leap it is important to consider both the advantages and disadvantages of buying a home. When you purchase, you are taking on the responsibilities of ownership, many of which are financial. You'll now have to pay the mortgage(s), taxes, insurance, maintenance and repairs, homeowners' fees for a condo, co-op, or association, and all utilities.

And there are other considerations. For example, when you own your home, you can't as easily pick up and move. There's no giving the landlord 30 days' notice. If you get a job in a new area or you simply decide you want to try living elsewhere, you'll need to sell your home or, if you can't or don't want to sell, you'll have to rent it out. That puts you in the position of being a landlord with a whole new list of responsibilities.

No, we're not trying to scare you, but it's important to understand the baggage that goes along with a house. Of course, millions of people each year feel it's all worthwhile. That's because the advantages of home ownership are both personal and financial, and, with careful planning, you'll meet all the obligations without breaking your checkbook.

Let's first look at the several financial rewards: You get to deduct (in most cases) all your mortgage interest and your property taxes. That helps make the big monthly payments more bearable. Remember, residential rent is not deductible. In addition, assuming the property goes up in value, when you sell it you can exclude up to $250,000 per person ($500,000 per couple) of the gain, provided you've lived in the property for at least two of the past five years and it's your main home. In other words, chances are you won't be taxed on your profit. And if you have an office at home, you may even be able to take a deduction for it. Finally, there's the profit motive. Most people buying their first home can look forward to strong appreciation in the near future.

How Much Can You Afford to Spend on this Trip?

Okay. You've made the decision. You want to buy. Like everything else in life, homes come in all shapes, sizes, and prices. Before you set your heart on the deluxe tour, there are some things you should consider. It takes just three things to buy a house: some cash, dependable income, and good credit. If you're lacking any of these three, don't despair. Home ownership is still possible, because there are ways of overcoming each of these problems. Just be sure to level with your tour guide (the real estate agent) about your financial problems. A competent agent can recommend an appropriate financing strategy for your particular situation.

Before you set off down this road, you should have a realistic idea of your current financial status. The standard guideline is that mortgage debt should be less than 28 percent of your gross income, and that total debt should be less than 36 percent. These guidelines provide for a basic standard of living in addition to the mortgage, but do not account for your individual needs and circumstances, such as your desire to send your kids to college, vacation preferences, and retirement issues. From a financial planning perspective, it's important to factor lifetime goals into your affordability calculations.

Most of today's homebuyers may have some debts, but they may also have an investment portfolio to bring to the table. Most buyers finance homes with mortgages these days, and the interest rates fluctuate much more than they did in your parents' generation. The current trend is to concentrate more on the monthly costs of home ownership as they compare with income and debts.

Each lending institution and each loan program has its own guidelines. The debts that are considered excessive to one loan underwriter may be acceptable to another. Outstanding student loans, life insurance payments, or child support may affect your allowable mortgage payment—or they may not.

Step One: List Your Income. When estimating your allowable mortgage payment, include all the income of anyone who will be on the title to the house (see Roadmap 1.1). Unmarried persons may pool their income to buy a house together, just as a married couple can. If you are self-employed, average your past two years' income from that source. Do not include one-time events such as inheritances, insurance settlements, and capital gains.

Step Two: Calculate your current monthly expenditures. We've now moved down the road a bit to see how much is left over for a house payment. Roadmap 1.2 will help you calculate your real current expenses. Be honest here. Put down what you are actually spending, not what you wish you were spending or what you want to spend.

Don't Forget the Side Trips: Additional Expenses

Don't make the mistake of thinking that your only housing expense will be your mortgage payment. Homeowners face costs that renters do not (see Roadmap 1.3). In the next section, we'll be showing you how to calculate them. Once you do, add these expenses to your previous total.

If you're like most of us, the amount left over from your income will now seem terribly small. But we're not finished yet, so don't despair.

▶ Budgeting for Your Trip: Expenses + Savings = True Cost

Finding a home is often a compromise between what you want and what you can afford. You've heard the expression "champagne taste on a beer budget." Housing is no different.

Armed with the information in Roadmaps 1.1, 1.2, and 1.3, you are now ready to decide how much *you* really feel comfortable spending. You are the only person to decide if the discretionary income (what is left after you have paid your mortgage payment, regular debt payments, utilities, and other bills each month) remaining each month would be enough for you and your family to feel secure. You may even know what your lender says you can afford.

Roadmap 1.1

Your Monthly Income

	Owner 1	Owner 2
Salary (gross)	_____	_____
Self-employment income	_____	_____
Second job income (gross)	_____	_____
Dividends (not reinvested)	_____	_____
Interest (not reinvested)	_____	_____
Pension/401(k)	_____	_____
Social Security/Disability	_____	_____
Rental income	_____	_____
Court ordered child support, alimony	_____	_____
Other	_____	_____
Total	_____ A	_____ B

Total Income (A + B) = $ _____

However, lenders use only formulas and profiles; you, on the other hand, must work in the real world of paying the bills. So let's dig and do the numbers to see what you can handle comfortably.

How Much Will This Trip *Really* Cost: Doing the Math

Taxes and Insurance. Sometimes when a lender preapproves a monthly "mortgage payment," that figure includes property taxes and fire and homeowner's insurance. (It's called PITI and stands for principal, interest (on the mortgage), taxes, and insurance.) But sometimes the preapproved monthly figure does not include taxes and insurance. If you put less than 20 percent down, the taxes and insurance are normally part of your monthly payment.

Roadmap 1.2

Total Expenses (Without Rent or Mortgage)

Groceries	$ _____
Utilities	_____
Telephone	_____
Insurance (auto and health)	_____
Medical payments, pharmaceuticals	_____
Car payments	_____
Car maintenance and repair	_____
Public transportation	_____
Alimony	_____
Child support	_____
Kids' expenses (clothing, school expenses, and so on)	_____
Child care	_____
Eating out	_____
Clothing	_____
Entertainment	_____
Big ticket purchases (furniture, computers, and so on)	_____
Vacations	_____
Hobbies	_____
Memberships	_____
Charitable giving	_____
Savings (10% minimum)	_____
Gift giving	_____
Other items	_____
Add 5 percent for extras overlooked	_____
Total monthly expenses (excluding housing)	$ _____

Roadmap 1.3

Calculating Additional Monthly Expenses

Property taxes (including trash collection, water, and sewer) and home insurance payments (if your lender hasn't figured these into your preapproval "mortgage payment")	$ _____
Yard maintenance and landscaping	_____
Home repair (buying a newer house helps here)	_____
Additional utilities (those that your landlord currently pays; possibly gas, electric, water, garbage, sewage, cable)	_____
Homeowners association dues (if any)	_____
Total monthly expenses less mortgage payment	$ _____

If you put more than 20 percent down, you can choose to pay taxes and insurance separately. If you will pay taxes and insurance separately, be sure to include them as an additional monthly expense.

A useful rule of thumb for calculating taxes and insurance is to find 2 percent of the likely value of the home if it is in a low-tax state, or 4 to 5 percent if it is in a high-tax state. Divide the result by 12 to find the monthly extra cost for taxes and insurance. (If you don't know whether the tax rate in your state is high or low, ask your real estate agent.)

Property Taxes. Make certain that you know the true tax figure for every house you are considering. Find out whether a tax assessment would be changed and how much the taxes would be if you bought at a given figure. Valiant efforts are made to keep taxes equitable, but the process is a constant challenge. Your agent can tell you what system is used in your community. New homebuilders must disclose to buyers the existence of extra assessments, such as school bonds, lighting and landscaping maintenance, and infrastructure improvements in some communities. They should be able to provide information on the duration of these assessments, what your monthly outgo would be, how they are collected, and under what circumstances they may be escalated.

Tollbooth 1.1

Escrowing Taxes and Insurance

If your home were ever seized and sold for unpaid back taxes, the lending institution would be left with no security for its mortgage. If the house burned to the ground, only the vacant lot would remain as security. So your lender has a direct interest in seeing that you pay your taxes and insurance premiums on time.

With some mortgages, including all VA and FHA loans, an escrow account (reserve, impound, trust account) is set up for you by the lender. Each month, along with your principal and interest payment, you send one-twelfth of your anticipated property tax and homeowner's insurance cost. As the bills come due, they are sent to your lender, who pays them on your behalf. Your lender is allowed to keep not only enough to pay the next bill due, but also a two-month surplus as a precaution. In about half the states, you are entitled to interest on your escrow account on certain types of mortgages.

You will receive regular reports, monthly or yearly, on the status of the escrow account, which is, after all, your own money. At regular intervals, usually yearly, the account will be analyzed and your payment adjusted up or down, depending on whether the account shows a surplus or deficit. This adjustment can be a surprise to the homeowner with a fixed-interest mortgage, who expected monthly payments to remain at exactly the same amount for the full term of the loan. It is, of course, taxes and insurance costs that change, not —with a fixed-interest loan—the underlying principal and interest portion of the payment.

Also, ask whether trash collection is included in the taxes or in a separate bill. Is it billed with water, sewer, and garbage, or is it a private matter? Inquire of owners about their heating and cooling costs. Ask to see past utility bills, or call the local utility company and ask for a recent street survey of bills.

Insurance. Insurance can be handled in one of the two ways: You may meet those bills on your own, or the lending institution will handle them for you, either by design or by request, as mentioned earlier.

Bonus Miles: Tax Incentives

So far we've been talking about money going out. But your first home can also provide you with some money coming in. Many people buy a home just for financial and tax incentives that can include mortgage interest tax deductions, property tax deductions, capital gain exclusions, and penalty-free IRA withdrawals for first-time homebuyers. Owning a home may also enable you to itemize your deductions, which opens up an array of other deductible expenses.

All property taxes and interest on your mortgage (up to certain limits) are deductible. You can view the total amount of your tax savings as additional monthly income.

Capitalizing on Those Tax Benefits

Most people think of taxes only in a negative way. However, when you own your own home you actually get some positive benefits. In fact, the home is probably the last, best tax shelter available to most Americans. We are now going to look at some of the tax-related possibilities of first-time home ownership.

Here's how to calculate your tax savings:

1. Ask the lender what the total interest on your mortgage will be for the first full year.
2. Ask your agent what the taxes will be on the property. (A good agent should be able to give you a pretty accurate guess.)
3. Now add these two figures together to generate an estimate of your total deduction.

For each dollar that you spend toward your mortgage interest and property taxes, you are entitled to subtract a dollar from your adjusted gross income (AGI). Use the following formula to calculate your potential savings:

> Annual Mortgage Interest Payment
> + Annual Property Tax Payment
> = Subtotal
> × Your Effective Tax Rate
> = Annual Tax Savings

> Annual House Payment
> − Annual Tax Savings (calculated above)
> = Real Cost of Annual House Payment

Let's assume your annual mortgage interest payment is $13,500 and your annual property tax payment is $3,500 for a total of $17,000, which represents your total deduction. To determine how much that deduction will save you in taxes, first check with your accountant to see what your marginal tax bracket is. Let's assume it's 28 percent, and do the math to find out approximately how much you would save:

$17,000 (Total Deduction) × 28% (Effective Tax Rate) =
$4,760 (Annual Tax Savings)

That's a large deduction, isn't it? Remember those high payments you were struggling over? Well, here's the sunny side of making those payments.

Hazard!
If Your Income Drops

As you add up those tax savings, it's important to remember, we're dealing here with your *marginal* tax bracket. If your income *decreases,* you may fall back into a lower tax bracket—that would reduce your tax savings.

On the sunny side, if your income *increases,* and you move into a higher bracket, your tax savings would go up.

In this scenario, by making payments on your first home, you will save roughly $400 a month on federal taxes during the first year.

Tax calculations, however, are complicated, and it's important that you don't take this chapter as a guide to doing your own taxes. You need a competent accountant for that. Check your specifics with a professional.

Keep in mind that here we're only considering federal income taxes. If you have to pay state income taxes, you should also have savings on them. Remember that as time goes by, the amount of your mortgage payment that goes to interest will decrease, and the amount that goes to principal will increase (in a standard amortized mortgage). This will affect your tax savings for subsequent years.

One important question is: How much mortgage interest can you pay and deduct in one year? Normally, you have 12 monthly payments and you deduct the interest paid on all of them. But what if you made the following January's mortgage payment in late December and it was cashed by the lender before December 31? Because interest is paid in arrears (after it's due), you would be entitled to deduct 13 month's interest instead of 12. That could give you a hefty extra deduction in that year, and indeed, many owners do take advantage of this. (The full amount of interest you have paid should show up on a statement from the lender that will probably be mailed to you in January.) The drawback, unfortunately, is that in the next year you would only have 11 monthly payments of interest to deduct (unless you again made the January payment early). Check with your accountant to see just how the timing works and how to avoid problems with the IRS if you want to do this.

Property taxes are deductible in the year paid. If, in December, you make the next payment (due the following March), you can take the deduction for both the payments on that year's taxes, again receiving a one-time tax deduction boost. This only applies, of course, if you make your own tax payments. If your tax is paid out of an impound (escrow account), then it's normally paid in two installments and you can't take advantage of early payment.

Interest and Property Tax Deductions Can Increase Your Take-home Pay. Because you now have mortgage interest and property tax deductions, you'll owe less federal income tax. You can take home that savings each month by increasing the number of personal deductions you take with your employer. Using the calculation above, you could tell your employer to reduce your federal withholding by $400 a month, thus increasing your take-home pay by a similar amount.

Calculations can be tricky. You want to get as much as you're entitled to, but if you take too much, you could end up owing more money (and possibly even penalties) when the taxes are due on April 15. We suggest you ask an accountant or financial planner to calculate it specifically for you.

When you consider your tax savings, you suddenly have more money that you can use to pay for a mortgage. That is one of the reasons that your lender may have calculated a higher affordable payment than you thought reasonable.

More Mileage: Interest Rates

It's important to keep in mind that the size of your mortgage depends not only on the monthly payment you can afford, but also on interest rates. The higher the interest rate, the smaller the mortgage you can afford; the lower the interest rate, the larger the mortgage. Because a substantial portion of the price of the home will be covered by the mortgage, interest rates indirectly determine how much you can afford to pay for your new home. Note the amazing difference in the size of mortgage you can afford depending on the interest rate. The higher the interest rate, the lower the maximum mortgage you will qualify for. This is why it is important to purchase when interest rates are low, if at all possible.

The monthly mortgage payment is, of course, the largest cost of home ownership for most people. If you buy at a time when interest rates are relatively low and you plan to stay in the home for a few years, you will probably opt for a fixed rate mortgage. In that case, you can calculate at the start exactly what you'll pay each month for principal and interest for perhaps 15, 20, or 30 years. When interest rates climb, more borrowers choose adjustable rate mortgages. If you know the lifetime cap or ceiling on your interest rate, you can calculate the worst case right at the beginning—the highest monthly charge you could ever have if interest rates shot through the roof

Hazard!

Home Equity Interest Deductibility

If, after you purchase your new home, you decide to take out a home equity mortgage and use the money for anything other than improvement or building, you are further limited in how much interest you can deduct. You are limited to a maximum mortgage here for other purposes of $100,000.

during the term of your loan. (These mortgage types are discussed in greater detail in Chapter 3.)

Extra Added Attractions: Tax Breaks for Qualified Buyers

Home ownership offers additional benefits in the form of tax savings; here are some of them:

Deductibility of Points. In the first year of home ownership, you may be entitled to an additional tax break if you paid any points (also called *origination fees*) to the lender to get your mortgage loan. The points are considered prepaid mortgage interest and can be deducted as additional mortgage interest. You can amortize them over the term of your mortgage or take them in the first year of home ownership.

Capital Gain Exclusion When You Sell Your Home. We hope you will make money on your home, but it's important to remember that homes do not always appreciate in price. Assuming yours does appreciate, there are a few requirements for taking advantage of this exclusion. When selling your home at a profit, gains of up to $250,000 per person ($500,000 for married couples filing jointly) are tax-free, if you have lived in your principal residence at least two of the last five years. If you have lived there for less than two years, you may still be able to claim some portion of the exclusion if you were forced to sell because of a change in the location of your employment, a health condition, or some other unforeseen circumstance. In that event, you would get only part of the $250,000 per person exclusion. And, the icing on the cake is that you can use this same exemption again after living in another home for at least two years of the last five.

Let's take an example to understand this better. Let's say you and your spouse buy your first home and live in it for at least two years. Maybe you bought your home in a great location for price appreciation and you've seen the value of your home skyrocket. At the end of the two-year period, it's gone up nearly $100,000. Your tax person tells you that you've got a capital gain of $97,000. How much tax do you owe on that gain? The answer: nothing! If the gain had been $197,000, you would still owe no taxes. Similarly, if it had been $497,000 and if you were married filing jointly, no tax would be due.

If, however, your gain was miraculously over $500,000, then you'd owe capital gains tax on the overage. For example, if the gain was $550,000, you'd owe tax on the $50,000.

What can you do with the gain? Anything you like. You do *not* have to reinvest it in another house. Of course, you can do that if you want, or you can add it to your retirement savings, buy a car, or take a vacation with it. *A word of caution:* You cannot take a write-off on your taxes for a loss on the sale of your home.

Penalty-Free IRA Withdrawals for First-Time Homebuyers. If you have an IRA, you may be entitled to withdraw funds from the IRA penalty-free for the down payment on a home. But the early withdrawal is subject to income tax on any previously untaxed distributions. A distribution from a Roth IRA is not subject to the early distribution penalty or income tax, but it must first meet a five-year holding requirement. Before withdrawing any funds, check with your accountant or financial advisor to be sure that you qualify for this distribution treatment and also to understand the potential effect on your retirement savings.

Tax Breaks for Refinancing. Since you are just buying, it is unlikely that this will affect you in the near future, but it's good to know that points paid on a refinanced loan are also tax deductible. In this case, they must be amortized over the life of the loan.

What You Can't Deduct. There are some things homeowners can't deduct. You can't deduct your fire or homeowner's insurance, and you can't deduct maintenance of your home. Your bills for gardeners and water simply aren't going to get you a write-off. You also can't deduct the cost of fixing a water heater or repairing the roof, no matter how much they cost, although you can add improvements to your basis.

Improvements (in real estate terminology) are considered permanent additions that increase the value of your home. You should keep a permanent file detailing all expenses for improvements, including bills, checks, and receipts. The Internal Revenue Service considers your cost basis for the house to include not only the original purchase price but also money spent on improvements. Repairs and redecorating are not considered improvements. Patching the roof is a repair; installing a completely new roof is an improvement. Repainting your living room doesn't count; painting a new addition to the house does. Other improvements are fences, driveway paving, a new furnace, new wiring, landscaping your backyard, adding a pool or spa, finishing a basement, and adding new rooms or bathrooms.

▶ Long-Term Benefits of Travel: Equity and Return on Investment

Equity represents the amount you'd have if you sold your home and paid off any liens (financial claims) against it—usually the mortgage and any past due taxes. Put simply, if you buy a $180,000 house with $25,000 down and a $155,000 mortgage, your equity the day after you move in is $25,000. Equity is the money you have invested in the house—it's like money in the bank. Home appreciation has become so tangible in our society that tapping that equity for revolving loan consolidation debt, paying for college tuition, or buying more real estate has become commonplace in recent years. It is very similar to tapping one's savings account for further investment or other debts.

If your house goes up in value by 10 percent the next year, your interest rate is 8 percent and your debt is paid down (amortized) by $1,240 that first year, your equity has grown to $44,240 (market value $198,000, less remaining debt of $153,760). Real estate prices may vary considerably from one area to another. The real estate market is cyclical: A drop in prices eventually attracts new industries and turns into recovery.

Return on Investment (ROI). Is the return on investment an incentive to own a home? Let's do the math. A typical down payment is 20 percent of the home's value. For a $150,000 purchase, that's $30,000. If that same home's value increases 2 percent next year to $153,000, the return (ignoring taxes) is more than 2 percent because of the leverage from the down payment. Divide that $3,000 (increase in value) by $30,000 (the down payment), and it leaves you with a 10 percent return.

As a general guideline, to cover the costs of buying or selling a property (mortgage, appraisal, application, inspection, moving, title insurance, legal costs, real estate commissions) plus the regular costs of home ownership, a property has to appreciate about 15 percent. That generally takes five years, depending on location and markets.

Of course, you need to consider other factors when calculating your total return, such as closing costs, mortgage interest, equity buildup in the home, repairs and maintenance, and tax savings. With a home purchase, this leverage can work to your advantage as long as the home appreciates.

▶ Crossroads: Decision-making Time— How Much Can You Spend Now?

The amount left over from your income may seem terribly small. This number is probably much smaller than the amount the lender says you need to qualify for a mortgage payment. Ask yourself what you might be willing to give up to own your first home. Remember, buying a home is not like purchasing furniture or a car—or even like renting. Furniture and cars decline in value the moment they leave the showroom. And paying rent is like throwing the money out of the window each month. On the other hand, your home will hopefully increase in value. If each month it's worth more than it was the month before, you've got appreciation. And there are many other great things about home ownership. Therefore, you may be willing to tighten your belt so that you can pay more for a home of your own than you would be willing to pay for a rental.

Think of your home purchase as an investment; you will no longer be throwing out the rent money. On the other hand, don't go overboard and commit yourself to a payment that will sink you.

▶ What to Expect on Your Voyage to Home Ownership

Because you're a first-time buyer, you may be completely unfamiliar with the procedure for a property transaction. It isn't, after all, quite like going to the store and buying a bottle of ketchup.

Navigating the Waters: Understanding the Transaction Process

Perhaps the simplest way to introduce you to the process is to follow a real estate transaction from the time the offer is made until the transaction is concluded—when you get the keys to your new home and move in.

The Beginning. You decide you want to buy a house. You find an agent to show you around or look around on your own (more about agents vs. do-it-yourself in Chapter 4). You look for a neighborhood and a house. The beginning can take anywhere from a few days to several months, depending on what's available, how much you can afford, and how choosy you are.

The beginning in many respects is the most important part of buying, certainly for the first-timer. It's a time of investigation and discovery. Often you really won't know what you want until you've been looking for quite some time. Finally you discover your house, you and the seller make your offers and counteroffers, and the seller accepts. Then all the paperwork starts.

The Paperwork. For the first-time homebuyer the paperwork phase can be the most traumatic.

> *I was asked to sign one piece of paper and then another. I gave them a check, then signed more papers and initialed others. They kept telling me what it was all for, but I couldn't make heads or tails of it. I just signed and initialed and eventually I got the house!*

Customs in real estate vary tremendously from one area to another. In some states, you may be told that no one uses lawyers for real estate transactions except when something goes wrong or you just want to seek legal advice about your purchase. In the states, located mostly in the west, midwest, and south, escrow companies act as neutral third parties, assisting both buyers and sellers in residential real estate transactions. Title companies sometimes clear title to the property and make sure that the deed is recorded so that the property is legally in your name. In other states, attorneys are used for handling the paperwork and the closing on your house.

The Documents. After the sales agreement has been signed by both the parties your first chore is to get your financing wrapped up. Ideally, you've

Hazard!

Advice Not *Legalese*

In the real world some attorneys tend to muck up real estate deals because when they do what they're supposed to do, namely protect their clients, they tend to go so far overboard that the other party, the seller, is loathe to accept the deal.

What you really need is someone who is legally competent to steer you to safe waters but who also knows how real estate deals are put together and can come up with something the other side will feel comfortable signing. Out west, there are many good agents who fit the bill. On the East Coast, there has arisen a whole class of real estate attorneys who can handle this for you. Yes, you want legal advice. But you don't want legalese. You want to be protected, but not to the point where no seller will touch your offer.

It is also during the paperwork phase that you must consider disclosures and a home inspection. (These issues are usually part of the offer process and are discussed in greater detail in Chapter 5).

already been preapproved (see Chapter 3), so it's simply a matter of going back to the lender and submitting the property for appraisal (see Chapter 5).

We suggest that you visit your lender immediately after finalizing the sales agreement to get the ball rolling. Then you should call the lender every week to keep abreast of any problems. When you talk to your lender, always ask if there's enough time for the lender to "fund the loan." The lender should be comforting you by saying yes. If the lender says no, it's an emergency situation. The mortgage is off track. Call the agent and/or your attorney and, if necessary, find another lender to get the mortgage back on track.

You will be asked to sign a document indicating that you received a notice of estimated mortgage costs (called a Real Estate Settlement Procedures Act, or RESPA, statement). The RESPA statement must be given to you within three days of the signing of the loan application. Read it carefully. You will have to pay for everything that's listed on it (and possibly some things that aren't).

The escrow holder, whether it is an attorney or an escrow company, will ask you to sign "escrow instructions." These reiterate everything on the sales agreement and instruct the escrow holder to gather all the documents, signatures, and money necessary to close the deal. This is usually a long form. Read it carefully with your attorney, making sure it accurately reflects what is in the sales agreement. Once you and the seller sign the escrow instructions, they are as binding, if not more so, as the sales agreement. If there is anything that's different, point it out and get it made right. Don't sign until it's right. The escrow holder may also ask for a variety of other documents.

The identification sheet will ask you everything about yourself including previous addresses, other names used, former spouses, and so on. This identifying information is needed so that the title can be recorded.

Your sales agreement may specify that certain items are to be paid out of escrow at the time the deal closes. These may include such items as the termite inspection fee, home inspection fee, and document preparation fee. The escrow officer may ask you to sign a separate payment voucher for each item or one voucher that covers all of them.

The escrow holder will usually receive a preliminary title report on the property. This details the title and, hopefully, proves that the seller is indeed the owner and has the right to convey title to you. Your signature just signifies that you've received a copy of the title report and have no problems with it.

You want title insurance because it guarantees that your title to the property is good. To get it, however, you have to pay for it. In most areas, buyers pay for title insurance. In some parts of the country, however, sellers traditionally pay or the fees are split. You'll be told what's common for your area.

If you're buying a condo or co-op, you'll receive bylaws and other documents of the association. You should also receive a current financial statement as well as a report on any lawsuits or other legal problems that the association faces.

The whole process of gathering and signing these documents and others that may be necessary to close your deal will take a number of weeks. When everything is completed, all documents are in, the loan is ready to fund, and the seller has signed (or is prepared to sign) the deed, you'll be asked to schedule a time to sign your final papers and turn in the money necessary to close the deal.

The Final Walk-Through. If your sales agreement provided for it (and it should have), you'll be given the opportunity to reinspect the property just before the closing, usually a day before. Accompanied by the agent and perhaps the anxious seller, you will visit your new home to see that the seller has moved out (or is completing the move out) and will be shown that everything is the same as it was when you first saw it. Don't accept a property with the sellers still living in it. If the sellers aren't out by now, when will they be out? Having the sellers as tenants is not a good idea. Now is the time to complain if something is amiss. But it's not time to try to back out of the sale, unless something is very seriously wrong. Look for recent damage and for missing items such as wall or floor coverings that were to be included in the sale, but are now gone. Has the yard been kept up? If not, perhaps the seller should pay for a gardener to get it back into shape. Make your feelings known if there is a problem. This is your last opportunity to check out the property before the sale is complete.

The Closing. The closing can be like a zoo, with paper after paper being put in front of you—and with check after check being written by you. Don't panic! You'll be fine if you're prepared. You're a first-time buyer; you don't know what you should sign and what you shouldn't. You don't have time to pick through and read each clause in every document. So what should you do? Don't go to the closing by yourself. Take your agent along, or even better, take your attorney. You want someone who's experienced, knowledgeable, and competent to check every document with you. If you go to the closing alone and don't know what you're doing, it can be frightening and it can be expensive, much more expensive than the cost of an attorney to represent you.

So don't try to wing it. Spend a few bucks to take someone along who knows what's going on. Most real estate attorneys will include this in their overall fees for handling the sale. Incidentally, many agents do not want to accompany you to a closing because they are afraid that if anything turns out wrong later on, you will blame them. That's not acceptable. Your agent should be there to assist you or should send a counsel instead. Don't assume that all the documents have been prepared correctly. They may not have been. Don't assume that the escrow officer is on your side. They just want to get this deal signed and finished so that they can get on to the next one. And don't assume that the sellers have done everything they were supposed to do. They might not have. The closing is the last opportunity to correct any mistakes, but as a first-time buyer, you might not recognize a mistake the size of a watermelon. With the help of your agent or attorney, be sure all the figures are right, and don't pay anything you aren't supposed to. (Normally, the escrow holder will ask for a few dollars more than necessary in order to meet any unexpected expenses, so if you notice this, don't worry about it. If there are no additional expenses, this money will be sent back to you later.)

What Needs to Be Checked at the Closing. All documents: Be sure that the correct documents are there and that they are filled out correctly. The mortgage papers: Be sure they are correct as well. The math: Don't assume that everything adds up accurately. More often than not, at least one math error is discovered at the closing. If you don't understand anything, ask.

Mileposts: Ten Steps to Buying Your First Home
- ▶ Mile 1: Decide that you want to buy instead of rent.
- ▶ Mile 2: Make a list of what you want in a new home.
- ▶ Mile 3: Get preapproved by a lender.
- ▶ Mile 4: Make a budget you can live with.
- ▶ Mile 5: Find an agent who feels right for you.
- ▶ Mile 6: Choose your location and begin your search.
- ▶ Mile 7: Make an offer to buy the home.
- ▶ Mile 8: Start the financing process.
- ▶ Mile 9: Go through the disclosures and home inspection.
- ▶ Mile 10: Close the deal and move.

Smooth Sailing: What to Do and When to Do It

By now you've figured out that buying a home is not something you should rush into, but once the decision is made, it is something you should move through with some deliberation. Speed is not of the essence—and certainly, don't let anybody rush you—but as a practical matter you should be able to accomplish this task in about six months. Of those six months you might have spent a few weeks looking through homes and might have taken several walking tours before deciding what you wanted to buy.

What follows is a general calendar that you can adapt to your own circumstances. It is a broad-brush schedule that is fixed on paper, not etched in stone. Once you get into your transaction, you are going to find that some parts will go more smoothly and quickly than anticipated—and others more slowly. Much depends on you. Much depends on the professionals you deal with. And, a little depends on luck.

If you think homebuying is a mathematical, paper-driven transaction that should have nothing to do with luck, you're wrong. Paperwork is going to get lost. Something always is going to need another signature. There is always going to be a missing piece of data. If you're lucky, appointments that have to be rescheduled can be reset in a matter of hours or days, not a matter of weeks. Remember, all real estate deals work on paper. It's only when you start plugging in people that things get bogged down.

Although the first five steps involve little or no money being spent by you, they are essential to the decision-making process.

Step 1: Make Sure You Want to Do This. At this point, the notion of home ownership is little more than a twinkle in your eye, but a twinkle you think you may want to pursue. It's the period when you prepare yourself mentally to make a yes or no decision about home ownership.

Step 2: Start Paying Attention. This is also a "Do I really want to do this?" step, but it comes as you've started getting used to the idea that some day soon you may want to be a homeowner. During this stage, if you don't already, start reading the local newspaper. Start on the front page. You are looking for a general idea of what's going on in the community where you want to live. Do people have jobs? Are new shops and stores opening up or closing down? Are the big companies hiring people or laying people off? Is the population of the community generally going up or down? Are there zoning changes in the works to allow more commercial construction? Is the local high school adding a new wing? Are local referendum bond issues being passed by the voters or turned down?

When employment is high in a community, it usually means there is a pretty stable housing market. It means that people are making money. And when people are making money, they can buy houses and builders can build new houses with relative certainty that they'll sell within a fairly short period. In that kind of market, there probably aren't going to be too many homes available at bargain rates. In fact, competition for housing may be fairly brisk, pushing housing prices up. A few months from now, that might mean you'll end up in a bidding war to get the home you want. Just be aware of it.

On the other hand, if people are being laid off, stores are closing, and builders aren't very active, it's probably a sign of a weak local economy. In times like that, housing prices are a little softer. People may be a bit more willing to negotiate price. There may be more houses on the market for you to look at. Odds of getting into a bidding war have significantly diminished. Think supply and demand.

Step 3: It Must Be the Money. You have reached a point when you need to figure out, generally, how much money you have, what kind of spender you are, what kind of cash flow you have (that's what Roadmaps 1.1, 1.2, and 1.3 were all about), and whether there is a reasonable expectation of maintaining that cash flow in the future or even improving it. When you get to the mortgage loan application, you are going to need details, but for this preliminary exercise, look at your household income per month and your household outflow. Ask yourself these questions: After all the addition and subtraction, do I have more at the end of the month than at the beginning? Am I prepared to make a commitment to a big-time financial obligation? Am I willing to curb my spending for a while to get it?

Step 4: Evaluate Your Future. You need to be honest with yourself about your future with your current employer. Is your job secure? Is your company secure? If the answer to either of these questions is no, you may want to delay your decision. Also, are there any mandatory big-ticket items in your near future? Are you going to have to buy a new car? Are there medical issues on the immediate horizon? Are there tuition fees? If your answer is no, that's a very positive sign that when the time comes to borrow money, the lender will smile.

Step 5: Evaluate Your Current Living Situation. This is the time to pull out the contract on your current living arrangement. If you have a lease, when is it up? What are the financial penalties for breaking the lease? Alternatively, if you are on the brink of renewal, have a conversation with your apartment manager or landlord and see if you can arrange a month-to-month lease. Be honest and tell them you are thinking about buying a home. See what you can work out. Conversation is good. If all the above come up as green lights, or at least no worse than yellow, it's time to take more serious steps forward.

Step 6: Stop Spending Money. Several months from now there is a good possibility you are going to be sitting at a closing table and writing checks. You want to be able to cover those checks, so stop spending money. Don't buy a car or new boat. Stop going to restaurants. Stop having a beer after work. For the next several months, cut back to basic necessities. Stockpile cash in your bank account. Keep all your bills current. Try to avoid adding more debt. Using ballpark numbers here, let's say you want to buy a house for $150,000. Even if you only put down 10 percent ($15,000) and pay closing costs (roughly another two percent), this means you are going to need $18,000 in the bank before you start the process.

Step 7: Get Yourself Two Yellow Legal Pads. On the first legal pad, start listing what you want and need in a home. Everyone in the house who will be making the move to the new house should participate in this list. Setting priorities will come later and tough decisions will have to be made, but for now it's a dream list. Everything goes on the list. Number of bedrooms, number of bathrooms, ideal commute time to work, school, movie theaters, favorite restaurants, everything. Priorities come later.

The other legal pad is for names, dates, and notes on conversations. In the course of this transaction, you are going to be talking to real estate agents, bankers, lawyers, home inspectors, movers, and other people. These are going to be important conversations and you need to write down the name of each person you talked to, the date you talked to them, what you talked about, and what everybody agreed to do. Get the names and contact information for real estate agents, bankers, title people, and movers. Write them down. It's important.

Step 8: Talk to Homeowners. Talk to people you know who own homes and ask them how they ended up where they are. Was it hard to get a mortgage? Where did they get it? Was it difficult to get homeowner's insurance? Who insures them? Did they use a real estate agent and would they recommend that real estate agent to you? (Do not let them say, "I'll have my agent give you a call." Rather say, "If you have the card handy, we may give them a call once we figure out what we're doing.") This is also a good time to pull out the classified ads in the real estate section of your local newspaper or the newspaper that serves the community where you want to live. What you're trying to get is an idea of how much existing homes are selling for and what new homes cost. Needless to say, you want to pay attention to houses that appear to generally match what you're looking for in terms of number of bedrooms, bathrooms, and amenities. (Check the list on your legal pad.) Also, it's good to do a little web searching now—just for practice. Without filling in any online forms or even bookmarking any sites, do a search for homes that fit your general criteria. Of course, most of the homes you see on the Internet today will be sold by the time you're ready to buy in a couple months. Right now, you're just trying to get a feel for what's out there.

Step 9: Determine What Neighborhood You'd Like to Live In. If your move is strictly local, drive through a couple of neighborhoods that seem like good prospects with your yellow legal pad in hand. Look for a variety of things. If playgrounds are important, be sure to note them. If schools are important, note their names—you'll be able to check them out later on the web. If commute time to work is important, look for the routes you'd probably take. This exercise will help you rule out some areas and concentrate on others. It's important to get that first blush of "I can live here" or "I can't see myself living there" out of the way. Within a few weeks, you're going to get serious about this. If you are moving to a distant city or are being relocated by your company, this is a good time to make an exploratory visit to your new destination.

Step 10: Prequalify for a Loan. Things start getting scary now. Remember the word is prequalify (which is free), rather than the words preapprove or loan commitment letter (which will actually cost you money). What you are looking for right now is a good approximation of how much a bank may actually lend you, which, in turn, will tell you approximately how much house you can qualify to buy. If you have a relationship with a bank or a credit union, call them and ask them to help you. The bank may have you come in or they may be able to do it over the phone. They may direct you to a Web site. Prequalification does not entail a commitment to work with that lender. You will need certain numbers: the amount of your income last year, your current debts—car payment, credit cards, etc. You won't have to document any of these figures too closely (that will come later when you go for the commitment letter), but you want to be as accurate as possible. If this bank won't lend you as much as you'd hoped, another lender might, but this is a good time to revisit your wish list.

Step 11: Talk to a Real Estate Agent. You should interview at least three agents to find one who fits your style, but anyone you interview should have credentials in representing buyers. (You don't want an agent who is only skilled in representing sellers.) If you have some agents' business cards, look for the letters ABR (Accredited Buyer Representative), CBR (Certified Buyer Representative), or CEBA (Certified Exclusive Buyer Agent). Those letters tell you these agents have had at least some specialized training in working with buyers. After you interview at least three, select the agent you want to work with. You may be asked to sign a buyer agency agreement, which is fine. If you haven't already done so, expect an hour or so of conversation with the agent about your dream list, your finances, your school preferences, and things like that. Before you leave that interview, ask for a blank copy of a

HUD-1 form. Months from now, at the very end of the transaction when you are worriedly sitting at a closing table and pieces of paper are flying by you, one of the most important forms will be the HUD-1. It will have numbers all over it. The time to begin familiarizing yourself with the HUD-1—and asking what's this and what's that—is now, while you're not under pressure to get things signed and there are no numbers in the blanks.

Step 12: Contact a Lawyer. If you have an attorney, let them know you are in the home-buying process. If the attorney you know is not a real estate lawyer, ask for a referral to one who is. Ultimately, you are going to want a lawyer to review your contract with the seller. If you don't have a lawyer, you might get a referral from your agent. You are going to want your own lawyer.

Step 13: Preapproval and Loan Commitment Letter. This is going to cost you some money, probably around $45 for a credit report and maybe $300 to $400 for an appraisal. Getting a commitment letter tells you exactly how much a specific bank will lend you and it guarantees that loan. That, in turn, makes you a very powerful buyer. It's the equivalent of having somebody standing right behind you with a suitcase full of cash when you are negotiating the purchase price, or if you end up in some kind of bidding war for a house, having the money ready means you can make the deal on the spot. If the other bidder hasn't arranged financing yet, that puts you in a very powerful position.

Step 14: Set Priorities. Review the wants/needs list on your legal pad. In one column, list the "must haves." In another, list the "should haves." Don't discard anything, but make sure the truly optional items are out of the way.

Step 15: Homeowner's Insurance. Start calling insurance agents. Your lender is going to require you to have homeowner's insurance. Make sure you can get it.

Step 16: Start Looking at Houses. Your agent will be on top of what's being listed that might interest you. For the next few weekends, depending on your schedule and your agent's schedule, you will be looking at houses. Now you need to decide whether you are going to buy a home or stay where you are. So far you've only spent a couple of hundred dollars getting a loan. After you've seen the first few houses—which the agent will have selected according to what you want and how much money you can spend—you should know whether you want to go forward or not. If the answer is no, tell the agent right away so that nobody wastes any more time. But if the answer is yes, then you need to be able to make a decision on a moment's notice. If you see the house you want, you need to be mentally prepared to make an offer. Keep your schedule open. Be available. You never know when your agent will call and ask you to meet at a house.

Step 17: Contact Movers and Your Landlord. Now that you've made the decision to a buy a house, you need to deal with a couple of ancillary issues. Get recommendations of movers. Don't be afraid to ask for discounts. Try to schedule an interview with at least three or four movers. They'll want to come over and calculate the weight of what you have. (You can get a rough idea yourself by going to Moving.com.) Get free estimates, and check their references.

Also, talk to your landlord or apartment manager and let them know, again, that you hope to be moving in the near future. Go over the details of giving notice. Talk about security deposit rebates. Be sure to write down the names of the people you talk to and summarize the conversation, dates, and times.

Step 18: Make an Offer. If everything is going well, you should be narrowing your choice of homes. You should have narrowed down to some good homes by now and may be ready to put in an offer. You should definitely be aggressive now. Call your real estate attorney and tell him what's going on. The attorney will want to review any agreement proposal before you sign it. Make no mistake, the lawyer can be a real pain for both you and your real estate agent—and the seller and their agent. But your lawyer also can save your behind.

Step 19: Negotiate the Purchase. With any luck, you should now be in negotiation to purchase a home. Offers and counteroffers will have been exchanged and you should be ready to reach an agreement. Keep your lawyer in the loop. At the moment the seller says yes and you say yes, a number of things should happen and your real estate agent should be there every step of the way. You need to be prepared to write an earnest money check that could be anywhere from a few hundred dollars to a few thousand dollars. This is good faith money that will tell the seller that you are a serious buyer. Discuss with your real estate agent and/or your attorney how much that should be. Call your landlord or apartment manager and share the closing date and when you plan to vacate your rental dwelling. Go over the rules of your departure—how clean does your apartment need to be, can you get back your security deposit? Remember the movers you talked to last month? Call the one you liked best and tell them when you need to move. Tell them everything you can and get a firm price in writing. Call the lender you have a commitment letter from and tell them the final price. They'll want to see the purchase agreement. Ask them what you need to do next to make sure everything goes smoothly. They will start the paperwork moving and order the appraisal. Make sure your lawyer has a copy of the purchase contract. Work with your real estate agent to decide when the home inspection will be scheduled and which inspector you will use.

Step 20: Work Out the Details of Your Move. Work with your landlord or apartment manager to figure out who will be in charge of closing out your current telephone, gas, water, electric, cable TV, Internet, newspaper, and other utility accounts. Work with your real estate agent to make sure all those same utilities will be working on the day you move in to your new place. (Many agents have services that are skilled at working through those bureaucracies.)

Step 21: Attend the Home Inspection. It will probably take a couple of days for the inspection report to come back to you. When you receive it, you will want to go over it with your agent as soon as possible. You may need to reopen negotiations with the seller if the home needs some repairs. If the deal is going to come unglued, now is the time it will happen. This is when paperwork disappears and when things you thought were going to happen don't happen. Be flexible, but also be deliberate and be ready to be forceful. At the very bottom line, this is a business deal and the deal isn't done until all the paperwork is completed and all the loose ends are tied up. Know where your break point is. Even now, you need to be prepared for the whole deal to go up in smoke.

Step 22: Stay on Top of Things. Keep in touch with your agent and your bank to make sure everything is as it should be. Notify your mover and emphasize the date you want your furniture delivered to your new home. Now is also the time to get rid of clutter in your current dwelling that will not be making the move. Give it away or throw it away. Get boxes. Start packing.

Step 23: Prepare for the Closing. The day before the close (and sooner if you can manage it), you should have the settlement papers available to you—the infamous HUD-1 with all the numbers should be filled in. Note the things you don't understand, and there will be several of them. Whoever closes your deal—a lawyer, a closing office, a title company—should be prepared to answer your questions. Your lawyer and your real estate agent also should be helpful. You should know how much money to bring to the closing table the next day and who will be getting checks from you.

Step 24: Closing Day. Paper everywhere. Be mentally prepared for this to be all fouled up. Be prepared to be delighted if it isn't.

Step 25: The Night of the Close. Celebrate in your new home. Unpack the necessities and leave everything else until tomorrow.

Step 26: Tomorrow. Start unpacking and start filling out change-of-address cards.

Learn the Language

Key Terms to Know When Buying a Home

Condominium (also condo): A system of real estate ownership wherein there is separate ownership of units in a multiunit project with each separate unit ownership being coupled with an undivided share in the entire project less all of the units.

Cooperative (apartment): An incorporated apartment building in which the tenants each own shares of the building, which entitle them to live in it and make decisions regarding the building as a whole.

Net house payment: A house payment minus the value of the tax deduction and principal payment.

Residual income: A monthly leftover income after deducting housing costs and fixed obligations from the net effective income in qualifying for a VA loan.

Tax savings: The value of the tax deduction you receive on your mortgage's interest and home's property taxes.

Choose Your Destination

Condo, Townhouse, Co-op, or Single-Family Home

▶ Planning a Dream Vacation: Buying a Home

Do you have a home of your dreams?

Interestingly, most people have only a partial idea of what they truly want in a home. For some, it may be a particular look: a colonial with shutters, a plantation style with pillars in front, a Tudor with those cute brown boards on white plaster, or a western-style ranch. Others simply want room to roam: lots of bedrooms, a big kitchen, and a bigger family room, all on a large lot. Still other first-time buyers are looking for good schools or a close-to-work location and aren't that concerned about the appearance of the house.

Do you know what you really want in a new home? There's an old saying that you can't get what you want until you first know what it is. That certainly applies to homes. Therefore, before you call your tour guide (real estate agent) or do anything else, it's important to sit down and create a list of your priorities.

You may be sure of the kind of home you want now, but think about the future as you begin your search. Unless you are willing to move every

Dear Son,

Mom and I are so happy that you and Suzie have decided to buy a home. I know we all have to make our own mistakes, but I felt I had to tell you about the fiasco our first house was. Mom was pregnant with you, and I was struggling with a new job. Of course, we liked the idea of having three bedrooms and a couple of bathrooms with a garage instead of a carport. But we didn't really talk much about it, and the "home of our dreams" came down to something we could get into fast that didn't cost a lot of money. And that's what we bought. It was a home that we quickly came to dislike. While the house itself was small but adequate, the neighborhood was horrible. Can you believe the neighbors across the street threw their garbage out onto their lawn? How could we not have noticed this!

Needless to say, we didn't enjoy living there, and, of course, we had a terrible time reselling it. Potential buyers would take one look at the neighborhood, and not even bother to stop and look at our house. After living there awhile, we discovered what we truly wanted in a home, and heading the list, for us, was a good neighborhood. We also wanted a bigger backyard and a separate family room. If only we had known this before we bought!

A word to the wise,
Dad

P.S. As it turned out, we did eventually sell and move into the home you and your sisters grew up in, and lived happily ever after!

few years, try to anticipate some of the changes that may lie in your future. Nature-loving newlyweds may come into the agent's office asking for "an old house—we don't care if it's rundown because we can do some work on it, but it has to be in the country on five acres." (There's something mystical about five acres; no one ever requests four acres or six and a half.) A few years later those adventure travelers may come back to the agent, having found themselves isolated with two infants and nary a babysitter in sight. "Please," they say, "this time show us something in the middle of a tract full of toddler playmates and baby-sitting teenagers."

On the flip side, Americans are more transient than ever before, with the average householder moving seven times during their life. Seeing your home as an investment that may be sold someday will make you want to retain its desirability and broaden its appeal so that if the time comes to sell it, you can get top dollar in the shortest marketing time.

Your ideas about housing design may also change: The couple with the toddlers will be delighted with a family room open to the kitchen so that the tots can be supervised while the cooking is going on. Almost 10 years later, they may be longing for a family room located down a flight of stairs, around a corner, and with a soundproof door. Every house is a compromise. Before you start looking, accept that you will eventually give up something you now consider important: the mature trees, the open fireplace, the guest room. You'll fall in love with one special house and suddenly decide you can live without a sunny backyard after all.

Traveling Together: Keeping a Relationship Together Through It All

The emotional aspect of buying a home can be extremely intense. Women view their homes as nests, men as their castles and investments. If buying a home with a spouse or partner, it may be wise to talk about what kinds of compromises may be in order, creating less room for conflict when the time comes to choose. Establish your own priorities: factors that are essential, those on which you will compromise if necessary, and those that don't matter at all. Okay, time for the first leg of your journey to begin, so let's put the pedal to the metal and start figuring out where you *really* want to go now. Remember, if you are like most of us, there will be other trips!

Compact, Mid-size, or SUV: Assessing Your Needs

Some first-time buyers just know they want a single-family home, no matter what. They were brought up in a house and are renting one now, and that's all they'll settle for. (If you're in this group, however, you might be pleasantly surprised by some of the features of "shared" living that we will discuss later in this chapter.)

Other first-time buyers are apartment dwellers and only know the lifestyle of living in proximity to other tenants. If you're in this category, you may not know whether you would like a single-family, detached home or would actually prefer to continue in some form of shared living.

What Kind of Travel Do You Enjoy: Choosing the Right Type of Home

As soon as you begin looking for a home and working with an agent, you'll be asked (or should ask yourself) whether you want a single-family, detached home or are willing to live in a condominium or co-op. This is an important question because single-family homes are the most expensive. You may not be able to afford a single-family home in the neighborhood you want. And, if neighborhood is important to you, to get into a particular neighborhood, you may have to opt for some sort of less expensive, shared living. Another reason for asking this question is that you may actually prefer some form of shared living. To understand the considerations involved in different types of homes, let's examine each separately.

Group Tour vs. Self-Guided Travel: "Sharing" a Home vs. Single-Family Living

In areas where land is at a premium, cooperatives, townhouses, and condominium apartments may be attractive alternatives to more expensive housing. Multifamily living offers the advantages of owning a home without the constraints of single-family homeownership. What's more, the Internal Revenue Service treats co-ops and condos exactly as it does single-family houses.

There are two key reasons why first-time buyers in particular may find a condo, townhouse, or co-op attractive:

1. *Price.* In any given area, a shared home usually costs less than a single-family home of roughly the same size. (In metropolitan areas such as Manhattan, where single-family homes are virtually unaffordable for most people, there is a premium on good co-ops.)

2. *Exterior Maintenance.* As with an apartment, there's no yard work (although town homes will often have a small yard area where you can plant a garden). Also, you don't have to worry about your neighbors taking care of their property. From the outside, at least, the Homeowners Association (HOA) will handle the upkeep of the entire development. It

is, in fact, this lack of exterior maintenance responsibilities that entices many first-time buyers.

On the other hand, there are several drawbacks to sharing a home. It is true that historically, the prices of shared homes (with certain exceptions, such as the co-ops in New York City) have been lower than those of single-family, detached homes. Part of the reason is that it costs less per unit to build condos or co-ops than to build detached homes, and the units themselves take up less space on valuable land.

However, a point not often mentioned by those selling shared homes is that they simply have not appreciated as well as single-family homes. Over the past 20 to 30 years, shared homes have generally been considered less desirable than single-family homes. One reason for slower resales is that some condos have an excess of renters. Perhaps some of the original owners wanted to sell and couldn't, so they rented out their units. Or maybe people bought the condos as rental investments. Whatever the case, renters tend not to make as good occupants as owners. Because renters don't have any real stake in the property, they tend not to take as good care of the units as owners do, yet studies have shown that they use the amenities (such as pools, spas, and recreation areas) more heavily than owners. As a consequence, the more renters and fewer owners there are, the less desirable the development. In fact, when tenants represent 25 to 30 percent of the overall population of a development, many lenders will withhold financing for resales. If you are considering a shared ownership development, be sure to check the renter/owner ratio. If over 25 percent of the units are occupied by tenants, consider this a red warning flag.

Another minus for condos when compared to detached homes is the density. As in an apartment building, you have a lot of people living relatively close together. Noise can be a problem. Finding parking can sometimes be a headache. And there's a condominium Homeowners Association (HOA) that seems to impose countless rules about conduct, which sometimes can be a real burden on the owner.

Yet another potential problem is that if one of the condo owners gets angry at the condo association, they can sue. If the lawsuit is successful, you can be docked for the costs. I belong to a condominium HOA that recently lost $100,000 to an owner's lawsuit over where a commercial vehicle could be parked. The HOA was responsible for that loss, which had to be shared among the 350 of us who were members. Fortunately, an insurance policy picked up the costs, but that's not always the case.

Finally, in a shared home, you may never achieve the "my home is my castle" sense that you get from living in a single-family, detached house. You can't go outside and bang on the wall or put up a swing or paint your front door (on the outside) without permission (which often is not forthcoming) from the HOA. Some people find these restrictions so stifling, they refuse to live in shared homes.

Condominiums. The term condominium refers not to an apartment, but rather to a form of individual ownership. The buyer of a condominium receives a deed and owns real estate, just as a single house is owned. In the case of a condominium, the buyer receives complete title to the interior of the apartment ("from the plaster in") and also to a percentage of the common elements—the land itself, staircases, sidewalks, swimming pool, driveways, lawns, elevators, roofs, and heating systems. The condo is classified as real estate.

The buyer may place a mortgage on the property and will receive an individual tax bill for the one unit. In addition, monthly fees are levied to pay for outside maintenance, repairs, landscaping or snow removal, recreation facilities, and the like. Townhouse ownership is a hybrid form of condominium and/or cooperative, and can take many forms. Typically, the unit owner has fee simple (complete) ownership of the living space and the land below it, with some form of group ownership of common areas. The individual may or may not own a small patio or front area and may or may not own the roof above the unit.

Cooperatives. The cooperative is an older form of ownership, found mainly in New York City, Chicago, and a few other areas. The owner of a co-op does not own any real estate. Rather, the buyer receives two things: (1) shares in a corporation that owns the entire building and (2) a proprietary lease for the particular living unit being bought. These shares and the lease are classified not as real estate but as personal property. They may be borrowed against, however, to assist with the purchase, and the IRS will treat the loan as a mortgage. The owner of a co-op owes no property tax on the individual living unit. Instead, the monthly payment includes a share of taxes the cooperative pays on the entire building. It also includes a share of the cooperative's payment on the one large mortgage on the entire building, as well as the usual maintenance costs.

Tenant-owners in a cooperative building depend on each other for financial stability. For that reason, most co-ops require that prospective buyers be approved by the board of directors. Because a large part of the monthly charge goes toward property taxes and interest on the underlying mortgage, the prospective buyer can expect a certain percentage of that expenditure to be income tax deductible at the end of the year. If you are interested in a cooperative, you will be told what percentage of the monthly charge is deductible. Inquire also about the dollar amount of liability you will be taking on for your share of the existing mortgage on the whole building. This will be in addition to any loan you place to buy your shares.

What to Check: Condos and Co-ops. Before investing in either type of living arrangement, you will receive a daunting amount of material to read. Look it over carefully. Enlist the aid of an agent, an accountant, and/or an attorney to review the material. You are particularly interested in six things:

1. The financial health of the organization you will be joining. Does it have substantial reserves put aside to cover major renovations and replacements?
2. The condition of the building(s). Is it likely to need a new roof, elevators, boiler, or windows, for which you would bear a share of the responsibility?
3. The covenants, conditions, and regulations you must promise to observe. Could you rent out your apartment, paint your front door red, have a roommate under the age of 55, or eventually sell the unit on the open market?
4. The percentage of owner-occupancy. Traditionally, more homeowners and few tenants are preferred.
5. Any liens or judgments against the property and their type. These make it more difficult to sell the unit when you are so inclined.
6. Any pending litigation against the builder. This makes it almost impossible to get financing.

Townhouses. They are usually bigger than condos, and while you share walls with other owners, you typically don't have anyone above or below you. Yet another plus is the amenities. A good shared property will offer recreational facilities that may include a pool, a spa, tennis and racquetball courts, bike trails, a weight-training room, and a large central room to rent for parties. Recreation facilities present the opportunity to meet new friends.

Roadmap 2.1

Checklist for Judging Condos, Co-ops, or Townhouses

	#1	#2	#3
Address	_____	_____	_____
Condo, co-op, or town house	_____	_____	_____
Square footage	_____	_____	_____
Number of bedrooms	_____	_____	_____
Garage	_____	_____	_____
Fireplace, extras	_____	_____	_____
Price	_____	_____	_____
Monthly charges	_____	_____	_____
Percent deductible	_____	_____	_____
Financial stability	_____	_____	_____
Reserves	_____	_____	_____
On a scale of 1-10:			
Floor plan, layout	_____	_____	_____
Condition	_____	_____	_____
Kitchen	_____	_____	_____
Bath	_____	_____	_____
View, windows	_____	_____	_____

In a well-developed property, your individual unit will be relatively isolated to maintain your privacy, yet the overall property will have many amenities should you choose to use them.

▶ Travel Options: How to Create a "Wants" List

How do you really know what you want in a home until you buy one? It is not very helpful to create a "dream" list—a list of everything you've ever dreamed of having in a home. It just isn't practical, or for that matter affordable. If we let our imaginations run away, pretty soon we'll be coming up with huge master bedroom suites with fireplaces, saunas, and spas; palatial grounds with tennis courts and pools; views of mountains, oceans, or lakes; maybe even a lovely European countryside setting! In other words, most of our dreams are just that—dreams, wishful thinking not grounded in reality. But there's nothing more real than spending close to $150,000—or more—on a home.

While most of us do not always know what we *do* want, we are pretty certain about what we *don*'t want. If you've been renting, there may be a variety of things you want to avoid when you buy your first home. So start by listing the things you want to avoid. Once you get those down, you can easily convert them into a positive "wants" list. A typical first-time buyer may want to avoid small bedrooms; a noisy location; a carport or any open parking; lack of laundry facilities; a location that's dangerous, far from work, or far from family and friends; no outdoor garden area; and no nearby recreation facilities.

Your list, of course, may be far different. But you get the idea. While it may be hard to realistically visualize what you would want in a home, it's not so hard to put down what you want to avoid. Create your own list and discuss it with your spouse, significant other, or with friends. What do you really want to get away from by buying your first home? This, after all, gets to the heart of why you want to buy in the first place. Once you develop a list of negatives, it's easy to change them to positives. Let's take our list and convert it.

 Negatives Converted to Positives

THINGS TO AVOID	WHAT I REALLY WANT
Small bedrooms	Large bedrooms
Noisy location	Quiet location
Carport or open parking	Garage
Off-site laundry facilities	On-site laundry facilities
Far from work	Close to work
No outdoor garden area	Yard or garden area
Far from family and friends	Close to family and friends
No close recreation area	Nearby recreation facilities
Dangerous area	Safe area

Roadmap 2.2

Your "Wants" List

Things to Avoid	What I Really Want
1. _____	_____
2. _____	_____
3. _____	_____
4. _____	_____
5. _____	_____
6. _____	_____
7. _____	_____
8. _____	_____
9. _____	_____
10. _____	_____

Notice how easy it is to first make a list of things you want to avoid and then to change them from negatives to positives. Of course, you may want to delete some of the items on my list, and add several of your own. Use Roadmap 2.2 to create your own "wants" list.

Mountains or Seaside: Establishing Your Priorities

If you ask people what items they want from a list of desirable things, and if they're honest about it, they'll tell you, "I want them all!" Of course, we all do. However, in the real world, particularly given the high cost of housing, it may not be possible to get every item on your "wants" list. Therefore, it's helpful to set priorities—to figure out which things you want most and which you can do without. To begin, weigh the relative value of different items. Which carry heavier weight with you and your spouse or partner and which lighter? For many people, the factor that carries the heaviest weight is location, which means such things as

▶ quiet
▶ close to work
▶ close to friends and family
▶ close to recreation, and safe
▶ close to schools
▶ close to shopping

That's the reason for the real estate maxim: location, location, location. Real estate agents know that the single most important consideration for the vast majority of people who buy a home is where the house is located. Even within the heading of "location," there are priorities. Is safety most important? Or is being close to relatives and friends? What if the two are mutually exclusive? Which one is more important? (More on location on page 43.)

After location, it's really a toss-up about what's most important to you. You should ask yourself about the current and future size of your family. Are you planning to have children? How many? If you're going to have several children, then you'll want to think about a house with more bedrooms if you plan to stay in your first home while your family is growing. Ask yourself just how important a garage or basement is. If you work on cars or have hobbies, it may be vital. On the other hand, maybe you can give it up for the sake of having more bedrooms. What you should do is come to a decision about what's more important and start prioritizing your own list.

Planning Your Trip: How Specific Should You Get?

Sometimes first-time buyers can get carried away when they develop their list of priorities; some go so far as to specify the exposure (southern, northern, and so on) they want. Others come up with a drawing of the layout of their ideal home. While it's important to know what you want, it's just as important not to get bogged down in details before you even begin to look. Remaining flexible is the key to finding the right home. Try not to be too specific. If you get too finicky about the specifics you might soon realize that either your dream home just doesn't exist or if it does, you just can't afford it.

▶ Getting Started: Examining Your Priorities

Once you begin looking in earnest, you will undoubtedly modify your list several times. One final word of advice, however: Don't change your top priority, whatever it is, no matter what. If you have to give up everything else,

Roadmap 2.3

What Matters Most to You?

Before you start house hunting, consider which factors are most important to you. Rate on a scale of 1 (unimportant) to 10 (very important):

Proximity to work	___	Storage space	___
Quality and proximity of schools	___	Room for hobby	___
Condition/age of house	___	Room for entertaining	___
Type and age of roof	___	Home office	___
Fireplace(s)	___	Ease of maintenance	___
Landscaping, view	___	Mature trees	___
Garage requirements	___	Light and sunshine	___
Number of bedrooms	___	Sidewalks	___
Number of baths	___	Lot size and usability	___
Pool or spa	___	Expandability	___
Computer wiring	___	Security system	___
Large kitchen	___	Breakfast nook	___
Deck, patio	___	Formal entry	___
Separate dining room	___	Workshop	___
Family room/great room	___	Formal living room	___
Community pool	___	Neighborhood park	___
Gate guarded	___	Ample guest parking	___
Active adult (over 55)	___	Tot lot	___
Neighborhood rules (CC&Rs*)	___	Other	___

*Covenants, conditions, & restrictions

get your top priority. If you don't, you'll never be happy with your first home. So, hop aboard and let's take a closer look at those priorities and what they mean both in terms of where and how you live as well as those all-important criteria—price, resale value, and appreciation.

At a Crossroads: Choosing a Location

We talked earlier about the importance of location in terms of price and appreciation. In one sense, finding the right location is easy. Because so many people want to live there, it stands to reason that the "best" location is going to be the most expensive one. So simply look for the most expensive neighborhood in town and you're there! However, most of us simply can't afford the "best" neighborhood. So instead of wishing for what we can't have, let's take a look at what we really can get in a neighborhood.

Safety. There are many ways to measure the safety of a community. Probably the most accurate gauge is the number of crimes committed each year. This information is available from a variety of sources, including the U.S. Department of Commerce and some chambers of commerce (although usually only those communities with the safest records make them readily available to the public). Real estate agents are often able to tell you off the top of their head which have the lowest crime rates, but are wary of answering questions that might imply racial bias.

Schools. Those who have children often insist on moving to neighborhoods that have good schools. Those who don't have school-age children often couldn't care less about the schools and are happy in neighborhoods where the schools are dismal. This is fortunate for the latter group only because

Hazard!

Schools—Close, But Not Too Close

By the way, while having good schools is important, it's also nice to be located fairly near the school so that your children can walk. Being close to a bus pickup is the next best thing. Beware, however, of living directly across from the school. You'll have noise and crowds of kids on your front lawn all the time, except summer. And, of course, that could affect the value of your home when it is time to sell.

homes in neighborhoods with bad schools are usually less expensive that those in neighborhoods with great schools. If you have children or are planning to have them, this should be a big consideration. However, even if you aren't planning to have children, you should also consider the schools since, from the point of view of long-term housing values, the quality of its schools can be crucial.

Shopping District. How important it is to be near a shopping district depends on whether you have a car. If you're a city dweller who depends on public transportation, then having a grocery store, pharmacy, and hardware store nearby can be crucial, especially because you'll probably be carrying (or wheeling) everything you buy. However, if you live in the suburbs and have a car, then having shopping close by is far less important. Even in the suburbs, it's very rare that shopping is going to be more than 20 minutes away from any neighborhood. (But it's a good idea to ask, just in case.) If convenient shopping is important to you, be sure to stress that fact to your agent.

Transportation. Public transportation is an important consideration for urban buyers as well as for suburban residents who work in the city. If you commute to work daily, you should know how close you'll be to one of the freeways.

Proximity to Relatives or Friends. If you have to look after your aging parents, or if you have young children and your parents help babysit, proximity to them must be high on your list. It's important to remember that while buying your first home is not a forever proposition, it is a long-term one. On the other hand, relationships—even relatives—tend to change. Or, surprise, friends and relatives move away! If you've made proximity to relatives or friends a high priority, you might want to reconsider that factor, unless necessity demands it.

Other Considerations. Some neighborhoods have additional features that are worth considering.

▶ *Green Belts:* Some communities are built with common areas around homes. These are green belts that often contain walkways and bike paths. A green belt is a valuable asset—it will add value to the price of your home and will also make it easier to resell.

▶ *Anchors:* One type of anchor is a community center with a swimming pool and spa available to all the local homeowners through a homeowners association. This is often considered a plus and helps boost the price of the property at resale time. For the buyer, it also becomes an added attraction. On the other hand, some neighborhoods have anchors that drag them down. For example, an industrial site that abuts a neighborhood is a drawback. Try to determine the anchor for the neighborhood you are considering. Then, ask yourself if the anchor boosts the location or drags it down. If it's enough of a drag, you might want to avoid putting your money there.

Choosing a Location within a Neighborhood. You've done it; you've found the perfect neighborhood. But before we move on to the next attraction, we must point out that certain locations within neighborhoods are more desirable than others, in terms of enjoyment as well as value. Here's a quick summary:

▶ *Corner Lot:* True, it is bigger, but contrary to belief it is less, not more, desirable. A corner lot has more public space, which means more time mowing the grass and trimming the hedges, and less private space in which to enjoy yourself. Because it is exposed to traffic on two streets, there is more noise, more congestion, and, to some extent, less safety. Most people prefer not to own a corner lot; therefore you'll have more trouble selling it later. Also, property taxes may be higher. Check it out before you buy.

▶ *Key Lot:* This lot abuts a corner lot on one side. While other lots will have two side yards and the backyard of only one other lot will abut them, a key lot will have only one side yard and two backyards will abut it. Some people aren't even aware of a key lot, while others avoid it. The problem comes when it's time to sell. Chances are you'll get less for your key lot than you would have for another standard lot.

▶ *Flag Lot:* This lot is surrounded on all sides, except for the driveway, by the backs of other lots, and normally sell for less because they are much less desirable and are difficult to dispose of. Don't be tempted by their low price. You could spend years trying to resell the property at an equally low price.

Condo Location. In terms of the overall location of the development, the rules for condos are the same as those for single-family homes. However, there are some additional considerations with regard to your unit's location within the development.

▶ *Top Floor:* Some people, particularly women who live alone, prefer to live on the top floor of a two- or three-story building or on an upper floor of a taller building. Usually this is a safety consideration: It's unlikely for a burglar to climb into top-floor windows. It is also desirable because there's less noise and, unless there's a neighboring building as tall as yours, people can't see in the windows.

▶ *Noise:* There are other factors that contribute to the noisiness of a location. Units that are near the street or parking lot, laundry areas, or the pool or open-air recreation area can be very noisy. Corner units (not the ones sandwiched between two other units) and units that are separated from other units by a garage or open area are generally quieter.

▶ *View:* Many condo developments have some units that face the parking lots and others that face a view, such as a mountain or lake. If you have a choice, take the better view. You'll enjoy it while you live there, and you'll sell quicker and for more money later on.

Grand Canyon or Plymouth Rock: Lot Size

Some people want a large lot with room to roam. The problem with a large lot, however, is upkeep. You will have grass to mow, shrubs to trim, and leaves to rake, plus a bigger watering bill. In addition, if you have a big house on a small lot (as is commonly the case where land is very expensive), then yard maintenance will be minimal. On the other hand, if you have a very large lot with an average-sized house on it (as is often the case in the country), then it will require a lot of maintenance. Extensive maintenance is costly if you hire a gardener or takes a lot of time and effort if you handle it yourself.

So while some people like a large lot, others don't. In fact, sometimes it is more difficult to sell a house with a very large lot than to sell one with an ordinary-size lot. What's large and what's ordinary? A great deal depends on the neighborhood. A typical suburban lot is between 5,000 and 15,000 square feet. Anything over 15,000 square feet (roughly one-third of an acre) is considered overly large, except in very expensive neighborhoods.

Cottage in the Woods or Villa on the Riviera: House Size

Today buyers at all levels are looking for more house for the money. That does not mean, however, that smaller homes will never sell. A small, well-located

800-square-foot co-op in Manhattan might quickly bring a half million dollars or more. It just means that given a choice, buyers are opting for more room. (One look and an agent can tell you roughly what the square footage of a house is. After you have looked at some homes, you might be able to gauge it pretty well yourself.)

Bedrooms and Baths. The rule is to have neither too few nor too many bedrooms and baths. If you can avoid it, never buy a home with only one bathroom. The least you need is two bathrooms, even if one is only a "half bath" with no tub or shower. More than two bathrooms is nice but not necessary, and it often only adds to cost. In very expensive homes, of course, the number of bathrooms is sometimes simply a measure of status.

The ideal number of bedrooms is three, although in a shared-living arrangement, two bedrooms often is enough. It works like this: There's a master bedroom (with its obligatory bathroom), a child's bedroom, and a second child's bedroom or guest room. If you don't have children, of course, it may not matter to you. But when it's time to resell, chances are it will matter to the buyer. Most parents like to put their children in separate bedrooms, or at least to separate the boys from the girls. That's why three bedrooms work out well. Four bedrooms are nice for bigger families, but often builders will put four bedrooms in the same square feet area as three. You get an extra room, but you will end up with smaller rooms.

Room Size. Big rooms are always better, particularly a large master bedroom, a large family room, a good-size eating area off the kitchen, and a kitchen large enough to work in. Although huge bathrooms—particularly master bathrooms—have become fashionable, they are not critical as a selling feature. Neither is the size of the other bedrooms and the dining room, although buyers will notice if they are particularly small. Because most people spend much of their time at home in the family room, its size is usually more important than that of the living room, although a larger living room "shows" the house better.

Modern Features. Often what separates a "fixer-upper" from a polished home in the mind of a buyer are the fixtures in the kitchen and bath. Modern, good-looking fixtures including basins, faucets, ovens, and countertops are a must. If you purchase a home without modern features, plan on putting them in yourself before it's time to resell. Not only will you get all of your money back in an increased price (assuming you do a good job), but the home will sell much faster.

Design. The design of the home needs to fit the neighborhood. If every house is a ranch style and yours is a southern plantation style, it will stick out like a sore thumb. Try to find a home that complements the neighborhood rather than clashes with it.

Condition. The condition of the property is going to be critical to your ability to resell. A worn-out roof will either kill a sale or cost you money (lots of it) to repair or replace. Old carpeting, dirty ceilings and walls, battered doors—all of these are important to buyers. That's why it's sometimes much easier to buy a newer property (under 10 years old) than an older one. It is always in a better condition.

There are, of course, other important features, such as the way traffic flows through the home, how nice the entrance looks, and "curb appeal," or how appealing the house is when potential buyers first drive up. A good rule of thumb is that what strikes you as very nice about the house will probably appeal to the other buyers. Similarly, what you find undesirable, others will probably find undesirable, too. You get what you pay for. Lower-priced properties often have problems. You may be willing to accept the problem in order to pay a lower price. However, unless you can somehow correct it, that same problem will keep you from attracting a higher price later on when you resell.

The condition of the house is an important consideration and we'll cover that further in Chapter 5 on home inspections.

Floor Plan. Consider traffic patterns. Stand in the entrance and try to imagine yourself going about your daily routine. Consider, for example, a hypothetical trip home with bags of groceries. Where will you park? Will you have to carry the load upstairs? Must you go through the living room? Is there a handy counter near the refrigerator for unloading?

If you have an infant and you sleep with your door open, you'll want to stay within earshot. For that reason, many buyers with small children reject floor plans with master bedrooms on a different level than other bedrooms. In a year or two, though, you may value a private, quiet bedroom. It may be desirable to have the master bedroom separated from the others by a zone of closets, hall, or baths. (The best floor plans incorporate such buffers for all bedrooms.)

If the front door opens directly into the living room, a house in colder climates may eventually need an enclosed foyer to shield the occupants and the thermostat from icy blasts. If you don't like the idea of visitors regularly checking out your living areas from the front door, that's all the more reason to buy a home with a true entry foyer.

Imagine yourselves in midsummer, eating out on the patio. Will it be easy to serve from the kitchen, without risking spills on the living room carpet en route? Check the kitchen for sufficient counter and cupboard space. Look again for places to put things down, not only next to the refrigerator but also at the stove, sink, and dishwasher. Even if you are resigned to a small Pullman kitchen and plan to eat in the dining room, look for enough space in the kitchen for a high chair, a bottled water dispenser, or a stool for a chatty guest. If there is a kitchen island, check out its use as an eating area as well. Make sure there is enough clearance for refrigerator doors to open, room for "help with the dishes," and enough overhead lighting.

Give a house extra points if you don't have to go through a living room or family room to reach other areas. A dead-end living area makes for better relaxation and tends to stay neat. Check out potential furniture placement in each room. Is there an entire wall of windows and doors, making furniture placement difficult? Can you face your bulkier pieces toward an entertainment wall without blocking traffic?

Garages and their dimensions have become extremely important in these days of SUVs, sophisticated recreational toys, and two- or three-car families. They are particularly important for breathing room in areas where basements are not prevalent, such as the southern and western United States. In many areas, three-car garages are the norm in all but the smallest of new homes.

Orientation is also important especially in the Sun Belt. Evaluating where the sun will hit during certain times of the day can mean the difference between faded carpeting, more costly energy use, a swimming pool that sits in the shade most of the day, or the need for solar screens. Look for the convenience of an outside entrance if the home has a basement and see if there is a service door to the garage. An engineer's inspection can help you evaluate conditions, which is particularly valuable when you are buying an older home. But you are the only one who can judge whether a floor plan fits your lifestyle.

Rest Stop: Assessing Your Personal Profile

Establish your own priorities by analyzing the ratings in Roadmap 2.3: Factors that are essential, those on which you will compromise if necessary, and those that don't matter at all.

▶ Mapping Your Trip: House Hunting

Inspecting houses is a tiring and confusing process. If you look at more than four in a morning or afternoon, you'll end up with your head in a whirl. And if you look at several new home communities, with three or four model homes each, you may lie in bed that night, trying vainly to remember whether it was the brick ranch, the two-story Mediterranean, or the Craftsman style tri-level that backed up to the busy street. You'll be totally unable to recall which house or model home had the kitchen with the center island.

It can be helpful to take along a Polaroid, video, or digital camera (often an agent has one or can borrow one from the office).

For your own peace of mind, prepare ahead of time for your house-hunting adventure. If possible, leave the little ones with a friend, relative or sitter for the initial house-hunting trips—at least until you have narrowed down your choices. This will save your sanity, and give you more quality time with your agent or for your search, and can eliminate pit-stops and bored little kids who inevitably get irritable while touring homes.

Fork in the Road: New vs. Preowned

At one point every home was new. Production (tract) homebuilders usually offer several floor plans, options to each floor plan, and several elevations (facades) for each one. Along with groups of speculative homes built by smaller builders, homes constructed on builder-owned land account for up to 80 percent of new single-family homes sold, according to the National Association of Home Builders. The remaining 20 percent or so are custom homes that are tailored according to the needs of individual landowners.

There are both positive and negative points to buying either a new home or a resale (previously lived-in).

Benefits of buying a new home

1. New homes are an original reflection of their owner's tastes. Brand-new appliances, heating and air-conditioning systems, roofs, carpeting, and energy-efficient windows are but a few of the attractive features.
2. New homes are built to stricter energy codes, resulting in more energy efficiency and cost-savings.
3. Many in the real estate industry believe that new homes tend to appreciate faster than homes in older, more established neighborhoods, where the bulk of the appreciation has already taken place.
4. New home areas sometimes offer newer schools, newer shopping areas, and newer infrastructure.
5. Common experiences can create a rapport between neighbors moving into a new neighborhood.
6. Areas where new homes are built can also offer more high-tech wiring for a growing number of telecommuters, home-based businesses, and home entertainment junkies.
7. New homes can be specially designed for handicapped homeowners with fully accessible elements.
8. Some new home areas are master-planned with carefully designed amenities, such as tot lots for kids, soccer and softball fields, hiking and biking trails, perimeter walls or security gates, and community pools and clubhouses.

Drawbacks of new home purchases

1. Taxes may be higher. Special bonds and assessments for schools, road widening, and common lighting and landscaping are more prevalent in new home areas.

2. New home areas might not offer lush, established trees and landscaping that you probably would find attractive in older areas.

3. Spending your first few years putting in some landscaping, buying window coverings, installing patios, and making your home livable to your own tastes can be costly.

4. Depending on the builder's schedule, the weather, and the availability of labor and building materials, you may have to wait up to six to nine months for a new home to be built from the ground up causing scheduling nightmares. Don't lose patience, be willing to roll with the punches.

5. If you change your mind on anything during construction, you'll run into construction cut-off times, after which the builder may charge for alterations to the original plan—these can be quite costly.

6. You'll pay full-cost for anything extra you do to a new home, unlike the purchase of a home that's even just a few years old, where a previous buyer put in the pool, enclosed the patio, installed built-in cabinetry.

7. You may spend the first year or so working through the kinks of a new home purchase by dealing with the builder's warranty department. Chunks of concrete in the plumbing, previously unnoticed anomalies in the paint, walls, trim, or installations may have to be dealt with.

When shopping for a new home, it's important that you or your agent do your homework, not only evaluating the criteria already mentioned, but also checking the reputation of the homebuilder, its new home warranty, and any applicable taxes that may apply.

Make sure you can live with neighborhood restrictions, such as those prohibiting RV storage, basketball hoops hanging from garage doorframes, cars regularly parked on driveways, or satellite dishes. These rules are usually referred to as the CC&Rs (Covenants, Conditions, & Restrictions) and should be carefully reviewed *before* you make a commitment to buy. Never buy a new home in an area where you have mentally planned ahead to ignore any or all of these rules. It might sound paradoxical, but it is true that the reason—say, too many rules—that deters some people to buy in a given neighborhood might become an attractive reason for others to move into that neighborhood. People define a "good neighborhood" in different ways.

Yellow Light: Should You Buy Direct from Builder?

Suppose you discover that there's a neighborhood with new homes where you'd really like to live. Should you deal directly with the builder? The answer here has to be both yes and no. Builders tend to be inflexible about financing and price. If you deal with a builder, you'll have to do your negotiating face-to-face. If you deal with the builder's salesperson, they probably will not have your interests at heart. In short, you could end up spending more money than you want to.

On the other hand, new homes in "good" areas generally tend to appreciate faster than older homes in the same area. That's because most people want a newer house. It's more desirable, so while it may cost more initially, it probably will not only go up in price faster, but also resell sooner. One alternative is to use a real estate agent to negotiate with a builder. Often builders, particularly in a slow market, are willing to pay a real estate agent's commission for the buyer. Look at the homes yourself, but then have the agent make the offer.

 Hazard!
Don't Sign In!

If you "sign in" when you first look at a new home (many builders have a sign-in sheet as you walk through the front door), you may be excluding yourself from the opportunity of having an agent represent you. By signing in, you give notice that the builder brought you in, not the agent, and the builder could refuse to pay a commission to the agent (depending on the listing agreement), even if the agent presents your offer. Remember, there's no requirement that you sign in when you look at new homes.

Beware of unfinished homes in unfinished developments. Spec builders —those who build without having presold the property—want to find buyers as quickly as possible. Thus, they will often begin selling as soon as the property is subdivided, sometimes even before streets and utilities are put in. They may, for example, ask for only a small deposit, say $250—to hold a lot. Or they may want $2,500 to hold a half-finished building. There's nothing wrong with putting up your money before the development or house is finished—as long as it does get finished. Too often, however, developers build more dreams than homes. The properties don't sell as fast as anticipated and the builder runs out of money. Construction stops, and many of the homes remain unfinished. If that happens, you may have to spend many months arguing with lawyers to get your money back.

Similarly, until the development is complete, you won't really know what it's going to look like. Parks and common areas shown on drawings may end up being far less attractive when actually built. What's worse, if the builder runs out of money, the half of the tract where you live could be finished while the other half is a wasteland of framed walls, rough plumbing, and dirty streets for months or even years. It won't be a pleasant place to live, and your home could be impossible to resell. Look for completed homes. You may have to wait, and it may cost a bit more, but you could save a fortune in headaches.

Bumpy Road Ahead: Buying a Fixer-Upper

The trouble with real estate these days, as any buyer will attest, is that it's too expensive. Everyone remembers how low priced real estate was just a few years ago. But for most buyers, that train has already left the station—and prices seem to be accelerating upward. As a result, many buyers, especially first-timers, who are finding that the neighborhood they want is just a bit out of their reach, are looking for alternatives. Frequently, they turn to fixer-uppers.

A fixer-upper is a house that has been neglected to the point that its condition has lowered its market price. While surrounding, well-maintained homes, for example, may be selling for $150,000, the fixer-upper may be priced at $135,000 or less because it's a mess. The seller wants out and realizes the only way to do it is to take less money. Many first-time buyers see purchasing a fixer-upper as a real opportunity. The lower price may get them into a neighborhood they might not otherwise be able to afford. But is it?

Economy Class: Opportunity or Money Pit?

What many buyers fail to appreciate is that fixer-uppers are cheaper for a reason: their poor condition. After you buy one, you have to fix it up, which requires a great many things, not least of which is money. But there are other important issues to consider before going down this road:

Money. Not only will you need the money to buy your first home, but you'll also need the cash to fix it up. How are you going to get it if you're strapped for funds? There are several options. You may be able to put less cash down and get a bigger mortgage, freeing cash to fix up the property. Or maybe you can get a home equity loan from a lender almost as soon as you purchase your home to finance the repair work. Credit cards will work for short-term financing. Some government loan programs are also available. Check out the Web site http://www.hud.gov.

Time. Fixing up a house can take months of hard, tedious work. Do you have the time? Are you willing to spend it? It's generally a mistake to think that you'll do the work gradually over many years, or even months. Few people can stand to live in a home that's under constant construction. The dirt, noise, and mess usually force them to get the job done as soon as possible. This doesn't mean that you can't do it. It can be done, if you're willing to make the sacrifices. The mistake is to believe that no sacrifices are necessary.

Supervision. Almost no one single-handedly does all the work of fixing up a house. You'll be hiring people to work with you, which means that you'll need to locate the appropriate people, be there when they come in to bid the job, determine whom to hire, and once they begin work, supervise to be sure that they do what you want them to do. (On remodeling jobs, watching is critical, because they're not building from scratch. Instead, they're frequently tearing down before they build. You want to be sure they tear down only what you want torn down, not what makes it easier for them to get their part of the job done faster.) You need to be able to say yes and no with authority and mean it. You need to be able to make decisions, sometimes quick ones. And you need to be able to live with the mistakes you'll make. It's not for everyone.

Workmanship. Do-it-yourselfers may discover after they've done the work that it didn't turn out quite as planned. What then? Do you rip it out and start again? Do you hire a professional to come in and do it right? Do you have the money? Once again, this problem is not insurmountable, but before you begin you should be aware of what's involved in getting your project done correctly. (See Appendix A: Resources for some useful books on remodeling and home repair.)

Before you head off on this adventure, ask yourself if all of this really pays. When you consider the money, time, and effort spent in fixing up, do you actually save money when compared to buying a home that's already fixed up and ready to go? It may shock many first-time buyers, but usually you don't save much money on a fixer-upper. Indeed, unless you buy very carefully, it may cost you more in the long run than it would to buy an already-fixed-up house!

That's because property is sold not so much on the basis of the improvement (the house) as on the location (the lot). In really fine neighborhoods, sellers realize that people are willing to do almost anything to get in. So although they may knock the price down a bit if the house is in bad shape, they may not knock it down enough to pay for fixing it up. In most cases, you can't get a fixer-upper cheap enough to warrant doing the work to repair it. On the other hand, if you're desperate to get into a particular neighborhood, you may be willing to do what it takes to get there, and, if the only way you can get in is with a fixer-upper, then the cost comparison really may not matter to you.

Flashing Light: How to Determine if a Fixer-Upper Makes Financial Sense?

This is where the tires hit the road. It's one thing to think about a fixer-upper in the abstract. It's quite another to actually find a property and then pencil out the figures to see whether a purchase makes financial sense.

Where Is It Located? There's that word again! For many first-time buyers, the whole idea behind purchasing a fixer-upper is to get into a home in a more desirable neighborhood. Unfortunately, most properties that are suitable for fixing up turn out to be in run-down sections of the city. Still, they do exist in virtually every neighborhood in every city. Where you need to look is in a prestigious neighborhood in an upscale part of town. What you need to look for is the bad apple in the barrel of good fruits. You want to find a dilapidated, run-down house in a great area. The problem here is that savvy sellers of such homes will often do the fix-up work themselves, if there isn't too much involved. This means that your chance of finding a house that is just a little rundown but has a significantly reduced price is not very bright. Most sellers realize that most buyers (who can afford to purchase a home) don't want to buy a house that is going to require a lot of repairs. Buyers want to move into a home that's ready to go. Consequently, if all it takes to get the house into shape is some cosmetic work—painting, recarpeting, and a bit of landscaping—the current owner will usually pop for the costs and then sell at full price (the price for which other homes in good condition in the neighborhood are selling).

But don't despair of ever finding a good fixer-upper in such a neighborhood. Houses that need more than cosmetic work often don't get fixed up by sellers. If it's going to cost a lot of money to fix up the property—say, more than $10,000 or $15,000—the current owner may not have the funds or may not be willing to commit the time and effort to doing it. They may sell the house "as is." This is your opportunity if you want a fixer-upper. You want to find a house in a location that's right for you, has problems too big for the current owner to remedy easily, but not too big for you to handle. You can then offer a lowball price and have a reasonably good chance of getting it. Keep in mind that you'll probably be looking for an older home in an older neighborhood. Unless there's poor construction or some sort of problem with the land itself (such as settling), you probably won't find a newer house that is a fixer-upper.

What's the Problem? Once you accept the fact that to get a fixer-upper at a reasonable price you're going to have to find a home with more than just cosmetic problems, the next task is to identify the problem and then determine whether you're capable of fixing it. Remember, when a house is priced sufficiently below market to allow you to add in all your costs and still get it for less than a fixed-up property, there is usually something severely wrong with it. But it can happen: If you use a sharp pencil when figuring your costs, get the property at a low enough price, and then get lucky.

Pricing a Fixer-Upper. When assessing a fixer-upper, never forget that your goal is not to buy for as low as you can get the seller to sell for, but to buy low enough so that you can afford to fix up the property. If the seller won't come down this low, then you're better off looking elsewhere. The issue is whether the price is too high for you, regardless of how fair it may seem to the seller. Here's a basic formula to help you evaluate the fix-up price for any given property:

Purchase price = Resale price – Total costs of fixing – 5%

The formula simply says that the price you pay for a fixer-upper plus the total costs of fix-up plus 5 percent for error must equal what you can resell the property for after costs of selling (commission, closing, and so on). The only true way to calculate is to determine the price of the property after it is fixed up and work back from there. Unfortunately, applying the formula is a

Dear Sis,

You won't believe it, but after four months of looking, we finally found our home just where we wanted it! You know, most of the houses were in the $200,000 range; they were asking $180,000 for ours, but still $10,000 more than we could afford.

You should see it— or maybe you shouldn't, yet. The walls are full of holes, with bare boards showing through the plaster, the floors are hardwood, in poor shape, of course, but 1 think (hope!) all they need is a superficial sanding and finishing. The kitchen and bathrooms are a mess. But the real problem—1 know, you thought the other things were real problems—is that the beams supporting the roof over the second floor are rotten, and the ceiling bulges downward and looks as if it might soon collapse. That's what scared off all potential buyers, who figured the house was a total loss.

1 know, it should have scared me off, too, but 1've called in several contractors, who tell me they can shore up the roof while replacing the rotten beams. Well, 1 offered $135,000 for the property. The seller, of course, was outraged, at least on the surface. But he owned the home free and clear, and he hadn't had a nibble, and we got it!

Wish us luck.

Sharon

bit more difficult than simply learning it. To apply the formula, you must determine two difficult-to-determine things in advance:

▶ total costs of fixing up
▶ future resale price

Calculating Your Fix-Up Costs. You must take a close look at the project and see what work needs to be done and what can be overlooked. You also must determine what you will do and what you will hire out. And then you must come up with solid figures that have to be pretty close to actual costs. No, it's not easy to do; but it's not impossible, even for a lay person with little or no experience. You'll just need to call in tradespeople to give you advice and to submit bids.

Locking in the Deal. The problem you'll run into here is that you'll want to know your fix-up costs before you lock in the deal (sign a sales agreement). However, the more people in the trades you call, the greater the chances that one or more of them will see the same opportunity and make an offer on the property. At the same time, other people searching for fixer-uppers may find this property and be eager to purchase it before you can finalize your offer.

One way to handle this is to use the home-inspection contingency (see Chapter 5) as a tool. Offer what you initially think is the right price based on whatever information you have. However, insert a clause that says that the deal is contingent on your approving inspections of the property within 10 days. If the seller signs, you now have 10 days to check out the property and get estimates on the work to be done. If it turns out that your original offer was in the ballpark, you may simply want to proceed with the purchase. If your offer was way off because of unforeseen problems, you may now reopen negotiations with the seller. You can point to your estimates from various contractors and indicate that in order to buy you need a better price. Reopening negotiations after a poor inspection report is done all the time.

The contingency offer is a way to try to get a good deal when you aren't sure of your estimating abilities. But it's not the best answer. The best answer is to be a good estimator of costs—including a margin of error. In our formula we included an extra 5 percent of the fix-up costs so that in case you're a little bit off, you won't get stung. You may want to make it 10 percent or 3 percent. Just be sure you leave yourself some room for error. How much is your time worth? The value of your time is difficult to calculate.

Most people who look at fixer-uppers, especially those who plan to live in the home for some time and have not bought it to fix it and flip it, simply don't figure in their time. That's a mistake. Time spent away from another paying job or away from relaxing is important, valuable time. How valuable? There are many ways to calculate this. Perhaps the best way is to apportion a set hourly rate for the time you spend on the fix-up. But do you charge the hourly rate of a professional who could otherwise do the work? Or do you charge a rate for what you yourself could make elsewhere? My suggestion is to take the higher of the two. You could probably get an extra job and make that money yourself. Or, if something goes wrong, you may need to hire professionals to do the work and pay their wage. If you choose the higher, you won't go far wrong.

What about a profit? Thus far, we're assuming you just want to live in the house; but you want to recover your costs in a resale. If you're also interested in investment—as well you should be—your result could be far different. On top of your hourly wage, you'll want to add a profit percentage to account for your risk on the deal as well as your return on money actually invested. You may want to increase the fix-up cost by 25 percent. Some investors totally overlook the hourly cost and simply add a percentage, often 10 to 15 percent or more of the purchase price, to the other fix-up costs.

Determine the Resale Price. Finally, you have to determine how much the property will be worth after you finish fixing it up. This may be the hardest prepurchase task of all. It requires that you make the assumption that the work will be done in a reasonable time, and that it will look good to buyers. The resale price is determined by what comparable homes in good shape are selling for in the neighborhood. For example, let's say similar houses in good shape are selling for $200,000. It's reasonable to expect that the most you're likely to get for your home after fixing it up is $200,000. You may get more because you will have added new features, which buyers like, but not much more.

Again, we're assuming you are buying this home to live in. Nevertheless you should be concerned about over-improving the property. (An over-improved home is one into which the owner puts too much money, more than is justified by the neighborhood comparables and more than what they can get back at resale.) If you do, do it for your own pleasure, but don't expect to make a profit (or even to get your money back) when you sell. That's because most people are very concerned about paying extra for an over-improved property. This is an important point to understand. For example, let's say that you purchase your home for $170,000 and put in an additional $50,000 to fix it up just right. Is the property worth $220,000? Not if the comparables are going for just $200,000. You can sell your home only for what buyers are willing to pay, and if you over-improve it, you may lose.

Why are we talking about selling when you're just buying? Because it is the best way to accurately determine how much to pay. Besides, although when you buy you may not intend to sell for many years, statistics show that people in the United States move around a lot, and you may actually end up selling sooner than you think.

Don't Forget Resale Costs. The issue of resale costs is controversial. Some experienced fixer-uppers say that you shouldn't worry about the costs of resale, such as agent commission and closing costs. They say that you're going to live in the home for several years, and by the time you get around to reselling, the property should have appreciated enough to cover the costs of the resale. Maybe. But not all properties appreciate. Maybe they will go up —but maybe they won't. We recommend that you figure in the costs of resale to know where you stand when your journey is over.

Adventure Travel: Manufactured Housing and Mobile Homes

Manufactured housing has come a long way since its "trailer" days. In fact, many consumers do not fully appreciate what they see when they are looking at manufactured housing. Modular can refer to anything from build-it-yourself log cabins to luxury homes that are factory-built as modules on an assembly line.

Modular manufacturing techniques sometimes have advantages over the sticks and mortar trades. They can be built year-round, installation times can be cut considerably, they are ideal for remote and rural areas, they can be easily customized, and they can cut waste and the environmental impact made by traditional types of home construction. Manufactured housing leaves the factory in a variety of stages, to be assembled and completed on the home site. Some are precut and paneled. Others arrive in modules that are joined together, complete with plumbing, floor coverings, cabinetry, and electrical and insulation systems installed at the plant. Manufactured housing is gaining in popularity in both the United States and Canada.

However, you may be limited in finding lenders who offer loans on manufactured homes. Check with a mortgage company or manufactured-home dealer about which lender can help. Not all neighborhoods permit manufactured homes to be placed on their home sites. Find out if the area you have in mind for a home of this type will permit this kind of construction.

Mobile homes are still popular in many parts of the United States. One attraction is the lower initial cost, as compared to a single-family home. Again, check zoning before considering the location of a mobile home, and investigate financing carefully. Mobile homes are regarded as personal property, and qualify for regular mortgage loans only if on a permanent foundation, and on land that is owned, not rented.

Choosing the community in which you buy may be more important than selecting the individual home itself. Talk with the occupants of the mobile home community that interests you, and find out how cooperative the management is. Carefully consider how the property is maintained by both its occupants and its management. Also inquire about current lot rental rates, historical increases, and what is covered with the lot rental. Often water, trash, and sewage are included.

▶ Future Travel Plans: Buy with an Eye toward Reselling

It is often rightly said that you make your profit on your home not when you sell, but when you buy. Buy right and you'll find it easy to resell. Buy wrong and selling for a profit can be almost impossible. Buying right means, of course, getting a good location. But it also means buying a home that others will want to own. For example, the most popular single-family home has three bedrooms; a two-bedroom home is usually too small (a one-bedroom home, except in the case of a condo, is very difficult to resell), and four bedrooms often push the price too high.

Don't think you won't move: You will move. Unless you're the very rare exception, within seven to nine years of ownership you will resell the home you're now buying and will buy another. That's a statistical fact compiled by the U.S. Department of Commerce. So you might want to remember when making your list of priorities that it's not for all time. If you don't get some special thing you want in this house, there's a good chance you'll get it in the next.

What Resells Best?

You need to consider what features most buyers look for—the ones described above, in Getting Started: Examining Your Priorities. Certain features in a home can make it more or less resalable later on. Remember, if you buy the wrong kind of home now, that could be a problem down the road.

Now take a deep breath and we'll move on to the next stop—where you are going to get the money to pay for this trip! So, fasten your seatbelts, we're about to take off.

Financing Your Trip

Coming Up with the Cash

▶ Know Before You Go: How to Avoid Sticker Shock

You've come a long way in planning this trip and are well on your way. The question now is how to finance your travel—the purchase of your home —with a mortgage. We're assuming you're not filthy rich and can't afford to plunk down the whole payment in cash. (Nor is that necessarily a good idea by the way, but that's too far down the road for this trip!)

When you buy a home, whether it is a single-family house, condo, townhouse, or co-op, you're almost certainly going to need a mortgage. For first-time buyers who don't have very much cash to put down and may be stretching to afford the purchase, getting the right mortgage is essential. Indeed, the mortgage itself often determines what you can purchase, and over-extending yourself with a mortgage you can't afford can result in turbulence at best, foreclosure at worst.

What Road to Take: Calculating the Costs

The first step to take before you actually house hunt is to determine how large a mortgage you can afford. To qualify for a home loan, you must pass certain tests that all banks will impose. Therefore, you might take those tests yourself before you ever meet with a banker.

Rule of the Road. If you plan to make a 10 percent down payment on a home, banks will typically approve a loan only if your monthly real estate obligation—which includes mortgage principal and interest payments, real estate taxes, homeowner's insurance, and maintenance costs (for a cooperative or condominium)—is 28 percent or less of your gross monthly income. In addition, all of your debt—including payments on credit cards, car loans, student loans, and revolving lines of credit, as well as mortgage debt—should not total more than 36 percent of your gross monthly income. Roadmap 3.1 will help you determine how large a mortgage you can qualify for using these rules. (The worksheet includes sample figures.)

How Much Can You Carry? To determine how much money you can borrow for the purchase of a home, you must assume an interest rate and a mortgage term. You must also estimate what's known as PITI (principal, interest, taxes, and insurance), which comprise the four standard components of a monthly mortgage payment.

With some mortgage plans, lenders collect these last two amounts each month on a prorated basis (one-twelfth of your yearly property taxes and one-twelfth of your homeowner's insurance premium), for an impound (trust or escrow) account. Those tax and insurance bills go directly to the lender, who will pay them with the money in your escrow account. Lenders want these bills paid to protect the security of their loan. (Note: If your lender does not require an escrow account, but you feel more comfortable having these expenses paid each month, ask that one be set up—some lenders charge a nominal fee.)

Property taxes and insurance differ from one house to another. Interest rates differ from one loan program to another, and, of course, the amount of cash available for down payment will affect that difference. Still, you can get a rough estimate at this point. You'll need information (available from any agent or by calling the county assessor's office) on average property tax bills in the price range and neighborhood you're eyeing. Homeowner's insurance is a simpler matter, because the whole calculation is a rough estimate anyway; 0.75 to 1 percent of the home value per month might be used.

Roadmap 3.2 lists factors for the two most popular term loans, 15 and 30 years, at various interest rates, from 7 percent to 13 percent.

Roadmap 3.1

Monthly Mortgage Worksheet

	Example	Your Loan
1. Percentage of gross monthly income available for total mortgage payment, including principal, interest, real estate taxes, and homeowner's insurance	28%	
2. Percentage of gross monthly income available for real estate taxes and homeowner's insurance	4%	
3. Percentage of gross monthly income available for mortgage principal and interest payments	24%	
4. Gross monthly income	$6,250	
5. Multiply item 3 by item 4	$1,500	
6. Percentage of gross monthly income available for principal, interest, real estate taxes, and homeowner's insurance, plus other debts (subtract item 2 from 36%)	32%	
7. Amount of monthly income available for principal and interest, plus other debts (multiply item 6 by item 4)	$2,000	
8. Amount of gross monthly income available for other debts	$450	
9. Subtract item 8 from item 7	$1,550	
10. Enter either item 5 or item 9, whichever is less	$1,500	

Roadmap 3.2

Monthly Payment Factors

Interest Rate Percentage	30-year Loan	15-year Loan
7	.00666	.00899
7.5	.00700	.00928
8	.00734	.00956
8.5	.00769	.00985
9	.00805	.01015
9.5	.00841	.01045
10	.00878	.01075
10.5	.00915	.01106
11	.00953	.01137
11.5	.00991	.01169
12	.01029	.01201
12.5	.01068	.01233
13	.01107	.01268

When you have located the proper factor, multiply the loan amount by this factor to arrive at a monthly payment. For example, a $200,000, 30-year loan at 8 percent interest would require a $1,468 monthly payment ($200,000 × .00734 = $1,468). If item 10 on your Roadmap 3.1 is greater than this monthly payment, you can qualify for the mortgage. Try different combinations of terms and interest rates to see how much money you can borrow by dividing item 10 by various factors to produce different loan amounts. The longer the loan term and the lower the mortgage interest rate, the higher the loan amount you can qualify for.

Roadmap 3.3

Purchase Cost Worksheet

	Example	Your Purchase
Start with the mortgage amount qualified for (assuming $700/mo., 7.5%, 30 yr.)	$100,000	_____
Add down payment cash	11,000	_____
Total price of home	111,000	_____
Add closing costs (at 4% of loan amount)	4,440	_____
Total Purchase Cost	$115,440	_____

Armed with the knowledge of how large a mortgage you can qualify for and how much you must pay each month toward that mortgage, you can now determine what price you can pay for a home. It is safe to assume that closing costs, which include points (prepaid interest charged by the lender —one point is 1 percent of the loan amount), legal fees, title searches, transfer taxes, and other charges, will amount to about 2 to 4 percent of your mortgage amount. You should deduct all of these closing costs from the cash you have available for a down payment.

Most sellers and lenders require at least a 10 percent down payment, though some will accept 5 percent. If you can make a down payment of 20 percent or more of the home's purchase price, you will save thousands of dollars of interest over the mortgage's life, you can avoid the cost of private mortgage insurance (PMI), and your loan will be approved much more readily. If you plan to make a 10 percent down payment, Roadmap 3.3 will help you determine how much home you can qualify for.

You've now answered the million dollar question: "How much can you qualify for?"

▶ Adjusting Your "Sites": How Much Will this Trip Cost?

It is very important to know how much you *can* actually afford. It's a waste of time, effort, and hope to look at homes in the $200,000 to $250,000 range when you can afford only $75,000 to $150,000. Before you invest too much shoe leather, miles per gallon, and day dreaming in finding the perfect home, it's time to prequalify for a mortgage. Mortgage lenders and financial planners often have different ideas on how much mortgage a person can afford. The planner will often suggest a lower amount. If you have a financial planner discuss your plans with him or her before making a decision. If you're doing it yourself, consider the other things you need or want to spend money on. Remember, it's important to factor lifetime goals into your affordability calculations.

Put yourself in the driver's seat, and sit down with your Realtor® or mortgage broker and determine what range they believe you can realistically afford. (Don't be surprised if it's different from what you calculated. Remember, lenders may be adding in tax savings and other things you're not yet comfortable counting on, or factoring in dependents and other variables.) This is no time to be shy or embarrassed about finances; everything will come out sooner or later. It's better to be fully informed up front before you waste a lot of time looking at the unobtainable. Lenders use a formula to determine what percentage of your income can be allocated toward purchasing a home. They also take a close look at your credit rating, which is why it's so important to take care of your credit—you can't build or rebuild it overnight.

Hazard!
What You Can Really Afford

Just because a lender says it's so doesn't make it so. The difference between what a lender says you can afford and what you will feel comfortable with may be worlds apart.

If you're the sort of person who's pretty good at budgeting and keeping track of your checkbook, chances are you'll find the lender's figure okay. If, on the other hand, your checkbook tends to be off each month, and you never can stick to a budget, then perhaps you'd best look for a lower payment.

Of course, the more you earn, the more you have in savings or assets, the better the financial picture you can paint, and two incomes are better than one. Still, regardless of what you think your situation may be, it's important to know for sure. Get prequalified to make sure you're not overreaching.

Fly Now, Pay Later: The Ins and Outs of Mortgages

When you purchase your home, you'll use other people's money in the form of a mortgage. A mortgage is a written instrument (contract) that allows you to use your newly acquired real estate as collateral against the loan you use to purchase that real estate. As the borrower, someone who pledges that property to secure the loan, you are the *mortgagor*. The financial institution, such as a bank, savings and loan, or mortgage loan company, providing the money for your purchase is the *mortgagee*.

> *Money talks and when you find, acquire, and put money to work buying your new home, you'll feel like the talk of the town.*

Traditionally, lending institutions did not loan the full purchase price of a property; the breakdown was 80/20. The loan covered 80 percent of the amount with the borrower responsible for the remaining 20 percent as a down payment. That's changing, however, and some lenders today are requiring as little as 5 percent down on a conventional loan.

Many people assume they can't wheel and deal with a real estate lending professional, but that's not always the case. In some markets that may be so, but in others brokers and lenders are more than willing to work with buyers. It never hurts to try a bit of negotiation. If your efforts don't work out, you're no worse off, so why not give it a try? Ask the lender or broker what it would take to lower the rate a point or two, or if some of the fees can be reduced or even eliminated. Make sure everything is in writing and that you fully understand it. You don't want to negotiate a reduced fee here only to have another fee raised over there.

Reserving Your Berth: Coming Up with a Down Payment

For most of us, buying a home still depends on our ability to put together a down payment. The inability to do so is the single most common reason that people are shut out of the housing market. Many people have enough income to make mortgage payments, but are never able to assemble that up-front lump sum. If this is your dilemma, you have options:

1. Borrow the money from your parents or other relatives. If they are in better financial shape than you, Mom and Dad or another family member might lend you the down payment, which you should repay as you pay off your mortgage.

2. Put securities or bank deposits in escrow to act as your down payment. For example, in the Merrill Lynch Mortgage 100 program (Telephone: 866-275-6522), if you can place a bit over 30 percent of the home's purchase price in escrow in the form of stocks, bonds, mutual funds, and certificates of deposit, Merrill will lend you 100 percent of your home's purchase price.

One advantage of this system is that you do not have to sell securities and pay capital gains taxes on any realized gains to assemble your down payment. As you pay down the principal of your mortgage or the value of your home increases, you will be able to take securities out of escrow, because you will have built up enough home equity (the amount you "have in" the property —roughly, market value minus mortgages owed).

If you do not have enough securities to participate in the Mortgage 100 program, Merrill also offers the Parent Power Program, which permits parents to fund the escrow account with their securities or bank deposits, allowing their children to get 100 percent financing for their home. As the children pay down the mortgage or as the value of the home increases, the parents' securities can be released from the escrow account.

What does Merrill Lynch get out of this? A brokerage customer and a mortgage customer. Keep in mind the fees you might be subject to.

1. Make saving a priority and invest it for growth, in order to accumulate the down payment. (Think of all those Chinese dinners you pick up on the way home from work and those spur-of-the-moment vacations as assaults on your down payment fund.)

2. Get a Federal Housing Administration (FHA) or Department of Veterans Affairs (VA) loan, both of which require lower or, in some cases, no down payments.

3. Obtain private mortgage insurance from your lender. If you are credit worthy, you will be able to reduce the size of your down payment because your lender is now protected against your default.

4. Borrow against your equity in your employer's profit-sharing, thrift, or 401(k) plan. Most firms allow you to borrow at the prime rate or at a little more than prime and repay the loan through payroll deductions.

5. Buy a foreclosed home. Local lenders, as well as the FHA and VA, will often accept low down payments to induce buyers to buy foreclosures. You might have to fix up the property and it might not be located in a prime area, but the investment can get you into the housing market.

Payment Plan: Choosing the Best Mortgage

The entire process of uncovering and qualifying for a mortgage is crucial to making the most of your real estate dollar. To find the best possible deal, you should understand the various sources and types of loans available and shop around.

Loan Sources. The first step in shopping for a mortgage is to identify likely lenders:

1. Savings and Loans (S&Ls) are the largest traditional lender to the home mortgage market. They have great expertise in this area and frequently offer the lowest rates.

2. Savings banks, largely the same as S&Ls, are found mostly on the East Coast and specialize in mortgage lending.

3. Commercial banks have been aggressively pursuing the S&L's bread-and-butter business of making mortgage loans; they may offer the best deal around, particularly if you combine your mortgage with your checking, savings, and investment accounts at the bank.

4. Credit unions, nonprofit organizations designed to serve its participants, may offer the best mortgage terms, but are often overlooked. If you belong to one, tell the broker with whom you are working, and investigate for yourself whether your credit union offers mortgage loans.

5. Mortgage banking firms have become a large part of the lending industry. They borrow money from banks or investors, make mortgage loans, and resell the loans to investors at a profit. They may be able to tap into mortgage pools created by insurance companies, pension funds, and other institutional lenders you would not normally have access to on your own. Frequently, mortgage bankers collect both your monthly payments and a fee from the lender for providing this service. You can find a mortgage banker through a local real estate agent, the Yellow Pages, or

the Mortgage Bankers Association of America (1919 Pennsylvania Ave., N.W., Washington, D.C. 20006; Telephone: 202-557-2700; http://www.mbaa.org). Don't assume your real estate agent's recommendation of a mortgage lender will be the most competitive.

6. Mortgage brokers find the best loans for homebuyers for a fee paid by the lender. They get these good deals because they bring in many loans to a particular lender and therefore can obtain better terms than you, individually, could from the same lender. In addition to the loan fee, you normally must pay the mortgage broker an application fee. Generally, mortgage brokers do not lend any of their own money. You can locate a broker through a local real estate agent, the Yellow Pages, or the National Association of Mortgage Brokers (8201 Greensboro Dr., Suite 300, McLean, VA 22102; Telephone: 703-610-9009; http://www.namb.org).

7. Sellers may offer the best financing option if you are not able to qualify with another lender and the seller is desperate to move. The amount of seller financing rises sharply when interest rates at traditional lenders shoot up.

In addition, most lenders will make loans guaranteed by the FHA or VA, which set certain standards for the kinds and sizes of loans and borrower qualifications to qualify for their guarantees. Many VA loans require little or no down payment for qualified veterans. Many states also sponsor housing finance agencies that offer below-market mortgages for low- or moderate-income homebuyers.

When you shop for a mortgage, compare not only the interest rate but also the closing costs (points and other fees), which can significantly add to your total cost. A few services—such as the Home Buyer's Mortgage Kit run by HSH Associates (237 West Parkway, Pompton Plains NJ, 07444; Telephone: 800-873-2837; http://www.hsh.com)—can, for a small fee, give you a current comparison of rates and terms for lenders in your area.

Booking the Trip: Preapproval Process

If you want to impress a seller (and maybe negotiate a concession on the purchase price), consider obtaining a loan approval before you've even found the house. Being preapproved for a loan differs from the prequalifying process you may go through with a real estate agent, or on your own.

Why Get Preapproved? As we discussed in Chapter 1, before you begin you should ask yourself these questions: How much money can you afford to pay for a home, how big a monthly payment can you comfortably make, how much money will you need to put down? You will need to find answers to all these questions before you can realistically go house hunting. But don't worry, the work you did preparing for it will stand you in good stead now. You can quickly, easily, and, most important, accurately answer your financial home-buying questions, and, in the process, acquire a tool that might allow you to leverage a better price.

To get preapproved, you go through the process of applying for a mortgage from an actual lender even before you've found a home. You fill out an application and put up the fee (usually under $50) for a credit report, and provide the same documentation on your finances as you would when applying for a mortgage (see What to Pack: Applying for a Mortgage), except you won't have a sales contract and other information pertaining to a "real" home. The lender then looks at the application and sees how much money (if any) you have for a down payment, and will investigate and verify your credit, assets, debts, and income to determine the maximum loan you can get.

If all is in order, you'll receive a written statement that the institution stands ready to make a mortgage loan, assuming that the house you choose meets its standards and that a last-minute check on your financial status when the loan is to be made does not hamper an approval. The letter may state that you can borrow up to a certain amount of money at a specific interest rate, or it may state that you are preapproved for a maximum monthly payment. Lenders prefer to name a maximum monthly payment because although the most you can qualify for won't change, interest rates may, and as interest rates go up, your maximum loan amount will go down; as they go down, your maximum loan amount will go up.

Of course, this appeals to a seller, who can be certain from the start that you're as good as gold. You'll be as welcome as an all-cash buyer. In short, preapproval will tell you

▶ your maximum monthly payment
▶ your maximum loan
▶ your minimum down payment
▶ that you are virtually guaranteed a loan

A preapproval letter can be heavy artillery with which to motivate sellers. Consider the position of the sellers. They want a good price for their home, but they also know that most buyers must get a mortgage in order to

What to Pack

Applying for Mortgage

Some of these items, if not available, can be obtained later during the application process—VA eligibility certificate, for example, or legal description of property. To expedite your application, though, take as much as possible to your initial interview. *Make copies of everything for the lender; don't give away your originals!*

▶ Original purchase contract signed by all parties. It will be copied and returned to you
▶ Cash or check for application fee, to cover appraisal of the property and credit report. Additional points or origination fee, if required
▶ Social Security numbers
▶ List of all income
▶ List of debts, credit cards, account numbers, payments, balances
▶ Addresses of out-of-town creditors
▶ List of two years' past employment and two years' past addresses
▶ Seller's agreement to pay points (if not in contract)
▶ If self-employed, two years' signed income-tax returns. If on job less than two years, copies of previous W-2s
▶ Expense and income statements on property presently rented out
▶ Leases signed by tenants
▶ Account numbers and balances on checking and saving accounts, branch addresses
▶ Donor's name and address for gift letter
▶ Explanation of any credit problems. Copies of bankruptcy papers
▶ Certificate of Eligibility, if applying for VA loan
▶ Legal description of property, survey (not required for all loans)
▶ List of stocks and bonds, current market value
▶ List of other assets
▶ True property tax figure on the projected purchase
▶ Name and phone number of person who will give access to the lending institution's appraiser
▶ Copy of divorce decree or separation agreement if paying child support or alimony; same documents if claiming them for income, along with proof that payments are being received

purchase. That introduces an element of uncertainty. Will the buyers be able to get a mortgage large enough to make the purchase?

The sellers won't know whether the sale can be completed until they have signed a sales agreement and you have spent a few weeks trying to find a mortgage. On the other hand, when you are preapproved, it's a sure thing. You've already been to a lender. The lender has already said yes. What's there to be uncertain about? When you're competing against buyers who don't have preapproval, you're the one most likely to win; and if there's no competition, it's a good way to get a better deal.

Your Passport: The Preapproval Process

The lender's process of analyzing a mortgage application (looking over the loan package appraisal and/or inspection of the property, verification of employment, credit report, etc.), and making a decision about making the loan, is known as *underwriting*. When you look for preapproval, of course, the lender won't be able to appraise or inspect a property you've not yet chosen, so the preapproval is contingent upon satisfactory completion of both.

Lenders consider your employment stability and prospects, present assets, credit history, past mortgage experience, and present debts. Most lenders will consider other *compensating factors* that may tip the scales in your favor: future verifiable salary bonuses or the drop-off of child-support payments by a certain date.

The lender judges two things: your ability to meet your obligations in the future and your willingness to do so, as evidenced in the past. Lenders will ask you to furnish a list of documents (see What to Pack: Applying for a Mortgage). Some types of loans and some lenders require more than others. Over the past few years, some lenders have streamlined the process by dispensing with employment verifications, using only buyer-furnished paycheck stubs and verified credit scores.

Assets. You may not borrow elsewhere for the down payment (secondary financing) on most loans. You will be asked to prove that you have enough on hand for a down payment and closing costs. Many institutions will credit you with only a limited amount in cash—as little as $200, perhaps. They also want an explanation for large sums of money that have turned up in your savings accounts within the past few months. (Maybe, they figure, you borrowed it somewhere, thus taking on too much debt.)

Bring in all details on your assets: numbers and balances on savings accounts (the lender will check with the bank), list of stocks and bonds owned, income tax return if you anticipate a refund. Your earnest money deposit counts as an asset; the lender will verify it with the person holding it. You may have assets you've forgotten about: cash surrender value on your life insurance policy, valuable collections, jewelry, boats and RVs, IRA accounts, other real estate. If your loan agent says you are a borderline qualifier, ask if you should list your free-and-clear furniture, appliances, and automobiles.

A gift letter from a relative, promising to furnish some of the funds you need for closing with no repayment required or anticipated, can sometimes be used at mortgage application. Many lenders require the letter on their own form, and most want to verify that the relative does indeed have the funds.

Income to Qualify. The lending institution will analyze your income and will accept only figures that can be verified and are claimed on your tax returns. More than one borrower (husband and wife or unrelated buyers) may pool their incomes to qualify for the loan.

The usual rule of thumb is that two years' continuous employment in the same field indicates employment stability. Exceptions are made for recent college graduates or those who have just left military service. Lenders are nervous about those who jump from one sort of job to another; employment changes that show upward movement within the same field are more acceptable. Bonuses and overtime count toward qualification if your employer will verify them as dependable. Part-time and commission income count if they have been steady for the past year or two. Alimony and child support can be considered as income, but you must be able to show that they are being paid dependably and are likely to continue for the next five years or so.

Older applicants will not be asked their ages, but they will be asked to prove dependable Social Security and pension income if they anticipate retirement within the next few years. Disability income counts if it is permanent. Seasonal income may count if applicants can prove at least a two-year history of such a cycle, and you may even be able to count unemployment insurance income. The self-employed will be asked to furnish income tax returns for two years past and profit-and-loss statements.

Other sources of income might include dividends and interest, and net rental from other properties (leases signed by your tenants may be required). If you will have rental income from the house you are buying (a duplex, for example, with the other side to be rented out), half or even all of the anticipated rent may be counted as further income.

Debts. Lenders give careful consideration to your present liabilities. Depending on the type of loan, they may count any debt on which you must pay for more than six, 10, or 12 months. Car loans are among the most common liabilities in this category.

Before you arrive for the mortgage application session, list your debts, including loan numbers, monthly payments, balances, and time left to run. Student loans are considered obligations if payments are presently due. Child support or alimony you pay is considered an obligation; so is childcare if you are applying for a VA or FHA loan. (If you fail to earn approval, see below to find out how to overcome qualification problems.)

How Long Will It Take? It's wise to start the preapproval process early because it can take some time to complete. The lender has to evaluate your application, secure a credit check, and perhaps verify your employment and savings (for your down payment). Then your application must be sent to underwriting where secondary lenders (Fannie Mae or Freddie Mac for most loans) will check it over and give approval. Only then will the lender issue the preapproval letter. The process might take only a few days (if the lender does it electronically), or it might take a month or more if a problem is discovered that you must correct.

Some lenders will offer you a preliminary preapproval letter, which means that they have taken your application and have completed a credit report, but they have not yet obtained underwriting approval. A preliminary preapproval letter will say that you're preapproved subject to underwriting. It's not as good as an actual preapproval letter, but it is easier to get, particularly if you're short on time.

What If There's a Problem? If a problem arises while you're getting preapproved, you usually have time to do something about it. If you wait until you're in the midst of a deal, the delay could cause you to lose the very home you want most.

What sorts of problems can occur? A credit check might turn up unpaid bills, late payments, or even a bankruptcy. True, you should already be aware of these. But we're only human, and sometimes we forget—or choose to forget. Or there could be an error at the credit bureau. Perhaps they've mistaken you for someone else. Or they didn't receive word that a loan was paid off. Or a lender improperly states that you haven't paid when you have. In short, almost anything can go wrong, and until you check it out you won't know. This is why we recommend that you check your own credit in advance (see below for how to do it). Problems other than credit sometimes crop up. You might not have enough income to warrant a mortgage as big as you want. Or perhaps in order to get a mortgage, you'll need to put 20 percent down instead of 10 percent. In short, the problems that can—and often do—arise are endless, and you won't know about them until you actually apply for the mortgage, which is why sellers are so worried about buyers who don't have preapproval letters.

Where Do I Get Preapproved? Any legitimate lender can preapprove you (see above). And remember, it should cost you nothing except the $50 or so for the credit report.

While today relatively few mortgages originate on the Internet, you can get preapproved and find some of the best financing available, but you must choose your e-lender wisely. Some online lenders to check out as of this writing are

- http://www.lendingtree.com
- http://www.eloan.com
- http://www.chase.com
- http://www.homefair.com.

Most of the loan sites will calculate your monthly payment if you simply input the principal, interest rate, and term of your mortgage. They also provide "wizards" that will recommend the type of loan to get if you input critical financial information. The mortgage calculators are usually excellent. However, most of the wizards leave a lot to be desired.

Using the Internet for preapproval is convenient; you can send in whatever documentation is needed.

Locking in the Rate. A lock-in holds the interest rate you are quoted for a set period of time to allow you to obtain the mortgage, and are most common when interest rates are rising. You may be quoted 7 percent, for example, but are worried that during the month or so it takes to close the deal, the rates may rise to 7.5 percent or higher. You ask the lender to lock in your rate, which guarantees that within the lock-in timeframe, you'll get the rate you were originally quoted. You will pay a premium to lock in a rate, but it's a good idea if interest rates are likely to rise. To protect yourself, get the lock-in offer in writing.

▶ Drive at Your Own Risk: Overcoming Qualification Problems

Despite what fly-by-night credit fixers say, you need lots of good credit to obtain a good mortgage. That means you need to have borrowed and promptly repaid many loans, such as personal and auto loans and credit cards. You also need to have an excellent history of prompt payment of all your bills (electricity, gas, rent, and so on). Just a couple of late payments can mean you won't get a good "conforming" loan. Default on payments, a bankruptcy, or a foreclosure can preclude almost any financing.

If you have bad credit, you can't fix it overnight. Before a mortgage is funded, the lender checks with all three of the national credit bureaus (Trans Union, Equifax, and Experian). If there's a problem, it will show up.

Check the Radar: Your FICO Score and Your Mortgage

When you apply for a mortgage, your credit report is run. Lenders are interested in your FICO score, which is a credit-scoring system, developed by the Fair Isaac Corporation, used by many lenders to determine a borrower's ability to repay a mortgage.

Your score, which measures the degree of risk you represent to the lender, is based on the information listed in your credit report. It does not include your income, assets, or bank accounts. It doesn't use age, sex, race, color, religion, marital status, occupation, homeownership status, length of time at present address, or zip codes to calculate a score.

Fair Isaac Credit Bureau Score models are available through the three national credit reporting agencies, and all three are referred to as FICO scores, although Equifax uses Beacon, Trans Union uses Empirica, and only Experian uses the Fair Isaac Model.

The FICO system uses a scoring range of 300 to 850: the lower your score, the higher risk you are to the lender. Acceptable scores vary according to the type of credit you are trying to obtain. Scores fall into three categories:

1. *750 or above.* You are considered the cream of the crop.
2. *700 to 749.* Okay but room for improvement.
3. *620 to 699.* You are in a questionable category. This doesn't mean you won't be approved, but you will have to provide more documentation to the lender to satisfy its requirements and you'll pay a higher interest rate.

4. *Below 620.* You may get a loan, but you'll pay a *much* higher interest than someone with a higher score.

Keep in mind that a person who has a perfect credit report with no derogatory information can still receive a low FICO score by having too much debt. There can be different FICO scores from each of the agencies.

To understand why a credit report scored the way it did, listed next to the score are four codes and underneath the codes is an explanation. They represent the top four reasons, in order of severity, for the score.

It is important to know what your FICO score is; however, the only way to get your score out is by asking a credit grantor what the score is. You will not receive your score when you request your credit report from any of the three credit reporting agencies.

Improving a Low FICO Score. If your FICO score is too low to get the best interest rates offered, you can improve your score and reapply at a later date. Here are some ways to raise your FICO score:

1. Review your past payment history on your credit report. Bankruptcies, foreclosures, collection accounts, and delinquencies will cost you big points. Contact the credit bureaus about any incorrect or inaccurate entries on your report before you apply for credit. Your payment record carries the most weight on your score.

2. Scores are lower for consumers with no bank credit cards and those with five or more bank credit cards. A good balance would be two to four cards. If you decide to close any accounts, do not close your oldest account. The longer you have held an account, the better it is for your score.

3. Keep your balances well below your credit limit. The amount of debt you carry on all accounts is the second biggest factor in determining your score. If your total debt is more than 75 percent of the total credit limits, your score will suffer.

4. Avoid frequent inquiries. According to the score models, the risk of default appears to rise after two to four inquiries within six to 12 months. Inquiries are not picked up when consumers check their own credit report.

5. Don't open several new credit card accounts or take out loans over a short period, because this can hurt your score. If you have high balances

on those new cards, your score will be lowered. Have one or two lines of new credit established within the past two years maximum.

6. More recent negative entries on your credit report are worse than problems that occurred years ago. An account that has been delinquent in the past six months will hurt you more than a bankruptcy five years ago. Problems more than two years old have less impact on your score.

7. Avoid obtaining loans from finance companies; these also lower your credit score. Finance companies are lenders of last resort and they charge extremely high interest rates.

If you are having problems paying your bills, prioritize them to avoid damage to your credit report. Pay your mortgage first, then your car payment, followed by payments on your credit cards and other revolving accounts. Don't make partial payments unless the credit grantor agrees to it, and will not report the payments as late.

Once you have tried to raise your FICO score, wait four to six weeks before reapplying for your loan. It takes at least that long to have the creditors update your credit files. Have your loan officer run another credit report to

---

Hazard!

Make Sure Your Credit Reports Are Up to Date

When you apply for a mortgage, the mortgage company will run "a standard factual" report on you: This combines information from the three credit bureaus, and it's part of the qualification underwriters look for to approve a loan.

Frequently, errors are found in these reports. If negative entries surface, the mortgage company will either ask you for a letter of explanation or will contact the creditor who made the report to verify it. If it's incorrect, the creditor will submit a letter acknowledging their error.

This will help you get mortgage approval; however, most often, the credit bureaus have **not** been notified, and if it's not changed in their systems, that error can reappear on your credit report. Send a copy of the creditor's letter to the mortgage company, with a letter to each credit bureau, asking them to update their files.

Always check your credit reports before you apply for a mortgage so you can solve any problems **before** you make an application and risk being denied credit.

see the results. If the FICO score is still too low, continue looking for ways to improve it.

Don't allow several creditors to run inquiries on you unless you have first requested your credit report directly, and made sure there were no problems that needed to be corrected first.

Check Your Rearview Mirror: Bankruptcy and Your Mortgage

If you have filed for bankruptcy in the past, it's still possible to get a mortgage. However, you must wait at least two years since the bankruptcy before you can qualify. There are a few lenders who will give you a home loan prior to the two years, but you would have to go through a mortgage broker who has access to different lenders offering these programs. The lender will want to see two to three new open accounts with a good payment pattern since the bankruptcy or credit problems.

There is a question in the loan application for a mortgage that will ask you if you have ever filed for a bankruptcy. It is important that you inform the loan officer about your situation before you apply. A bankruptcy is a public notice, so if for some reason it is not on your credit report, it is filed at the county recorder's office, and it could easily be revealed. Have the lender prequalify you before you look for a home.

The lender wants to see that you have been able to reestablish good credit since your bankruptcy. Job stability, income, and your down payment will play an important role in your qualification.

▶ Choosing the Right Packager: Mortgage Brokers and Lenders

As mentioned, sometimes home financing is arranged through a third party called a mortgage broker. Some lending institutions do double duty and act as a broker. It's important to know whether a broker is involved in your transaction, because brokers charge a fee that may be in addition to fees charged by the lender. If a broker is involved, find out how this individual or company will be compensated.

Frequently, brokers' fees are in the form of points, a percentage of the loan principal, whereby one point usually equals 1 percent of the amount of the principal. Obviously, it's important to know the extent of your financial obligation, but it is equally prudent to know how those funds are distributed in the form of principal, interest, charges, fees, and possible penalties.

Few of us have the financial strength to purchase a home on our own. Fortunately, we have access to organizations that not only have money but are more than willing to lend it to worthy individuals and families.

Before You Book Your Trip: Shop Around

Most of us compare prices before we buy clothes, cars, computers—just about everything. It's only prudent to apply the same principle to acquiring a mortgage. Although what you'll find at one lending institution is pretty much the same as what you'll find at another, differences do exist. Almost every lender will offer you the same dollar-for-dollar deal. If market rates decline, so will the rates charged by the lenders. If rates move upward, so will lender rates. Still, a small percentage saved here or there can make an enormous difference in real dollars over time.

Also, by shopping around you'll meet a lot of different real estate lending professionals; and as in any business, some folks are better at their jobs than others. Different real estate lending professionals have different skills, levels of experience, willingness to go the extra mile, people skills, and other qualifications. It's important to find someone you like, trust, and believe has your best interests at heart. They're out there, lots of 'em. You just have to do a bit of looking and interviewing to find them, but why not seek out the best?

Another reason to shop around is that there are predatory lenders who will take advantage of inexperienced borrowers. It is unusual to find lenders who stray too far from the pack, but they do exist. Carefully investigate people and companies offering loans that appear too good to be true; there's a good chance they require more stringent conditions than do other lenders. The market for borrowing money is like any other market. To be competitive you have to work within normal limits for your economy and geographic area, and according to local market conditions. Some predatory lenders charge as much as twice the norm for their market. Shopping around can help you make necessary comparisons.

The cost of a mortgage to the borrower depends on the state of the economy. When there's a lot of competition, costs can be as little as zero; banks and lending institutions will absorb the costs (appraisals and other related fees, for example) that at other times are passed along to borrowers. The situation you face will be dictated by your local market at the time you apply.

Comparing Travel Offers: Qualifying the Lender and the Loan

There are thousands of mortgage lenders throughout the country. One of them is as close as your nearest bank or savings and loan association. Banks, savings and loans, credit unions, mortgage brokers, and mortgage bankers all offer mortgages. In addition, some insurance companies dabble in direct mortgage lending, offering mortgages through their real estate affiliates.

All kinds of lenders offer nearly all of the various types of mortgages that are available. However, interest rates, points (which we'll discuss later), and terms will vary from lender to lender. As a first-time borrower seeking to get the best mortgage, you will probably need to check with several lenders.

One way to check is to go from lender to lender and ask what their mortgage loan programs are. They will be happy to tell you and to give you an application. The best way to begin is to pay a visit to at least one major bank, preferably the one with whom you have a checking or savings account, to see if it will give you preferential treatment. Visiting many lending institutions can be exhausting and unnecessary. You can kill several birds with one stone by simply checking with a mortgage broker.

Guided Tour: Using a Mortgage Broker

A mortgage broker is often a real estate agent who is licensed by the state to deal in mortgages. The broker is typically a highly sophisticated agent who has specialized in mortgages for a long time and has contacts with a variety of lending institutions.

Wholesale vs. Retail Mortgage. If you think you, as a first-time buyer, have a problem locating an appropriate lender, put yourself in the lenders' shoes. They have a variety of mortgage packages that are suitable for different borrowers, including some suited exactly to first-time buyers, but how do they find you? In brief, by "wholesaling" their mortgages.

The mortgage brokers are the department stores. They handle mortgages for a variety of lenders, sometimes just for four or five, and sometimes for a hundred or more. When you borrow through a mortgage broker, you pay a retail price for your loan. The mortgage brokers have to make a profit to stay in business, so they in effect pay wholesale. Typically markups average around $1,500.

An active mortgage broker can offer you mortgages from the bank and the savings and loan (S&L) down the street as well as from banks and S&Ls across the country. In addition, insurance companies and other companies that wish to make mortgage loans can form their own "pools" and deal wholesale through the mortgage broker. Thus, the mortgage broker is your window to the world of real estate finance. They can offer you the widest possible options for financing.

Can You Buy Wholesale? Why can't you go directly to the bank and ask for the $1,500 or so that goes to the mortgage broker? You can't because the bank will not undercut the mortgage broker by lending wholesale to you. If the bank undercuts the mortgage broker, the broker would stop finding borrowers for the bank. The mortgage you will get from the bank will be exactly the same as the mortgage you would have gotten from the broker.

Problems Working with Mortgage Brokers. Unfortunately, not all mortgage brokers are created equal. Some will work diligently to get the right mortgage for you. Others, a small minority, charge extra fees (on top of what the lender pays them), don't always deliver (because the lender refuses to fund at closing), and equivocate on the interest rate and terms. This is a greater problem when interest rates are low and there are a great many borrowers. A hyperactive market leads to abuses: Fly-by-night operators will jump in and even a few established mortgage brokers will seek to take advantage of eager borrowers. However, as rates rise to more normal levels, most of the abuses die out and the worst elements leave the field.

Not every mortgage broker is going to treat you wonderfully. As a first-time borrower, you have to be on your guard. Ask several real estate agents for recommendations. Agents are very concerned that the mortgage broker performs well. Try calling on two or three different mortgage brokers. Interview them. See what they have to offer and what they say. Don't sign anything, and don't give them any money until you are comfortable.

Mortgage Broker vs. Mortgage Banker. Whereas a mortgage broker lends other institutions' money to you, a mortgage banker lends its own money. It's similar to a bank. Yet even that definition is not wholly accurate. A mortgage banker is like a wholesaler acting on the retail level. The mortgage banker usually has several million dollars with which to work, and it usually keeps very good track of what's happening in the secondary market (more about them in the next section). The mortgage banker puts together several of what it considers to be highly competitive mortgage plans and then tries to find borrowers like you. When you borrow from a mortgage banker, it will fund the loan with its own money, and will then take your loan, put it in a package with a dozen or a hundred other loans from other borrowers, and sell the package on the secondary market. (Actually, it gets a commitment in advance from a secondary lender, but that's more detail than is necessary for our purposes.) Because it's able to do this, it usually gets a higher return than a mortgage broker.

The benefit of dealing with a mortgage banker is that sometimes, but not always, they can offer you an interest rate and terms that are substantially better than you can get elsewhere. While you are hunting for a real estate loan, it is a good idea to call at least one mortgage banker. A word of caution: Some mortgage bankers themselves only deal on the wholesale level. That is, they only deal through mortgage brokers, just like banks. When you call, the first thing you should ask is if they offer direct mortgages to consumers. If they don't, try elsewhere.

▶ Negotiating with a Packager: What They Look for in a Borrower

Today lenders qualify borrowers on the basis of profiles. As we all now know, airport security officers use profiles to apprehend potential terrorists. Lenders do something similar: They use sophisticated programs and a huge database of existing mortgages to determine what a successful borrower looks like. If you fit the profile, you get the mortgage. If you don't, you'll have trouble getting one.

Not all lenders profile borrowers, but lenders of conforming loans do. A conforming loan is one that conforms to the underwriting policies of Freddie Mac and Fannie Mae, the two major secondary lenders, who lend money to your lender by "buying" your mortgage. Other direct and secondary lenders, such as insurance companies, also use profiles. But their profiles are sometimes different from the Freddie Mac/Fannie Mae standards.

Some portfolio lenders (typically a bank that makes the loan out of its own funds and then holds it, not selling it on the secondary market; more about them later) use their own methods (usually the old formulas) for making loans.

Are You a Good Traveler: Do You Fit the Profile?

What goes into a lender's profile? Actually, no one but the lenders really know. The profiles are considered top-secret financial information. Lenders worry that if the content of profiles becomes widely known, retailers will mold borrowers' applications to fit the profile. Lenders would then lose the benefits of profiling.

One thing is certain; to obtain a mortgage, you must be creditworthy. This is the reason for the credit report. However, a credit report by itself isn't all that helpful. It needs to be interpreted. For that lenders rely on several specialized organizations, the largest of which is FICO (Fair Isaac Corporation). FICO evaluates your credit report (usually a unified report from all three major credit reporting bureaus) and gives you a rating between 300 and 850. The lender relies heavily on that rating.

For example, a rating of 660 might get you a loan. A rating of 620 might not. You may be surprised at what makes up your rating. For example, if you apply for credit more than three times in six months, it could lower your rating. If you have a lot of maxed out credit card debt, your rating could be lowered, even if you've never missed a payment. On the other hand, if you have established credit cards with a lot of unused credit on them, it could help your rating.

Your track record is another big factor. How well have you managed money in the past? Late payments, defaults, and bankruptcy show poor money management and lower your rating. On the other hand, taking a course in money management at a local college might raise your rating.

Another consideration is income. Lenders don't like it if you spend more than a quarter to a third of your gross income on housing. As we mentioned, in the past lenders had formulas that were cast in stone and used income to determine how big a monthly mortgage payment a buyer could afford. With profiling, however, those formulas are now secondary. Depending on your creditworthiness, you might be able to get a mortgage that represents as much as half your gross income or as little as 20 percent.

Finally, there's the matter of how much can you put down. The more you put down, the more lenders like you. The idea is that the more money you have invested in your home, the less likely you are to let it go to foreclosure, no matter what the circumstances. Lenders just love a borrower who will fight to the death to keep making those mortgage payments.

▶ Negotiating with a Packager: What You Should Look for in a Lender

Remember, negotiating a mortgage is business. You're there because you need a mortgage. The lender is there because it needs to loan money. Neither of you is doing the other any favors. It's business. So even though you're a first-time mortgage borrower, don't go to the lender with your hat in your hand. Walk tall, sit straight, and negotiate as an equal. It's business.

The first person you deal with will probably be a salesperson, who may work with you throughout the lending process, but who may have limited room to maneuver if you ask to waive certain fees, for example. Therefore, it's usually to your advantage to talk directly to the mortgage broker or to a bank or S&L officer. If you ask to do this upfront, there usually isn't a problem, and in the long run you'll get better service.

What's the Deal? Questions to Ask

Consider your meetings with lenders as interviews. You're interviewing them to see what they have to offer you.

> *Be sure to ask for an interest rate quote that is based on a fixed-rate, 30-year, conforming loan with zero points.*

Interest Rate. The interest rate is going to be of greatest importance. That will determine how high your monthly payments are going to be. Be careful that you understand the answer. The standard for quoting interest rates is for a fixed-rate, 30-year, conforming loan with zero points. Be sure that's the quote you get, so you can use it for comparison purposes.

Sometimes lenders will give a low interest rate based on high points; this is a detour; don't take it. If the lender begins quoting rates on adjustable mortgages, then you'll have a much more difficult time in comparison shopping. Each lender's adjustables are going to be slightly different.

When comparison shopping, start with a 30-year fixed rate, but also get quotes on ARMs so you can compare apples to apples. Remember, each lender's adjustable rates are going to be slightly different. To assess an ARM, you'll need to know the current rate plus the index margin, annual cap, and fixed lifetime cap. A lender with the best fixed rate will not necessarily offer the most attractive arm and vice versa.

You want to be sure you're getting an interest rate that has a fair market value. To get a good idea of what interest rates really are at the time you're looking for a mortgage, there are at least three independent sources you can check:

1. http://www.bankrate.com. This is my favorite national source.
2. Your local paper. Many large city newspapers list the current mortgage interest rates charged by the largest lenders in the area. Typically, this will appear in the Sunday real estate section of the paper.
3. Real estate agents. Many large real estate offices keep a list of interest rates charged by various lenders and make it available to clients. Sometimes this list is published by local escrow or title insurance companies. Find out who has the list and get a current copy

Annual Percentage Rate (APR). You should be aware that the APR is going to be different than the rate quoted by the lender. The APR required by truth-in-lending laws demands that the lender include many costs. That means that the points and other costs are added in when determining the rate. The interest rate usually quoted on mortgages, however, is just the interest rate itself; the additional monies that you pay are not figured in.

Both figures are useful. Remember, the APR tells you the true rate you will pay, based on most costs. The quoted rate usually tells you the interest rate that will be used to determine your monthly payments. The APR can be useful when you are comparing different types of mortgages, but you should use the quoted rate when you want to know what your monthly payments will be.

Points. You'll also want to ask how many points the lender charges. As with everything else, there are good points and bad points. Bad points are the ones you pay; good points are the ones someone else pays.

Points are the fees charged by lending institutions as extra upfront, one-time lump-sum interest when a new loan is placed. Each point is 1 percent of a new loan. If you buy a house for $150,000 and borrow $120,000, one point would equal $1,200 (not $1,500). Two points would be $2,400. The term is sometimes used interchangeably with percent, as in "You'll have a two-point cap," which means that you'd have a 2 percent cap. Points are usually paid at final settlement when the loan is actually made. Most first-time home buyers do not pay points; they pay a higher interest rate.

Zero point loans, however, are not uncommon, with the points financed into the loan, giving you a slightly higher debt. Don't assume in this case that points magically disappear, unless they are paid by another party entirely. Arranging for a zero point loan is not a bad option if you are short on closing funds, and don't mind the higher monthly payment.

Often the points charged will be based on a sliding scale depending on the interest rate. If you are willing to accept a slightly higher interest rate, you should get lower points. If you pay more points, you should get a lower interest rate. For example, if you're quoted 7.5 percent at two and a half points, you might also be able to get 7.25 percent at four and a half points or 7.75 percent at half a point. (The change in the interest rate can vary between .125 and .25 for each point.)

Sometimes you can pay extra points in return for special favors; for example, a lock-in that guarantees that you'll receive the rate in effect when you apply for the loan, no matter what has happened to rates in the meantime. Or you may be charged extra for an extension if you don't close within a given period after the bank commits to making the loan.

Points may be paid by the buyer or seller, depending on their agreement. Points paid by you as the buyer of your own residence are income tax deductible as interest, in the year they are paid. Points you pay to purchase rental property must be amortized (deducted bit by bit over the years) along with other costs of placing an investor's loan.

Points paid by the seller are one of the expenses of selling, and reduce the seller's capital gain on the sale. The buyer, however, is allowed to take points paid (even those paid by the seller) as an income tax deduction for interest expense for that year.

Terms. You will also want to know what the terms of the mortgage are. Is there a balloon payment? (In other words, when the remainder of the loan falls due on a certain date, will the final payment be larger than all the others?) If it's an adjustable-rate mortgage, what are the "steps," the "margin," the "index," and other features? In short, you want to obtain all of the data about the mortgage so that you can determine if it's the right mortgage for you.

Fees. Lenders always charge fees. Normally, you will not be presented with a list of these until you formally apply for a mortgage, so it's a good idea to ask

Tollbooth 3.1

What Will It Cost?

Normal Fees

▶ Credit report fee: usually under $50
▶ Appraisal fee (for the property): usually $300 to $400
▶ Points
▶ Tax and insurance impound fee: usually under $100
▶ Lender's title insurance policy: amount depends on the value of the property
▶ Lender's escrow fee: the amount depends on the individual deal
▶ Interest and tax proration

Additional Fees

▶ Tax and insurance impound fee: required on all mortgages for which there is less than 20 percent down; optional for others.

Miscellaneous Fees

▶ Document fees: from $50 to $300
▶ Underwriter's fee: usually around $300
▶ Loan application fee
▶ Loan origination fee: up to one point
▶ Loan processing fee: from $75 to $350
▶ Commitment fee, lock-in fee, loan evaluation fee, etc.

about them upfront. That way, if they seem unwarranted, you won't waste a lot of time and can quickly go elsewhere.

When you're offered a loan at a particularly favorable rate, inquire about closing costs. Certain costs are standard: appraisal of the property, credit check, and other legitimate charges. Most lenders charge an origination fee, which covers their cost of doing business; paying it upfront or seeing it absorbed into the interest rate is the trade-off you'll usually face. Any other fees should be questioned and compared with other lenders.

Private Mortgage Insurance (PMI). PMI allows people to purchase a home with a smaller-than-usual down payment by providing your lender security for its funds when you have little or no equity in the purchased property. In return, the borrower pays a premium (included in the monthly mortgage). Therefore, although your down payment is lower, your monthly payments may be higher (about $70 on a $100,000 loan) because of the added cost of the insurance. In essence, you pay the lender to carry an insurance policy on your mortgage loan in the event you default. Note: While mortgage interest is tax deductible, PMI is not.

As with most things, there's an upside and a downside. The down is the additional cost of the insurance, which is not too bad when you consider the up, which is that PMI allows those who don't have a down payment a way to purchase a home. It allows many people, especially young families, to own their own home earlier than possible before PMI.

Even though PMI is a great advantage in helping you get into a new home, it's an advantage you should work to get out of as soon as possible! There's no reason to pay for something you no longer need when you could put that money in checking and savings accounts, investments, college or vacation funds, or toward a bigger and better home. As you build equity, you will reach a point where you no longer need the insurance; many people reach this point after only a few years, at which time you should investigate the possibility of dropping your PMI. Contact your lenders for more information if you feel you are approaching 20 percent or more in equity.

Rack Rate or Discount: Negotiating Fees

Should you negotiate fees? Yes, absolutely! Challenge any fees you're not sure of. Ask if they're normal and standard. Then ask another lender in the area the same question. By interviewing three lenders you can quickly determine which fees are excessive. After you've gathered your information, contact the original lender and ask whether they are willing to drop the excessive fees if you take the mortgage. Explain that other lenders aren't charging them. You may be surprised at how much lenders will bend to get your business, especially in a tight market.

When rates are fluctuating rapidly, some borrowers have been known to apply at two different lenders: one with the rate locked in, and one without. For whichever loan isn't eventually chosen, the wheeler-dealer will owe some upfront money for appraisal or credit report fees. Lenders are less than pleased at the prospect, but it could give you a chance to choose the more favorable loan at the last minute. This can be an expensive and time consuming proposition and is not recommended.

"Good Faith Estimate." Under RESPA (Real Estate Settlement Procedures Act), the lender is required to give you a "good faith estimate" of your costs within three days from the time you make a loan application. You can ask

Hazard!

Lock Ins and New Construction

On new construction, builders usually will not permit their own in-house or preferred lenders to lock in an interest rate until they have received a firm completion date for the new house, so that you are not left with expired rate locks if construction is delayed. This is usually within 30 days of completion.

If you are using your own lender to buy a builder's home, be extremely careful that you don't lock your rate too soon, or you may be out of luck if there is a delay in the home's completion (unless, of course, interest rates fall while you're waiting).

for it when comparison shopping. (You'll probably be given the form at the time you bring in your completed application.)

Usually all the items you've previously discussed with the lender will be on this form along with an estimate of their costs. If the lender agreed to waive a particular charge and it still appears here, challenge it. Also keep in mind that the costs listed are estimates. They may go up (but will rarely go down) by the time the loan is funded and the deal closes.

▶ Choosing the Tour: Selecting the Right Mortgage

There is an alphabet soup of mortgages out there. According to an estimate from a large mortgage banker, at one time in the late 1990s, there were close to 700 different mortgage variations available nationwide! There are far fewer variations today, although the number is still in the hundreds. Still, dozens of terms describe particular mortgages: FHA, VA, assumable, portfolio, conventional, convertible, and adjustable-rate mortgages (ARMs), just to name a few.

Granted, most of these fall within a few broad categories, but as a first-time buyer, you're up against a daunting task in learning which mortgage is the best for you. Indeed, with so many different mortgage opportunities, you might let the best slip by because you are simply unaware that it exists. Choosing the right loan involves taking into consideration the following:

- ▶ Proposed down payment
- ▶ Your income and future prospects
- ▶ Current interest rates
- ▶ Type and condition of the property
- ▶ Costs and fees
- ▶ Price range of homes you want to consider
- ▶ Your personal debt portfolio
- ▶ Your credit scores
- ▶ How long you plan to stay in your home

In looking for the right mortgage plan, it helps to understand the difference between portfolio loans and those intended for sale on the secondary market.

Group Travel: The Secondary Market

Most mortgages are bundled into large packages and sold to big investors in what is known as the secondary market. Among the buyers are large insurance companies, banks and pension funds, and, most important, organizations specifically set up to warehouse mortgages, like the Federal National Mortgage Association (Fannie Mae). Borrowers may not know that their mortgages have been sold if the original lender retains the servicing —collecting payments, handling paperwork, and forwarding the money. In other cases, particularly when the buyer of the packaged mortgages is another bank, borrowers may be instructed to send their payments directly to the new mortgagee.

Lenders are required to notify you, before commitment, how likely your loan is to be sold on the secondary market. When Fannie Mae, which owns perhaps one out of every 20 mortgages in this country, announces that it will buy packages of certain types of loans, lenders around the country quickly bring their loan programs into compliance. Other national standards are set by the Government National Mortgage Association (Ginnie Mae) and the Federal Home Loan Mortgage Corporation (Freddie Mac).

All of this can affect your search for the perfect mortgage. When you find that most lenders have identical upper limits (this amount changes frequently) on the amount they'll lend, or analyze your income in the same way, they are probably conforming to the requirements of the secondary market in order to sell your loan. Whether the lender actually disposes of a particular mortgage in the secondary market is not really relevant. What's relevant is that the mortgage qualifies to be sold to the secondary market.

Special Tours: Portfolio Loans

Portfolio loans are sometimes called nonconforming (because they are not tailored to the requirements of the secondary market), or jumbo loans if they are for larger amounts than the secondary market will buy. The bank that uses such a system keeps the mortgages as assets in its own portfolio.

If you have an unusual situation (complicated self-employment income, for example, or the desire to pay your own property taxes and insurance instead of through the lender's escrow account), find out which local lenders are currently making portfolio loans. On these loans, underwriters can be more flexible, making exceptions to their usual rules, subject only to state laws and their own judgment.

Jumbo Mortgages. Jumbo mortgages are very big mortgages that are frequently found in high-cost areas, but any mortgage above the secondary market limit is considered a jumbo. It's made by an individual lender (usually a bank or S&L), and can be for any amount. These mortgages carry slightly higher interest rates (depending on the qualifications of the buyer), and for that reason, lenders love them.

If you need a jumbo mortgage, check with a bank or S&L in your area. Some mortgage brokers handle them, too. Loan programs vary enormously and sometimes can be set up to specifically meet your needs. These are really custom loans tailored for specific needs and properties.

How Long Will this Trip Take?
15, 20, or 30-Year Mortgages

The 30-year mortgage loans are still the most popular, even though borrowers often choose 20-year and even 25-year mortgages. Monthly payments on a 15-year loan can run about 20 percent higher than on the same loan figured on a 30-year basis. You would need about 20 percent more income to qualify for the shorter loan. On the other hand, you'd make payments only half as long and cut your total interest cost considerably.

The 15-year mortgage operates like enforced savings, because it requires you to pay off the debt faster. It may be appropriate if, for example, your children will be starting college in 15 years. At that time you'd like to have your house free and clear. It does tie up your money, however. If you have the discipline, there's nothing to stop you from putting that extra money, each month, into your own investment plan, where you can tap it as needed and where it will possibly earn higher returns.

Talk to your loan consultant about how to make a 30-year fixed-rate loan give you the same (and even better) benefits as a 15-year loan by making extra principal payments, or by tacking a certain amount onto your monthly payment. By opting for the 30-year loan, you won't be forced into the larger monthly payment, and you'll have the flexibility of paying down your principal and interest on your own terms.

All-Inclusive vs. Self Directed Plan: Fixed vs. Adjustable Rate Mortgages

Although a number of mortgages are on the market, it is most likely that you will be involved with only one of the two: a fixed rate mortgage or an adjustable rate mortgage.

Which is better, an 8 percent, fixed-rate loan for 30 years with payment of one point plus a half-percent origination fee, or an adjustable rate mortgage for 20 years, currently at 5 percent, with four points upfront? First, of course, you must decide whether you have a gambler's instinct and want to take a chance on next year's payment being higher or lower. If rates are currently at the lower end of their inevitable cycle, you might prefer a fixed-rate loan, especially if you're planning to stay in your new home for 5 years or more.

But trying to compare rates on such different loan programs, with varying closing costs, is like comparing apples to oranges. To aid the consumer, lenders are required to quote you an APR, which takes into account points and certain closing costs. Not all lenders calculate it in the same fashion, but it is useful for comparison shopping.

Some borrowers fear rates skyrocketing at a moment's notice, forcing them into a financial panic as they try to come up with the extra cash to make the end-of-the-month house payment. But it doesn't happen that way. Rules and regulations are in place governing how high and in what timeframes rates can climb, and by keeping an interest rate low, a borrower can pay down more principal at a time when cash is more readily available.

Still, most people prefer the peace of mind found in a fixed rate mortgage, but peace of mind has a price tag, one that can be determined only by an individual borrower. Most fixed rate mortgages are payable on a 15- or 30-year amortization (payback) scale. A 15-year mortgage has a lower interest rate, but your reduced monthly discretionary income is balanced by the fact that you'll be paying that money for fewer months—half as many to be precise.

Fixed Rate Mortgages. A fixed rate mortgage is just that: The rate of interest you pay is fixed at the origination of the loan and remains at that figure until the loan is paid off. Regardless of the ups and downs of the economy, the rate remains the same, fixed in place. If interest rates go up, the borrower is protected. Of course, it's too bad if rates drop because the fixed rate can't follow that market trend. (But, if it goes down sufficiently—usually 1 to 2 percent is considered enough—it might pay to refinance.)

The traditional 30-year fixed-rate mortgage is still the industry standard because it offers long-term predictability. Your total payments are spread over so many years that your monthly payments are lower than they would be on a shorter term loan.

In the long run, however, you will pay thousands of dollars more in interest on a 30-year loan than on a less extended obligation. This interest is usually tax deductible, though, which lowers your actual after-tax cost of paying it. Lately, 15-year loans have become popular. They usually offer slightly lower interest rates than 30-year loans, but you must make substantially larger monthly payments. If you want to prepay your mortgage on such a faster schedule, contact your lender to arrange a prepayment schedule, and make sure that you will not be assessed any prepayment penalties. In the early years of either a 30-year or a 15-year fixed-rate loan, you mostly pay interest. By the end of the loan, you pay almost all principal. Therefore, over time, ownership in your home gradually shifts from the lender to you.

Growing Equity Mortgage (GEM). A growing equity mortgage, often known as a rapid payoff loan, offers a fixed rate and a changing monthly payment. Formally, the loan is for 30 years but, in fact, may be paid off in 15 years or less because your payments reduce the outstanding principal quickly. Your payment amount is usually tied to some index, such as the Commerce Department's per capita income index. In this case, as income rises, your payments increase.

You can also create your own GEM by sending in extra principal payments or by paying your mortgage biweekly instead of monthly, but check to make sure there are no penalties for early payment. All of these methods of payment will help you build equity faster and pay off your mortgage sooner.

You don't need to pay anyone to set up a biweekly mortgage plan. You can do this yourself. Contact your lender for instructions.

Interest-Only Loans. One of the more recent entries into the home mortgage field and a possibility for a first-time homebuyer is the interest-only loan. This is a fixed-rate mortgage. As its name implies, instead of paying back interest plus principal each month, you pay back only interest. However, because of the mathematics of amortization of loans, this is only a small monthly savings, generally less than 5 percent of the monthly payment. (Most of the interest is paid at the beginning of a mortgage, most of the principal repaid at the end.)

If you're not planning to keep the property long and want a slightly lower fixed-interest-rate mortgage, this is an option you might consider.

Adjustable rate mortgages. Instead of offering an interest rate fixed for the life of the loan, an adjustable-rate mortgage (ARM) features an interest rate that moves up and down with prevailing rates. Early in the ARM's term, its rate will almost always be significantly less than that on a fixed-rate loan. Because the borrower agrees to risk fluctuating rates over the life of the loan, they are rewarded with a low initial rate.

ARMs come in many varieties. Some adjust their rates every year, while others alter them after three or five years, on an annual basis. Loan rates are tied to a number of interest rate indexes. A bank will charge a margin, or spread, over the underlying index of up to two or four percentage points. You can learn these rates from most lenders, from publications like *The Wall Street Journal* or from Web sites such as http://www.bankrate.com.

In general, the more short term the index that your ARM is tied to, the more volatile your payments will be. That's good if interest rates fall, but can cause trouble if interest rates rise. Rates on T-bills and one-year Treasuries and the prime rate will fluctuate much faster than the cost of funds rate or the national average mortgage rate. If you hesitate to take the risk of short-term rates, consider an ARM tied to the more slowly moving indexes.

Most ARMs offer two built-in caps to protect you from enormous increases in monthly payments. A periodic rate cap limits how much your payment can rise at any one time. For example, your loan agreement might stipulate that your rate cannot go up more than two percentage points a year. An aggregate, or a lifetime, cap limits how much the rate can rise over the life of the loan. The same loan that limits increases to 2 percent a year may also impose a 6 percent cap for the duration of the loan. Such caps can also apply to rate decreases.

In addition to rate caps, many ARMs feature payment caps, which limit the amount your payment can rise over the life of the loan. Therefore, if the underlying index shoots up, your payment would increase only to the limit of the payment cap. Even though you do not pay the difference now, you owe it to the lender over the long term. When your mortgage payment does not cover the full interest and principal due, this is called negative amortization. The lender will apply more, and possibly all, of your payment to interest, which means that your home equity will grow more slowly or, in the extreme case, will actually shrink.

Automatic rate cut (ARC): A variation on the adjustable-rate mortgage is called the ARC loan. The rate starts off a bit higher than current mortgage rates, but every time mortgage rates fall by a quarter point or more, the rate automatically adjusts downward with no closing costs, points, or fees for the borrower. These adjustments can occur as frequently as every 90 days. The best part is that the rate never rises after it has fallen. It's a one-way street in your favor! For more information about ARC loans, call 888-ARCLOAN or log on to http://www.arcloan.com.

Convertible: A convertible mortgage is an ARM that can be changed to a fixed-rate mortgage at a specified rate. You may have one chance or several to make the switch. The conversion feature gives you the opportunity to start with a low adjustable rate, then lock into a low fixed rate for a long time.

Advantages of ARMs: An adjustable-rate mortgage can cut your mortgage payment by a third or more, at least in the early days of the mortgage. This has two important ramifications, especially for first-time buyers. First, with a lower monthly payment, you may be able to buy a house in a neighborhood that you would not otherwise qualify for. Second, because you're making a lower monthly payment, it will be easier for you to maintain a higher-quality lifestyle.

An ARM is particularly useful if you're planning on living in the home for only a short period of time—say three years or less. During that time you could save a considerable amount on monthly payments compared to a fixed-rate mortgage.

The ARM is also useful during periods of temporarily high interest rates because it allows you to buy a property at a lower than-market rate when market rates are high. When rates have fallen, you can refinance to a lower-rate fixed mortgage if you plan on staying in your home for several more years.

Disadvantages of ARMs. On the other hand, ARMs have some very significant drawbacks. The most important of these is that the low monthly payment could last a relatively short time—months or, at the outside, a few years. After that, the monthly payment could rise very quickly to a point at which it's actually higher than if you had opted for a fixed-rate mortgage initially. But remember, you were hundreds of dollars ahead each month during the initial period of the loan, so it could take a few years of these higher interest rates to make taking out the ARM a bad idea.

The key part of this arrangement is that when you first get the mortgage there is a very low teaser rate. This rate, which is designed to get you interested in and hooked onto the mortgage, may be two-thirds of the market rate! That means that the interest payments for the ARM, at least initially, are going to be two-thirds the interest payments on a fixed rate mortgage. That's a lot of incentive.

How high the interest rate can go is determined in part by the index used and the margin. Common indexes include T-bill rates, federal funds rates, and even LIBOR (London Interbranch Bank Borrowing) rates. Be sure the lender shows you a 20-year history of each index. Depending on your need, you might want to select one that has been stable or one that has been volatile.

Caps. Many ARMs offer caps on the interest rate. This means that the interest rate cannot rise beyond a certain maximum. The cap is typically 4 to 6 percent above the current market interest rate, so there's relatively little chance the mortgage will get that high (unless there's suddenly runaway inflation in the country). The cap is a "feel good" sort of thing, but it's rarely going to be helpful.

Other mortgages offer caps on the monthly payment. They guarantee that the monthly payment will not rise beyond a certain point. Again, this is designed to make you feel good about taking the mortgage. The problem is that if the interest rate rises to the point where the monthly payment should be higher than the cap, the difference that you're not paying is usually added onto your principal. Because the difference is added to the mortgage amount, you pay interest on that interest in the future! This is called negative amortization and should be avoided by first-time buyers. It is a perfect definition of an "ugly" mortgage.

ARMs are complex mortgages, and of necessity the description here is brief. ARMs can be a real boon to first-time buyers, and you should seriously consider them. But you should also take into account their drawbacks.

Budget Travel: Low Down Payment Mortgages

Because coming up with cash is usually the hardest part of most real estate purchases, let's consider those mortgages that allow you to put up a minimal down payment. (Note that some low monthly payment mortgages can be combined with low down payment mortgages. For example, you can combine an adjustable rate mortgage with a PMI mortgage.)

Veterans can place VA loans with nothing down and do it on houses valued up to $203,000, if they qualify to carry the payments. If the seller agrees, a VA loan could even be placed with the seller paying all the buyer's closing costs. For those with limited income who want to live in rural areas, the Farmers Home Administration (FmHA) makes no-down-payment loans on modest properties, discussed later in this section. Monthly payments with FmHA can be subsidized, depending on family income, with as low as 1 percent interest.

Then—particularly with rental property, where the owner doesn't need to get the money out right away—you can always look for a seller who will turn the property over to you and carry the mortgage—and if you look really hard, perhaps do it with nothing down.

FHA Mortgages. The Federal Housing Administration (FHA), an agency of the Department of Housing and Urban Development (HUD), was established to help homeowners buy with low down payments. Lenders can safely make loans of up to 97 percent of the value of property, because the FHA insures them against loss in case of foreclosure. If FHA loans are used in your area, they can be a fine way to go. The money comes not from the government but from local lenders, so if no one in your locality is handling FHA mortgages, you're out of luck. Although maximum FHA loan amounts vary depending on the area, they range between $172,000 and $313,000 for a single-family house.

VA loans are given to members of the armed forces, veterans, and widows of veterans. The loans are not intended for expensive property, but upper limits in high-price areas are raised from time to time.

For inexpensive property, down payments can be lower than 3 percent; in any case, it runs less than 5 percent. FHA loans may be placed on single-family to four-family dwellings and are intended for owner-occupants.

Insurance premiums (to protect the lender in case of default) are due in a lump sum at closing and can run up to 1.5 percent of the loan. Because most FHA buyers don't have extra cash at closing, the mortgage insurance premium (MIP) can be added to the amount of the mortgage loan. If you pay off your FHA mortgage within the first few years, a portion of your MIP is returned. In addition to the one-time MIP, borrowers pay one-half percent of the outstanding balance each year. The number of years this extra premium is charged depends on the size of the down payment; minimum-down loans require the extra charge over the longest period.

When a first-time buyer agrees to go through mortgage counseling, some special FHA programs discount the original MIP. The FHA bases its loans on the value found by authorized FHA appraisers and sometimes requires certain repairs (items concerned with the preservation of the property and with health and safety) before the loan will be granted. In addition to the standard FHA program, #203-b, others are available in certain areas. FHA 203-k, for example, lends money to cover both the cost of a home needing rehabilitation and the money needed for repairs.

One of the additional benefits of an FHA mortgage is that it is partially assumable, meaning you can take over, or "assume," the seller's existing loan. The new buyer must qualify for the mortgage in order to assume it. (In the old days, anyone could simply take over an FHA loan without any qualifications.)

FHA loans are available from banks, savings and loans (S&Ls), and mortgage brokers. Just ask about them and almost anyone in the lending field can explain how they operate and if they are a viable option for you.

VA Is for Veterans. The most attractive benefit of VA loans is the possibility of no down payment. Beyond that, the loans are assumable, with some restrictions.

As with FHA mortgages, the money comes from a local lender; the Department of Veterans Affairs (VA) contribution is to guarantee the loan at no cost to the veteran. While FHA loans require some down payment, VA loans may be made for the entire appraised value of the property (100 percent LTV [loan-to-value ratio])—nothing down (unless the house costs more than the maximum mortgage amount). Additionally, the buyer can not pay any points for the mortgage; the seller has to pay them. This is another boon for you, although it's often difficult to find a seller who is willing to pay your points. The buyer must pay only some nominal closing costs.

To qualify, the veteran must have a discharge "other than dishonorable" and one of the following:

▶ 180 days active (not reserve) duty between September 16, 1940 and September 7, 1980

▶ 90 days service during a war (the Korean, Vietnam and Persian Gulf conflicts are considered wars)

▶ Six years service in the National Guard, and

▶ For those enlisting for the first time after September 7, 1980, two years service is required. In-service VA mortgages are also possible.

Dates change occasionally, so check with the VA, who will also provide a certificate of eligibility.

VA loans may be used for single-family to four-family houses, owner-occupied only. Eligibility for such mortgages does not expire. If one's first VA loan is paid off and the property sold, full eligibility is regained. At closing, a funding fee is paid directly to the VA.

There are, however, a couple of drawbacks. First, the VA guarantees just a small percentage of the mortgage (usually the top 10 percent or so of the loan, the first monies the lender is likely to lose) and only up to a maximum amount. (This maximum changes frequently—check with the VA for the current amount.) This means that, as with an FHA loan, you may not find a VA loan helpful in a more expensive area of the country.

Second, the buyer is held personally responsible for the payment of the mortgage. If the buyers default and lose the house to foreclosure, they are responsible to the VA for all the money it pays out as part of its guarantee to the lender.

Third, although these loans are fully assumable to anyone, you are not necessarily relieved of your liability to the VA when you sell on an assumption! If the subsequent buyer defaults, you are still liable for any losses the VA suffers. To avoid this future liability, you must either pay off the mortgage when you sell or get a "release of liability" from the VA. The VA, however, normally won't give this unless the next buyer is also a veteran and assumes liability for the mortgage.

VA loans are available from most lenders, such as banks and S&Ls. However, there is a fair amount of paperwork involved, so some lenders prefer not to issue them. Also, the fact that the buyer can't pay any points, a down payment, or many fees makes VA loans unattractive to many lenders.

Farmers Home Administration (FmHA). In rural areas, direct mortgage loans can sometimes be obtained from the Farmers Home Administration (FmHA, Department of Agriculture). If your income falls within specific limits (fairly low, depending on family size), you can buy a modest home on no more than one acre, with interest payments tailored to your income.

The program is intended for those who cannot obtain financing elsewhere. The money is allotted to local offices quarterly. At any given time, some offices will have money available; others will have waiting lists. The FmHA processes mortgage applications before you've found a house; it then notifies you as money becomes available.

Assumable Mortgages. An assumable mortgage is one that can remain with the property when it is sold. This results in considerable savings for the next buyer; no outlay for the costs associated with placing a new mortgage—items like appraisal of the property, mortgage tax, etc. A high assumable mortgage, or one at a low interest rate, is therefore worth a premium, and contributes extra value to property on the market.

FHA loans made before December 1, 1986, and VA loans made before March 1, 1988, are completely—freely—assumable. This means that you, or anyone the seller chooses, can take the loan along with the real estate, just as it stands. Neither you nor the house need pass any evaluation by the lending institution, which has no say in the matter. Closing costs are negligible, interest rates will not change, and the transaction can be closed and settled as soon as the parties wish.

In areas where prices have risen, of course, these older loans represent only part of the value of the property. You must pay the seller the rest of the purchase price in cash, unless you can persuade the owner to take back financing. The seller who does that agrees to hold a second mortgage for part of the purchase price, or even—in rare instances—for the entire missing amount (nothing down!).

You'd have to look pretty good financially before a seller would enter into such an arrangement, because even though you take over the payments on the loan and ownership of the property, the seller retains liability for that

FHA or VA debt if anything goes wrong. You can arrange to relieve the seller of future responsibility, however, if you are willing and able to prove to the lender's satisfaction that you are financially qualified to carry the mortgage payments on your own.

Newer FHA and VA loans are classified as "assumable with bank approval." To take over the newer FHA mortgages, the next borrower must be qualified (income and credit) to the lending institution's satisfaction. Once that's done, if payments are made promptly, the original borrower retains liability for only five years. With new VA mortgages, the person assuming the loan (who need not be a veteran) must always qualify with the lender before an assumption. A charge of no more than $500 may be made for the paperwork.

> The advantages of an assumable mortgage may include:
> no points, no change in interest rate, and low closing costs.

Besides FHA and VA loans, many adjustable-rate mortgages also have assumability features, which allow for considerable savings on closing costs. ARMs differ; most stipulate that the new borrower must qualify with the lender and that the interest rate may be adjusted upon assumption. Some charge is made for the privilege; one point might be typical.

Conforming Loans. Conforming loans conform to the underwriting standards of Fannie Mae and Freddie Mac, the "secondary lenders" that lend to the institution that lends to you. Both Fannie Mae and Freddie Mac have a wide variety of low down payment mortgages. Indeed, Fannie Mae has experimented with no down payment mortgages! Ask a mortgage broker for information on their various programs. You may also want to check out their Web sites, which are loaded with information on their various programs:

▶ http://www.fanniemae.com
▶ http://www.freddiemac.com

Land Contracts and Lease-Options. A land contract is a type of layaway installment plan for buying a house. Typically, it is sought by a buyer who does not have enough down payment to qualify for a bank loan or to persuade the seller to turn over title (ownership). You move in, make monthly payments to the seller and take care of taxes, insurance, and repairs exactly as if you owned it. Title does not transfer to you until a specified time, perhaps when you make the final payment. With some land contracts, you receive the title when you have made enough payments to constitute 20 percent equity.

A lease-option differs from a land contract in that you are not bound to buy the property. Instead, you move in as a tenant and typically pay a flat amount in return for an option—the right to purchase at a given price within a given time (one year, two years)—if you so choose. If you choose not to buy, you simply remain as a tenant for the duration of the lease. Who pays for what expenses, and whether any of your rent goes toward the purchase price, are negotiable items.

Any land contract or lease-option requires extra-careful consultation with your attorney since such contracts can vary widely. Either type of contract should be recorded—entered in the public records to notify the world at large of your rights in the property.

You will find many sellers willing to sell this way when the real estate market is down. They can't sell for a cash deal, so they take the next best thing. In a healthy market, however, you are not likely to find many legitimate sellers offering lease-options.

Budget Travel: Low Monthly Payment Mortgages

Shared Appreciation Mortgage (SAM). If you are willing to surrender to your lender some of your home's appreciation potential, you may want to opt for a shared appreciation mortgage. With this loan, you pay a below-market interest rate on your mortgage and, in return, offer the lender between 30 percent and 50 percent of the increased value of your home when you sell it in a specified number of years. If that day comes and you do not want to sell, you must pay the lender its share of the property's appreciation. If you don't have the cash to do so, you might have to sell the property anyway. On the other hand, if the property has not appreciated or has, in fact, decreased in value, you will owe nothing.

Graduated Payment Mortgage (GPM). A graduated payment mortgage is designed specifically for the first-time homebuyer. It has a low initial interest rate with steps at designated periods of time (usually every year or so) that raise the interest rate and monthly payments by predetermined amounts.

Eventually, the interest rate ends up higher than the market rate when you made your purchase. The idea is that as you get older and, presumably, your income grows, so too will the mortgage payment. You will have low payments when you first start out, and then, as you are more able to pay, you'll pay more.

Unlike an ARM, where the mortgage adjusts according to an index and it is impossible to know what the future payments will be, this is a fixed-interest-rate mortgage with a rate that changes at predetermined times and in predetermined amounts. The problem, of course, is that the payment schedule is inflexible, and if your career nosedives, you might not be able to make that ever-higher monthly payment. GPMs are often combined with FHA mortgages. Ask your lender for more information about them in your area.

Short-Term Mortgages. The short-term mortgage is recommended to first-time buyers. It combines the best of the adjustable rate mortgage with the best of the fixed rate mortgage because the mortgage has two different time periods: an initial loan period and a secondary loan period. Although the terms can vary greatly, generally during the initial time period you have a lower-than-market, fixed-rate mortgage. During the secondary time period, you have a rather ugly adjustable-rate mortgage. That's when you refinance or sell. (If you're like most people, you'll probably plan to sell before then, so you get the benefits without the drawbacks like the high adjustable interest rate.)

Short-term mortgages are available in a variety of terms, the most common being three, five, seven, and 10 years, all amortized over a 30-year period. The shorter the initial fixed interest-rate period, the lower the initial interest rate. The advantage is that you know in advance what your monthly payment will be for a fixed period of time.

Balloon. A balloon mortgage requires a series of equal payments, then a large payment (balloon) at the loan's termination. The mortgage term may be from three to 10 years. A balloon-payment mortgage will sometimes earn a first-time buyer a lower interest rate and, therefore, a lower monthly payment. Usually, balloon mortgages are offered at fixed rates, though some adjustable-rate balloons are also available. The payments on a balloon mortgage generally cover interest only, so you do not build equity in the home over time.

If you take on such a loan, you should know what you will do when the balloon arrives. Most homeowners refinance the payment. Some lenders will promise to refinance the loan when the balloon comes due, though they will not lock in an interest rate in advance. In many cases, sellers offer buyers balloon mortgage options to help the deals go through.

Budget Travel: Easy-Qualifying Mortgages

So far, we've been discussing mortgages that allow you to buy with less money down and those with a lower monthly payment. Sometimes the issue is not payments or cash, however, but credit. Sometimes because of a bad credit history or because you don't have a strong income, you cannot qualify for the types of mortgages we've been talking about. Again, this is frequently the case with first-time borrowers, who are often in the process of establishing their credit and growing their careers. Don't despair; there are several specific options available to you.

Family Financing. A family member may agree to lend you part of the purchase price. It is prudent to keep things on a businesslike basis, offering the property as security for a regular mortgage. Family members may offer low-interest or no-interest loans, but the Internal Revenue Service takes a dim view of them. It likes to see a private mortgage loan made at either the prevailing rate or the applicable federal rate, an index published monthly by the government, which follows current trends in interest rates. If the mortgage rate does not meet that standard, the IRS will impute the interest and tax the lender as if it had been received anyway.

Seller Financing. Seller financing is the oldest method of ensuring a small down payment. In addition to acquiring a new mortgage from an institutional lender, you get a second mortgage from the seller. For example, you get an 80 percent loan from the bank, and the seller lends you an additional 15 percent. You now can get the property with as little as 5 percent down, plus closing costs. And you don't have to be qualified for the second mortgage because it's coming from the seller.

The problem here is that very often sellers do not want to give mortgages because of the risk involved (you might not repay) and because they need the cash to buy another property. Thus, while you may find a seller who will "carry back" some "paper" (as these loans are referred to in the trade), it is not likely. The amount of the second mortgage is between you and the seller. However, many sellers are wary of anyone who wants to put less than 10 percent cash down.

Additionally, today many institutional lenders will set not only a maximum loan amount, but also a maximum combined loan amount. That means that you may get 80 percent of the price from the lender, and that same lender

will allow you to borrow only 10 percent from the seller for a combined total of 90 percent.

Low documentation (Low-doc), no-documentation, or express loans. These
loans have become popular with many who wish to minimize the amount
of personal financial information given to a lender in exchange for a sizable
down payment. If you are making a large down payment (usually 25 percent
or more), the lender may waive most of its usual paperwork for verifying income or employment, checking on reserves and credit standing only.

Roughing It: New Construction Loans

Financing new construction is easiest if you are working with a large custom
builder, who may finance the construction or may help you arrange a construction loan that later converts to a mortgage. If you are buying a home
site, you will find banks reluctant to lend on vacant land. You'll have to buy
for cash or persuade the seller to hold a mortgage. Once the land is paid for,
you can count it toward equity to help qualify for another loan. Construction
loans are most readily obtained after you have taken all the necessary steps to
have your plans and lot approved by local authorities, and if you are working
through a recognized contractor. Do-it-yourselfers, particularly those on a
shoestring budget, may find it very difficult to obtain financing.

In-House and Preferred Builder Mortgage Companies. Many large national
production homebuilders, and even some smaller local builders, have their
own lenders, often bearing the same name as the builders themselves. Those
builders who own their own mortgage companies may offer incentive credit
dollars (kind of like play money for upgrades, options or loan costs) for buyers to use if they keep their loan in-house instead of using an outside lender.
You cannot be forced to use their lender; no seller or builder can make you
use a particular mortgage company. They can, however, sweeten the pot by
thousands of dollars—so much that it may be difficult to walk away from
what they are offering. The in-house lender's first and almost only priority
is its builder's buyers, unlike other lenders who make loans for a variety of
other types of buyers. A preferred lender is usually one with which a particular builder has a partnership or business relationship and understanding,
much the same as the in-house variety.

In either of these scenarios, compare how much the builder incentive
money will help you to get into your new home, or whether their rates are
slightly higher than others and you may be paying more over 30 years than

Roadmap 3.4

Cost Comparisons of Different Mortgage Loans

| | Conventional | | | | | FHA 203-b | VA |
	Fixed 30-year	Fixed 15-year	Buy-down	Biweekly	Adjustable Rate		
Minimum Down	Some Plans 5% Down					3%–5%	0%
Mortgage Insurance	If Less than 20% Down					Upfront, Some Yearly	No
Maximum Loan	"Jumbo" Loans Sometimes Available					Moderate, Varies by Area	$203,000
Easier Qualifying	Somewhat		Yes		Yes	Yes	Yes
Faster Payoff		Yes		Yes			
Monthly Payment	Level	Level	Lower, Rises	Level	Lower, Can Rise or Fall	Level	Level
Assumability						Yes	Yes
Comments				Automatic Withdrawal from Checking		Repairs Sometimes Required	

you would ordinarily have chosen to do. If everything's equal, make your decision from there. If not, go outside, and pass up their offer of incentive money.

Buy-Down. If you buy a home from a developer, it may offer a buy-down, or mortgage subsidy, to help you afford the property. For example, to help you qualify, the developer may cut the interest rate on your mortgage by two or three percentage points for the first three years of your loan. In order to do this, the builder pays the lender the difference between the market rate and the interest rate you are paying, and because the builder pays the difference upfront, it amounts to less than it would be to you if you had to pay it monthly. But it still usually amounts to thousands of dollars.

Is this a good deal for you? Yes, providing the builder hasn't inflated the price of the home to compensate for the better financing! And providing that you can afford the payments when the subsidy lapses. If you count on a higher income in the future to help you meet those higher payments, you could be in trouble if your income does not rise sufficiently.

If you can afford the current interest rate, you may want to ask the builder to credit you with the money it would have cost him for the buy-down. The builder may be willing to take that much off the price or even to offer it to you as a credit toward the down payment if your lender will allow this.

Learn the Language

Key Terms to Know When Buying a Home

Adjustable rate A rate of interest that fluctuates up or down according to market conditions; *fully indexed rate:* maximum interest rate on an ARM that can be reached at the first adjustment; *initial interest rate:* the introductory interest rate on a loan; signals that there may be rate adjustments later in the loan; *lifetime cap:* the maximum amount of interest an ARM loan can reach during the life of the loan.

Annual percentage rate (APR) The rate of interest on a loan per year.

Amortization Regular payments that reduce the principal of a mortgage.

Assumption of mortgage An agreement by the buyer to take over the payment of the mortgage of the seller; the original holder of the note usually remains ultimately liable for its payment.

Balloon note A form of mortgage that requires a minimum payment of principal and the payment of interest at regular intervals, but requires a substantial final payment (all the remaining principal) on a specific date; *balloon payment:* principal sum coming due at a predetermined time (may also contain payment of accrued interest).

Biweekly mortgage A mortgage under which one-half of the regular amortized monthly payment is payable every two weeks, giving the benefit of 13 full payments per year; this allows a 30-year loan to be retired in approximately 18 years.

Blended rate The melding together of two rates to create a lower overall rate of interest.

Buy-down permanent Prepaid interest that brings the note rate on the loan down to a lower, permanent rate; *temporary:* prepaid interest that lowers the note rate temporarily on the loan, allowing the buyer to more readily qualify and to increase payments as income grows.

Cap (rate cap; rate ceiling) The maximum to which the rate can go in an ARM loan, specified in an interest amount; usually found on ARM loans; can be expressed as per period (e.g., annual or lifetime, meaning for the entire loan term).

Carryover interest rate Interest rate that is too great to add to the ARM adjustments because of the predetermined caps, so the interest amount is carried over until it can be applied. Note, however, that this amount is *not* added onto the principal balance, such as in negative amortization.

Cash on hand The amount needed for the down payment and closing costs.

Cash reserves The amount of buyer's liquid cash remaining after making the down payment and paying all closing costs.

Collateral Marketable property which a borrower pledges as security for a loan. In a mortgage, the collateral typically is the property itself.

Commitment period The length of time during which a loan approval is valid.

Conforming loans Mortgage loans that meet the FNMA/FHLMC underwriting guidelines in regard to loan type, amount, and other secondary market criteria.

Convertibility option A clause that allows the ARM loan to be converted to a fixed-rate loan during a certain period.

Convertible ARM Adjustable-rate mortgage containing a clause allowing for the rate to become fixed during a certain period (e.g., between months 13 and 60 of the loan term).

Construction loan A loan made to finance the actual construction or improvement on land. It is often the practice to make disbursements in increments as the construction progresses.

Conventional loan A mortgage or deed of trust for which the loan-to-value ratio is within an acceptable range for a particular lending institution; not backed by a government agency such as the Federal Housing Administration (FHA), the Veterans Administration (VA), or other government bodies.

Convertibility Describing the ability of the borrower to convert an ARM to a fixed-rate loan.

Credit scoring Numerically weighting various financial factors in the borrower's credit to determine the risk of lending to that borrower.

Debt ratios The comparison of a buyer's housing costs to their gross or net effective income (based on the loan program) and the comparison of a buyer's total long-term debt to their gross or net effective income (based on the loan program used). The first ratio is termed *housing ratio;* the second ratio is *total debt ratio.*

Earnest money (escrow) A deposit of funds by the purchaser of a piece of real estate as evidence of good faith.

Equity The market value of real property less the amount of existing liens and mortgages.

Fannie Mae/Federal National Mortgage Association (FNMA) A privately owned part of the secondary mortgage market used to recycle mortgages made in the primary market; purchases conventional, FHA, and VA loans.

Federal Housing Administration (FHA) A part of the federal government's Department of Housing and Urban Development; underwrites insured loans made by lenders to provide economical housing for moderate-income persons.

FICO Fair, Isaac & Company credit-scoring system used by many leaders to determine a borrower's ability to repay a mortgage; uses a scoring range of 300 to 850—the lower the score, the higher the risk.

Fixed rate mortgage A conventional mortgage having a rate of interest that remains the same for the life of the mortgage.

Floor The lowest possible payment if interest falls deeply during the life of the ARM.

Freddie Mac/Federal Home Loan Mortgage Corporation (FHLMC) A part of the secondary market, particularly used to purchase loans from savings-and-loan lenders within the Federal Home Loan Bank Board.

Funding fee The origination fee on VA loans, usually equal to 1 percent of the amount financed.

Ginnie Mae/Government National Mortgage Association (GNMA) A governmental part of the secondary market that deals primarily in recycling VA and FHA mortgages, particularly those that are highly leveraged (e.g., no or low down payment).

Graduated payment mortgage (GPM) A type of conventional loan containing a fixed rate for the life of the loan, but the initial monthly payments are too low to satisfy interest payments at the stated interest rate, and payments increase in accordance to a schedule.

Growing equity mortgage (GEM) This mortgage has a fixed interest rate for the life of the loan; but payments increase 3 percent, 5 percent, or 7.5 percent (depending on the program) for a period during the loan (usually not to exceed 10 years), with all payment increases applied directly to reduce the principal. The 30-year amortized GEM loans are typically paid off between 13 and 15 years.

House payment Total of principal, interest, taxes, and insurance paid per month for your home; insurance includes PMI and homeowners.

Income qualifications The amount of either gross income or net effective income (depending on the loan program) required by the lender for loan qualifying.

Index An indicator used to measure inflation.

Initial interest rate With most ARM loans, the rate during the first year or the first adjustment period.

Interest only Payments received are only applied to accrued interest on the loan; therefore, there is no principal reduction.

Interest rate The cost of acquiring a loan, expressed as a percentage.

Interest-rate cap Maximum amount of interest that can be charged on an ARM loan.

Jumbo loans Mortgage loans that exceed the loan amounts acceptable for sale in the secondary market.

Lease option A lease with an option to buy; said option can be either exercised to culminate in a purchase or forfeited by the optionee.

Lender A bank, company, or even an individual that actually risks money in making a loan.

Lender's title insurance policy An extra policy that protects the lender.

Lender's escrow fee A fee charged if the lender requires a separate escrow.

Leverage The use of a small asset to purchase a larger asset; allows a buyer's down payment to go further.

Loan application fee Loan origination fee (up to one point or more).

Loan origination fees Fees the lender charges, usually expressed as a percentage of the loan; charged for handling the loan.

Loan-to-value ratio (LTV) The amount of the loan as compared to the appraised value of the property.

Lock-in A written agreement guaranteeing a specific interest rate for the buyer; there is usually a time limit on a lock-in, such as 30, 60, or 90 days.

Long-term debt For qualifying purposes, debts that cannot be paid off within a certain amount of time, which varies depending on the loan type.

Margin A specific percentage above the index.

Mortgage A written agreement between the borrower and lender whereby the lender gains the right to take possession of the property should the owner default on the loan.

Mortgage amount Total amount of loan.

Mortgage broker Someone who helps homebuyers sort through loan packages offered by various lenders.

Mortgagee The holder of a mortgage; the party to whom a mortgage is made, generally the lender.

Mortgage insurance The protection against loss incurred by a mortgage default, the mortgage lender thereby enabling the lender to lend a higher percentage of the sale price. Not title insurance.

Mortgagor A person who mortgages property, generally the property owner.

Negative amortization Occurs where monthly installment payments are insufficient to pay the interest accruing on the principal balance, so the unpaid interest must be added to the principal due.

PITI Principal, interest, taxes (real estate), and insurance.

Points (discount points) The fees paid to a lender or broker; 1 percent of the principal loan amount equals one point; generally, the more points you pay, the lower your interest rate.

Portfolio lending Instead of selling the mortgage into the secondary market, the lender keeps it in portfolio (in the in-house file) for the life of the loan.

Prepayment penalty The charges the borrower pays for payment of a mortgage debt before it is due.

Prepayment privilege The right of the borrower to prepay the entire principal sum remaining on the loan without penalty.

Private mortgage insurance (PMI) This indemnifies the lender from the borrower's default, usually on the first 20 percent of the loan.

Prohibited costs Certain costs that cannot be paid by a particular party to the transaction, as determined by a certain type of loan.

Principal (1) The amount of money owed on which interest is payable. (2) A person who empowers another to act as his representative or agent. (3) A person having prime responsibility for an obligation.

Principal payment The total of the principal paid per month on your mortgage.

Purchase money mortgage A mortgage given by a purchaser to a seller on the subject property to secure payment of a part of the purchase price.

Qualifying ratio The percentages used to compare the amount of housing expense and total debt to that of the buyer's gross income or net effective income (depending on the loan program).

Ratio A percentage; used as a qualifying guideline in mortgage lending.

Real Estate Settlement and Procedures Act (RESPA) A federal law; establishes under what conditions referral fees may be paid when brokerages send business to lenders and title companies, and what kind of disclosures must be made to the consumer if the lender and title company have either common ownership with the brokerage or some other affiliation.

Secondary market Recycles lent funds from the primary market comprising FNMA, GNMA, and FHLMC.

Seller financing A seller allows the borrower to finance the property, using a portion of the seller's equity in the property.

Shared appreciation mortgage (SAM) A loan having a fixed interest rate set below the market rate for the term of the loan; provides for contingent interest by the lender based on a percentage of the appreciation in the value of the security at the sale or transfer of the property. Facetiously called the CYD (call your dad) loan.

Shared equity mortgage (SEM) A co-borrower mortgage by which the equity of the property is shared when the property is sold.

Simple assumption A no-qualifying assignment with the lender; the original obligor remains secondarily liable should the assumptor default.

Subject to The transfer of rights to pay an obligation from one party to another, with the first party remaining secondarily liable should the second party default and potentially responsible for any deficiency judgment caused by the second borrower.

Tax and insurance impound fee The setup fee for an impound account that allows the lender to pay your property taxes and your fire (or homeowners) insurance.

Thrift institution A bank or savings and loan.

Total for down payment All funds remaining for down payment.

VA (Veterans Affairs) loans Direct loans to veterans by lenders that are guaranteed by the Department of Veterans Affairs, enabling veterans to buy a residence with little or no down payment

Variable interest rate A "flexible" interest rate, an interest rate that fluctuates as the prevailing rate moves up or down. In mortgages, there are usually maximums as to the frequency and amount of fluctuation.

Wraparound The original loan obligation remains stationary, while a new amortizing obligation wraps around the other loan.

Self-Directed or Guided Tour

Finding Your Dream Home

▶ Before You Go: Beginning the House Hunt

At last, it's time to begin. You know where you want to live (the all-important location), the size and style of the home that best suits your needs, and you understand the ins and outs of financing (you may even have a preapproved mortgage commitment—although probably not quite yet), so let's hit the road.

As you might expect, there are many ways to find your dream home.

1. Tell relatives, friends, co-workers, and neighbors you're in the market for a home. They might know of a good deal.
2. *Contact a real estate agent.* Or, better yet, a buyer's agent (or broker as they are sometimes called). (See below for information on selecting agents and buyer's brokers.)
3. *Read classified ads in newspapers.* With practice, you will learn to scan the thousands of listings with an eye for a bargain. If the ad has been placed directly by the homeowner, you will avoid an agent's commission, (Although the seller pays the broker's fee, that fee is built into the price you pay.)

Roadmap 4.1

Deciphering the Ads

A/C, A.C.–air-conditioned, air-conditioning

appl.–appliances

appt.–appointment

apt.–apartment

attch.; att.–attached

ba.–bathroom(s)

bsmt.–basement

bdrm.–bedroom

beaut.–beautiful

bung.–bungalow

b/–by; buy

cln.–clean

cond.–condition

const.–construction

crpt.–carpet

cprtd.–carpeted

dec.; décor.–decor; decorated

din. rm.–dining room

elec.–electrical

ext.–exterior; extension; extended

exc.–excellent

excep.–exceptional

excl.–excluded; excluding

fam. rm.–family room

fin.–finished

flr.–floor

gar.–garage

immed.–immediate

incl.–includes; included

kit.–kitchen

laund.; ldry.–laundry

liv. rom.–living room

lrg.; lge.–large

ma.; m;–master, as in "master bath/suite"

m/l–more or less (used for approx. measurements)

O.A.C.–on approved credit

o/c–owner carry (seller financing)

occ.; occup.–occupancy

sac.–sacrifice

ste.–suite

sq. ft.–square feet

twnhse; twnhs.–townhouse

vltd.–vaulted (usually vaulted ceilings)

w/–with

yd.–yard

4. *Check the Internet.* There are numerous sites offered by local and national Realtors as well as newspapers. Many offer photographs and virtual tours of the homes listed. These sites are particularly useful if you're traveling to another city, state, or even country and want to get the lay of the land. To begin you might want to have a look at http://www.realtor.com.

5. *Visit open houses and tour new home communities.* Open houses are usually held on Saturday or Sunday afternoons; new home communities set their own hours, so check before you go. Both are invitations to the general public. You won't need any advance appointment or research; you can tour the neighborhoods that most interest you, stopping in at one house after another. It's a great way to get a feeling for prices. Don't hesitate to visit even if you're not ready to buy. Some agents sit on open houses primarily to find buyer clients, so be prepared for questions and chitchat.

   If you are in the market and have an agent, your agent will leave his or her business card, if he or she is with you. Community practices differ in the matter of open-house and new home tour etiquette among brokers. Ask your agent the best way to visit on your own when they aren't available. You don't want to find your dream house only to discover that you've stepped into jurisdictional disputes.

6. *Place a classified ad.* If you can't find a home you like through the newspapers, place an ad explaining what you are looking for. You may hear from a seller or real estate agent who can tell you about a property that you don't know about.

7. *Stalk the wild FSBO (for sale by owner; pronounced fizz-bo).* These are properties that the owners are selling without the help of a listing agent, almost always to avoid paying a real estate agent a commission. Anywhere from 15 to 25 percent of homes are sold every year without the aid of a full service real estate brokerage. (In many cases, discount brokers or fee-for-service agents may have helped the seller set the price of the home, may have rented the seller a sign for the front yard, and may have even collected a fee for putting the listing in the local Multiple Listing Service.)

   When approaching a FSBO, use caution. The seller is thinking of "making money" by keeping the commission. You are thinking you can lowball an offer because you know the seller is "saving" the commission.

Even if you find a FSBO, you should consider using an agent because FSBO sellers typically neither know nor understand things like property defect disclosure or fair housing laws.

While pure FSBOs are not for the novice, there are some situations that are conducive to FSBO purchases:

▶ The property is unique and you feel strongly attracted to it.

▶ The home seems underpriced for the area (the owner may not have had an appraisal or advice on pricing it properly). In that scenario, be prepared to act promptly; some investors lie in wait for unwary FSBOs and jump as soon as an underpriced property hits the market.

Hazard!

FSBOs: Not for Beginners

It may be difficult to begin house hunting searching primarily for FSBOs, particularly if you are a first-time buyer. And until you have a good grasp of the values in your area and the entire homebuying process, dealing with principals instead of professionals can be frustrating. If, however, you think you've found your dream home in FSBO clothes, try to gather as much information and advice on the property as you can, and see how comfortable you feel with this type of arrangement.

8. *Look for vacant homes.* By driving or walking through the neighborhood you are interested in, you may spot a vacant home. With or without a "For Sale" sign, it may be owned by a motivated seller who would be overjoyed to receive your bid.

9. *Look for foreclosures.* The ultimate motivated sellers are those who are about to lose property to the bank because they have not kept up with the payments. You can buy from the owner before foreclosure, from the trustee at foreclosure, or from the bank that holds the property after foreclosure. Foreclosed-upon properties are frequently offered at auctions; however, you will probably do better if you can buy the property directly from the owner before it gets to auction.

As you evaluate various properties, write in a notebook the location, layout, features, and financial details—such as price, taxes, and maintenance costs—of each home you consider. When you look at many homes, you may have difficulty keeping all these details straight.

▶ Travel Guide: Working with an Agent

You should expect utmost professionalism from your agent—no less than you would from your accountant, your lawyer, or your doctor. Most real estate people are professionals who can't afford to have you waste their time because time and expertise are what real estate agents are truly selling. One of the first things they are going to ask you is, "What's your timeframe for making a purchase?" You owe it to your agent to answer that question as honestly as you can. At your first meeting, the agent will work hard to figure out how serious a buyer you are. Before we move down the road and talk about what an agent does, let's review some of the basic ground rules for working with your agent.

1. The agent is someone who is going to help you accomplish a specific task and only succeeds when you succeed, so be straightforward and expect the same in return.

2. The first time you meet your agent, meet in their office. Be prepared to interview the agent and be prepared to be interviewed. Don't be afraid to ask for a real estate license number and don't be afraid to show your driver's license and let it be photocopied.

3. Don't be embarrassed. You are going to have lay out your finances eventually and you might as well start now. Don't gloss over the blemishes and problems. Neither you nor your agent wants to spend weeks looking for a house, only to have you fail to qualify for it financially because of a problem you "forgot" to mention.

4. Be honest about who is making the homebuying decision. If Mom and Dad have veto power, everybody needs to be aware of it upfront.

5. Work out a schedule. Talk about when it is a good time for you to tour homes and when it is good for the agent. Work out the best way to contact one another. Is the agent easiest to reach by telephone, by beeper or cell, or by e-mail? If you need to speak with your agent as quickly as possible, which method of contact does the agent prefer? Ask how often you can expect to hear from your agent about new listings and how promptly you can expect the agent to return your calls. Be blunt about your expectations.

6. Work out what you are going to do when you are out on your own look-ing at houses (and you will go out on your own and look at houses) and see something that interests you.

7. Work out what you should do if you attend an open house without your agent. The agent would always prefer to be with you but if they are unavailable, what information should you gather and what information should you give the seller's agent sitting at the open house?

8. Work out whom you will be dealing with. Will you always be working with the agent or sometimes with their assistant? Is that OK with you? You want to work directly with the agent most of the time.

9. Don't expect a free ride all of the time. Yes, the agent will probably drive you around in a very nice car, but if it's mealtime and you are still out looking at houses, don't expect the agent to foot the bill.

10. When you go through a house, your agent will urge you to talk about what you like and don't like. This helps your agent refine what homes to show you in the future, so be honest—and brutally so. It will make things easier in the end.

Again, the whole idea here is for you and your agent to work as efficiently as possible with each other. Eliminating surprises is a good place to start, so let's take a look at what you can expect from an agent.

Not Your Average Tour Guide: What the Agent Does for You

The average person assumes that a real estate agent's job is to help find a house, but that's only the tip of the iceberg. The typical broker will spend a considerable amount of time bringing you into agreement with the seller and, most important, helping you arrange financing for your purchase. In a new home purchase, your agent can research the builder and the new home war-ranty, offer advice on choosing a home site and floor plan, and help with your design center choices and loan application. You can expect a fairly lengthy list of services, even if you are using the seller's broker.

Analysis of your financial situation. We said it before, but it bears repeat-ing: Don't be offended by what appear to be personal questions. A good agent asks them at the beginning because a lending institution will ask them later on. Your agent is trying to assess if you are financially ready to purchase a home, and deciding whether to take you on as a client. During a first conversation, the broker is already forming a strategy for financing your purchase. In a resale (used home) purchase, don't reveal the top price you're prepared to pay, even though the agent may already have figured out just how much house you are qualified to buy based on your income, debts, and down payment information.

Education in basic real estate principles. Brokers expect to spend extra time with first-time homebuyers. Some seasoned homebuyers have not been through the purchase of a home in quite a while, making the same explanations necessary. You have a right to insist that every step be made clear so that you feel comfortable with the process.

Recommendation of a specific price range. Without those figures, all of you —sellers, agent, and yourself—may be spinning your wheels.

Orientation to a new community. If you are moving to another town, send for the local newspaper (the weekend papers are usually where most real estate ads appear) or find their community Web sites. You can also contact a few firms you find in the process and ask about what part of town may be best for your price range. You may receive long-distance phone calls, e-mails, maps, or new home brochures. Your agent can set up motel reservations for a visit. At that time, your agent can chauffeur you around, checking out neighborhoods, schools, and shopping, while also arranging a time-efficient tour of potential homes in your price range.

Information about different locations. The agent is prohibited by law (the federal Fair Housing Act) from answering questions regarding race, religion, familial status, or handicap of residents in any given area. They may, however, offer school test scores and expenditures, or guide you to Web sites with demographic information or crime statistics.

Screening of listings. The agent will show you any house on the market, being careful not to limit your choice by the use of subtle steering based on any of the prohibited criteria mentioned above. A good agent is a skilled matchmaker, however, who listens instead of talking and then helps you narrow down available listings. The agent should make efficient use of your time.

Showing property. The agent will set up appointments for house inspections and (unless representing a discount broker) will accompany you. During the tours, don't be afraid to ask questions. The agent will have a wealth of data on each house you see, including knowledge of lot size, property taxes and assessment figures, age of the house, square footage, heating and air conditioning systems, and the like. If you are also looking at new homes, the agent will have researched the new home communities, be able to discuss their amenities, understand the options in each floor plan, and know how to get information on the future of the area. The agent may also have knowledge of home construction and make recommendations on some of the technical aspects of your purchase.

Estimation of ownership costs. When you are seriously interested in a specific house, your agent will sit down to help you figure out how you could buy it and what it would cost you each month. If your proceeds for the down payment are coming from the sale of a previous home, they can discuss the timing of your move and the readiness of the next property.

Contract negotiation. The agent will prepare either a binding purchase contract or (in some areas) a preliminary memorandum of agreed terms, including provisions for financing, contingencies, or special terms. The broker negotiates differences between what you want and what the seller wants until you and the seller reach a meeting of the minds. In a new home purchase, your agent can try to negotiate for builder incentives (seller-paid credits used for financing or upgrade options) or even haggle over the price of the home if the builder is enticed by a quick reduction of inventory. Depending on whether it is a seller's market or a buyer's market at the time, it may be difficult to get the builder to negotiate. Except in, perhaps, a custom home purchase, most new homebuilders have their own purchase agreements, which are computer-prepared and presented by their own consultants. Your agent will be present for this and help advise and guide you along the way.

Set up the various inspections and help clear contract contingencies. Your agent will make sure you have all the necessary inspections arranged that are specified as part of your negotiated contract, such as the pest, roof, pool, and electrical or structural inspections. The agent will make sure that you have resolved all of your buyer-related contingencies within the timeframe allowed in your purchase agreement.

Liaison with your escrow officer, loan consultant, or attorney. The broker works closely with your lender, attorney, or escrow officer, keeping a watchful eye on the progress of the transaction from the moment you sign a purchase agreement.

Financing Insight. Some agents don't even consider looking for homes for their clients these days without a lender's loan prequalification or preapproval of their buyers (see Chapter 3), giving them even more bargaining power when the time comes to make an offer. After the purchase, the agent should help you with your loan application and keep in close touch with the lender, checking the status of your loan approval frequently to be able to point out any red flags along the way. You'll want to personally check in with the lender as well. Your agent may recommend several lenders and suggest a variety of loan programs that suit your needs, but you need not feel tied to the same lender who gave you your original prequalification letter or certificate if you find another more suitable later on. And don't feel obligated to use a lender referred to you by your Realtor; that lender may not be the most competitive. The choice of which loan consultant and which loan program to use is ultimately up to you.

Closing escrow/settlement. Local customs vary, but in many areas the broker attends the closing session. In a few places, agents even effect the transfer of title (ownership).

Recommend local services. Agents network with a variety of local businesses and can be a resource for their buyers. Your agent can locate moving companies, day care providers, housekeeping services, and gardeners, and help you set up utilities. Consider your agent your new neighborhood's "ambassador" and let them roll out the red carpet for you.

On-Site Guides: Listing and Seller's Agents

The law of agency clearly sets out the broker's duties to the principal (also known as the client), the one who retains and (usually) pays the agent. These fiduciary duties are complex, but they boil down to one thing: The agent must put the principal's interest first, above anyone else's, including their own. Among the specific duties involved are

1. Obedience to the principal's instructions unless they are illegal.
2. Loyalty to the principal, which strictly interpreted (it sometimes isn't) includes obtaining the highest possible price for the property and never suggesting any offer under the listed price.
3. Confidentiality, which prohibits the seller's agent from sharing with you details of the seller's financial or family situation, unless of course the seller has authorized such action to encourage offers. Whether the

seller has received previous offers, and for how much, is also confidential information.

4. Notice, a duty that obliges the seller's agent to forward to the principal (seller) any fact that it would be in the seller's interest to know, whether or not the seller knows enough to inquire. This one is of vital importance for you to understand. Unless you specifically hire your own buyer's broker to represent you (more on that later), none of these duties is owed to you. This is true for listing as well as selling agents; both work for the seller. Technically, you are a third party in that relationship, a customer rather than a client.

It sounds scary, but things aren't as bad as they seem. The law does require the broker to be honest, straightforward, and trustworthy with third parties. Your questions will receive honest answers. In addition, agents and sellers have an obligation to volunteer information about any serious (material) hidden defects you aren't able to see for yourself. State laws differ, though, on whether they must also tell you about past problems that don't technically affect the real estate, such as suicide or murder on the premises, illness of the seller, and the like. (Some buyers do have phobias against buying properties for these and other nonhouse related reasons. If you are one of them you must tell the broker in advance; most will be sensitive to your issues.)

> *When house hunting, keep in mind that a seller's agent is obligated to tell the seller anything known about you that could benefit the seller.*

Also, you will receive a great deal of service paid for by the seller, because without this service to buyers, the property might never be sold. And finally, you can take heart from the fact that, as a practical matter, many seller's brokers end up violating their duty to the seller. A good agent empathizes with you, wants you to find what you want at a price you can afford, and may emotionally adopt you. If brokers didn't to some extent identify with the buyer, not much real estate would get sold!

How to Protect Yourself. If the agent is dutybound to put the seller's interest first (and there's only one first place), how should this affect your relationship with the broker? First, realize that no confidentiality is owed to you.

It's practical to reveal your financial situation if you expect to get effective service, but you may want to keep some information to yourself, such as the maximum price you are prepared to pay. The broker who knows that you would pay more "if we have to" is, strictly speaking, obliged to convey that information to the seller. Assume that whatever you say will be (or at least should be) transmitted to the seller.

Take advantage of the fact that you must receive honest answers to your questions. In a few states you are entitled to a seller's written disclosure of defects, but elsewhere, "Are you aware of any defects in this house?" is a good all-purpose query to ask of both the seller and broker, preferably in front of witnesses.

Co-brokers. Agents "co-broker" virtually all the properties in an area, which means that the agent who listed the property will split the commission with any agent who brings in a buyer. In most cases, the other agent now becomes a "seller's agent" as well. In other words, even agents who didn't personally list the properties they're showing you represent the sellers.

Personal Tour Guides: Buyer's Brokers

What's to stop you from retaining your own broker, someone obligated to put your interests first and legally bound to help you obtain the property at the lowest possible price? Nothing.

Almost unheard-of in years past, brokers who represent buyers are now found in every real estate market, and you should have no trouble locating one. When you have specifically engaged a buyer's broker, those fiduciary duties are now owed to you, and sellers are now the customers. Your agent must keep your information confidential and obey your instructions, and is duty-bound to tell you anything that would be useful to you and to help you obtain the property for the lowest price. In addition, the buyer's agent will do some of the legwork for you. They go out and examine all the properties available, and, ideally, show you the ones that are best suited to you.

Use a buyer's broker, especially if you've never searched for a house before; it is always better to have a buyer's broker on your side. These brokers are unlike traditional brokers whose job it is to get the highest price for the seller. Buyer's brokers are fully licensed real estate professionals, with total access to all multiple listed, unlisted, and "for sale by owner" properties. Note: Buyer's agents come in two types: exclusive buyer's agents who work only for buyers; and nonexclusive buyer's agents who will sometimes work with sellers but promise to never work with both buyer and seller in the same transaction.

A buyer's agent is not a hired gun, and not someone you hire to beat up the seller on price; a buyer's agent is a skilled professional with whom you can discuss strategy in confidence. They assist you with the entire homebuying process, from helping you define your wants and needs to making price comparisons and offering strategies. They will help you objectively look at a property's strengths and weaknesses. During negotiations with the seller or the seller's agent, the buyer's broker will do the best to help you get the best price and terms. One strategy that can save you thousands of dollars is not to disclose your highest price intentions, or how motivated you are to buy the house. Buyer's brokers can help you by acting as an intermediary with the seller, only divulging the information that is needed to seal the deal.

You may be asked to sign a buyer agency agreement, and you should. It means the agent will expect you to be loyal. The logic is that if you are not willing to sign a buyer agency agreement, it means you are free to use other agents to help you find a house. However, if you are not willing to commit to an agent, can you expect an agent to commit to you? If a great house comes on the market, whom will your buyer's agent call first? Someone who has agreed to be loyal or someone who has decided not to commit?

To find a buyer's broker near you, look in the Yellow Pages, or you can contact the national Buyer's Homefinding Network at 800-500-3569 for a local referral.

Compensation. The buyer's broker may ask for a signed contract and nominal retainer to compensate for time invested; sometimes the retainer applies against eventual commission or even the purchase price of the property. If no property is purchased within the contracted time, the retainer may be forfeited. Before you sign a buyer agency agreement, have your lawyer or other qualified advisor look at it. Be sure that you are clear that under some circumstances you may be obligated to pay part or all of your agent's fee.

Sometimes, however, the buyer's broker maintains a verbal agreement with buyers, with a commitment to inform them of available properties and show them everything in the areas and price ranges they seek. The broker does this with the understanding that the buyers will not engage the services of any another agent for that purpose and that they will use the buyer's agent to represent them no matter what property they buy. It's pretty much a matter of trust and loyalty, based on faith in the agent's professionalism and expertise, and the buyer's willingness to use them exclusively.

In theory, the buyer who specifically hires a broker should pay for the service. In real life, however, it usually works out that the seller pays the originally agreed-upon commission, a designated amount of which goes to the buyer's broker, so that the house gets sold. In essence, your buyer's agent co-brokes with other agents, which means you may not have to pay your agent anything. Isn't this a conflict of interest? Interestingly, it's been held that the fiduciary relationship isn't necessarily determined by who pays the agent, but rather by who the agent declares is the client. In other words, a buyer's agent can be loyal to you even when receiving payment from the seller.

Proponents of the system like it because it sets up an adversarial situation similar to that in which the parties retain two different attorneys, each working on behalf of their client.

Special Tour Guides: Sales Consultants— Buying a New Home

In the usual production (tract) home purchase, the sales consultant represents the seller, who, in this case, is the builder of the home. Many builders offer a co-op fee, or commission, to any broker who introduces them to a buyer on the first visit to the builder's community, should that introduction lead to a closed sale.

If you tour new homes without an agent and opt to buy one on your own, there is an implied (but not official) responsibility on the part of the builder's sales consultant, even though they represent the builder. This means that the sales consultant works diligently to assist both you and the builder, addressing the concerns of both sides. The builder's agent is not ultimately obligated to take your instructions, however, because the agent does not, in fact, represent you.

Builders often post signs on their sales office doors warning buyers who are working with agents to have their agents come along on their first visit. The builder believes that its elaborately decorated model homes, signage, advertising, builder Web site, or on-site agent can also be the procuring cause of an eventual sale, saving them an agent commission. Some builders will refuse to compensate any agent introduced after their buyer's first visit for this reason. If you wish to remain loyal to your agent, make sure that they are available to escort you personally to any new home communities unless you've agreed otherwise.

Self-Guided Tours: Discount and FSBO Brokers

Some sellers who are willing to perform part of the brokerage work themselves list their property with discount brokers, or fee-for-service brokers. These agencies offer a seller a limited list of services for a reduced commission or per job fee. You'll need to understand this relationship because if you run into one, you, as a buyer, will be expected to do part of the work yourself. The discount broker may assist by making viewing appointments for you, but will probably send you to tour these FSBOs on your own. You may also be offered less help with mortgage financing, and end up viewing homes while the owners are present. It can be an uncomfortable experience, so try and avoid it.

Other types of discount brokers include those on the World Wide Web who offer both buyers and sellers "cash back at closing," such as e-Realty. com or ZipRealty.com. These sites will list states in which they are permitted to operate.

Fee-for-service brokers are those who sell individual services, such as a market analysis, represent the buyer or seller at closing, or recommend pricing all at a set fee, with no other obligations involved. This is a very new form of real estate professional, and is probably more popular on the seller side than the buyer side, but they certainly are available to buyers. As the name implies, you might hire a consultant just to drive you around for one afternoon and provide their professional opinion on five different houses, or if there are, for instance, 12 elements to a real estate transaction, and you feel comfortable doing seven of them yourself, a consultant would help accomplish the other five. Some real estate consultants charge by the hour, some charge by the task.

This form of professional is catching on and you may want to consider it. Just be sure to have a long interview with the consultant to make sure you know what you want, you understand how the consultant is to be paid, and how the consultant works.

When sellers engage the services of a discount FSBO brokerage, the primary responsibility of selling the home is left in the owner's hands. Some owners who engage discount brokers may also offer a buyer's broker a commission (broker co-op) or flat fee for bringing them a real buyer. In this case, as the buyer you can have the services of your own agent to help you through a possible purchase of this type, if you are so inclined. FSBO agencies usually offer owners the option of listing their homes in the Multiple Listing Service for a set fee. And, even though the discount brokers offer a list of other services, owners generally do their own marketing, such as placing classified advertising, creating flyers, and holding open houses.

Local Guides: Yet Other Arrangements

We're not quite finished with the roles real estate agents can play. Known in different states by different names, the transaction broker (TB) works to fill in the blanks where other types of agents don't. When someone is needed to represent neither the buyer nor the seller, but remain neutral, the transaction broker may be selected. This broker usually has no fiduciary duties, but can offer expertise and negotiate between parties. The law, in states that provide for this status, usually requires simple, honest, straightforward dealing, but may set up varying other duties as well. Find out, if considering the use of a TB, whether confidences are kept and just what the agent's duties would be.

The dual agent is allowed to represent both parties, as might take place if you visited an open house without any agent representing you and bought the house through the seller's agent, who, by the way, would be more than happy to help. In essence, you may surmise that a dual agent can represent both the buyers' and sellers' interests, but as mentioned earlier, true representation of a buyer is almost impossible when the seller directly or indirectly pays the commission for both. The role of the dual agent and whose interests are represented has been hotly debated and is still a controversial issue in many

Hazard!

Experience Required

Non-agents, facilitators, coordinators, and the like do have a place in this world. Buyers and sellers who have been through many transactions may feel quite comfortable dealing with a middleman.

Also, if parents are selling their home to their children, a simple middleman might be fine. In those cases, whatever questions arise are going to be resolved outside the presence of the agent anyway.

real estate markets. However, there are many competent agents who fill these shoes regularly, representing the interests of both the buyer and seller with professionalism and appropriate confidentiality.

Selecting an Agent

Okay; you know about the variety of guides available to you, but how do you find one who is right for you? You can meet agents by answering advertisements, calling the phone numbers on "For Sale" signs, searching the Yellow Pages, and visiting open houses. You will see advertisements about them on bus stop benches, in supermarkets, and in real estate Web sites, and hear about them through direct mail campaigns.

Another way to find an agent is to walk into any real estate office. Just like in an auto dealer's showroom, you'll immediately be introduced to an agent. However, if you're a walk in, you normally get the person who is "next up," or next in line. Agents are assigned "floor duty," or time they spend in the office answering calls on ads and responding to prospects who drop in. In a larger office there's a list, and you get the next person on the list, which is not necessarily a good thing. It is the newer agents who want floor time; often the more experienced agents have enough referrals to keep them busy. So if you are just walking in you might not get the better agent.

The best way to go about it is to pursue the agent whose name has been suggested by a relative or a friend who has had a good experience. But don't just go by the recommendations; it is important for you to know whether the agent in question specializes in the area and type of house you want. Call the agent and set up an interview. Get a list of the properties the agent sold over the past six months and the names and phone numbers of the buyers or sellers they represented. Then call those people and see what they say. Are they satisfied as well? If so, you've probably got a winner.

In a strange town, you can write or e-mail queries to the local chamber of commerce asking for maps and information; you will probably hear from several local real estate brokers interested in working with out-of-towners. If you study the local newspapers, you will discover which agents are active in the areas you like. If you are relocating with your company, chances are they will put you in touch with agents who are part of their relocation network and probably have a proven track record with their relocation department in your target area.

If you don't hire a buyer's broker and you deal with sellers' agents, you might be tempted to play the field, thinking that you'll get many people out there looking for your dream house. In reality, though, the buyer who works with many brokers is working with no one. If you plan to use sellers' brokers and find a good one, stick with that one.

Assessing the Broker. You've now compiled a list of names, and it's time to get serious. Create a list of the names and numbers you've collected for the past several weeks. At the top, put the names of the agents referred to you by friends or family members. Further down, list those whose names caught your attention for one reason or another. Be sure to write down not only the names of the agents but also how you got their names: Friend of Barbara, interesting ad in the newspaper, great Web site, or listed house on Cherry Street. Whatever.

Now you are going to have to make some decisions. You do not want to call 10 real estate agents and set up appointments. You probably don't even want to call five. But you should talk to at least two and a maximum of four such agents. Remember, you will get smarter with every interview you do. Your questions will get better and you'll understand the answers better.

The Appointment. Whether the interview is at the agent's office, in your apartment, or somewhere else, be prepared. Review the questions that follow and be prepared to take notes on the answers. It is actually far more important that you listen to the agent talk than write down the answers. As long as you keep in mind what you need to know, you'll be able to figure out whether this is the agent you want. The questions are automatic "kick-out" questions. You are sorting candidates, not disqualifying them.

You will want to get a feeling for the agent and whether or not you will be comfortable working with that individual. Questions to ask include

1. How long have you been in the residential real estate industry? Do you work full-time in real estate or part-time?

   You want a full-time agent.

2. Are you a salesperson, broker, or associate broker? What are your credentials and/or industry-recognized designations?

   This will give you an idea of their level of education in real estate.

3. Do you specialize in any specific area of town, type of housing, or price range? Briefly describe your real estate experience. How long have you lived in the area? What is your community involvement? How knowledgeable are you about the area I'm seeking?

   You are making sure that what the agent does is what you need.

4. How involved are you within the industry? Do you sit on any industry committees, such as for the local, state, or national Realtor association? If not, why not?

   You want a feel of how the agent interacts with other agents in town. If you get into a bidding war for a home, how well your agent is respected by peers could be a plus for you.

5. How experienced are you as a buyer's representative? How many buyers do you represent each year? How many buyer clients are you currently working for?

   Here are a few tests to apply when judging a broker:

1. Does the broker explain your state's law of agency at your first meeting and make it clear for whom they are working?

2. Does the agent return phone calls promptly?

   This is a good screening device. In these days of cell phones, pagers, voice-mail, and e-mail, there is no excuse to be out of touch.

3. Does the agent explain things so you can understand them?

   This is especially important for first-time buyers. If you find an agent who is a born teacher, you are in luck.

4. Does the agent seem ready to invest time in you?

5. Is the agent Internet savvy?

   Some agents carry a laptop computer with them wherever they go and are able to pull up pertinent information and new listings on the spot. If Internet communication is important to you, ask agents if they e-mail their clients with information on new listings as they appear.

6. Does the broker suggest an initial session in the office, rather than simply meeting you at the house you called about?

   To get good service, you need a sit-down financial analysis and discussion of your whole situation in a confidential and professional setting.

7. Does the agent ask questions about your finances soon after meeting you?

   This may not be proper etiquette in ordinary society, but it's the mark of an efficient broker who aims to give you good service. Suggesting a prequalification or a full loan preapproval is better yet, so that you have placed yourself in a position of strength and credibility as a buyer. If you haven't already spoken to a loan agent, the agent may suggest someone with whom they have a track record of success.

8. Does the broker explain upfront whether they are acting as a seller's agent?

   In most states, this information must be given to you in writing upon first contact.

9. When suggesting potential houses for the first time, did the agent show you listings that convince you that they have been listening and understand what you are looking for?

   If you're shown houses with the wrong number of bedrooms or ones clearly out of your price range, this may not be the agent for you.

10. Does the agent seem familiar and up-to-date on local conditions? Do they have maps of the area, handouts about schools, local activities, property tax rates, and other information that shows knowledge and interest in the area?

    The worksheet in Roadmap 4.2 will help you evaluate brokers.

    No matter what else happens, no matter how well or how badly the interview goes, do not leave the agent's office without a few forms. You would like to receive a blank copy of a buyer agent agreement (so you'll know what the agent is talking about when they ask you to sign one), you would like a blank copy of the purchase agreement (so you'll know what to expect when you finally find the house you want), and you want a blank copy of the

Roadmap 4.2

Worksheet for Evaluating Brokers

YES or NO	Agent 1	Agent 2	Agent 3
Returns phone calls/is accessible			
Follows up on contacts			
Uses office for interview			
Understands your needs			
Runs financial analysis			
Suggests a meeting with a lender			
Uses an interview sheet			
Seems computer/Internet savvy			
Uses Multiple Listing System			
Cooperates with other agents			
Knows the community			
Inspires confidence			
Knows both new and resale home markets			

HUD-1 form (so you won't be completely lost on the day you finally close on your house).

Once you find a broker with whom you feel comfortable, one who inspires confidence, stick with that one. Tell your broker about other firms' ads that interest you, Web sites (URLs) with homes that caught your eye, even about FSBOs, so that the agent can investigate and report back to you. Ask for advice before visiting open houses on your own. And if you have the agent's phone numbers, don't hesitate to use them. Real estate agents are accustomed to evening and weekend calls. Service is what they sell, and they welcome any sign that you intend to utilize it.

Getting the Best Tour: Working with Your Broker

Once you find an agent you're happy with, you need to help that agent as much as possible to get you just the house you want. Begin by showing your agent your "wants" list (see Roadmap 2.2: Your "Wants" List). This should immediately help the agent determine what you're looking for or at least narrow down which neighborhood you're interested in. Then by looking at a number of houses, you should be able to quickly get a feel of the market and narrow down your choices.

How Much Should I Tell My Agent? You need to tell your agent enough so that they can effectively help you get the house you want. Your broker needs to know how much you are preapproved for, and you should tell them about any potential problems that might crop up; for example, if there is something in your credit that didn't show up when you got preapproved, but that might appear along the way and sour the deal.

You also need to let the agent know just how much you really want to pay. Perhaps you are preapproved for a loan of $400,000, but you don't want the high payments that a mortgage that big involves. Indeed, you want a mortgage under $200,000, along with its lower payments. Let the agent know. That way they can show you properties that are within the price range you want.

Be aware, however, that as soon as an agent knows how much financing you are preapproved for and how much you can put down, the natural tendency is for the agent to show you the highest-priced properties you can qualify for. These properties will tend to be larger and to have more amenities, better locations, and so on. If you really want to pay less, you'll have to struggle both with the agent and with yourself to look at less expensive properties. On the other hand, maybe you really do want a more expensive property; you just want to "lowball" the price and try to get it for less. If that's the case, then you need to know whose side your agent is really on (are you working with a buyer's agent or a seller's agent?) and decide how much of your strategy to share.

To some extent the agent can act as your coach in these matters, but be sure you know who the agent is working for, and if it's a seller's agent, don't reveal your bottom line. Unless you negotiate directly with the seller, something we don't recommend for a first-time buyer, the agent will have to try to get your price for you. Therefore, sometimes it helps if you can do a little innocent acting for the agent's benefit. It's important to properly prepare your agent for the negotiations.

Stay in Touch with Your Agent. Of course, you'll read the ads avidly while you are house hunting. Particular real estate terms common to each area may puzzle you; don't hesitate to ask your agent to explain them. If you work through a seller's agent who gives you good service, or if you have retained a buyer's broker, don't answer ads yourself. Phone the agent and mention the items that catch your eye. The broker can do a little investigating, particularly where the Multiple Listing Service is involved. Then you'll receive a call back. If you're working with your own buyer's agent, they will follow up on discount broker, FSBO, or Internet ads as well.

Changing Agents. Your commitment to your agent need only be as strong as the service you receive. If your agent makes a big effort to find properties to show you every weekend, keeps calling to let you know as new properties come on the market, and is helpful in showing you homes you want to see, by all means continue working with that agent. But if your agent neglects you, doesn't call you, and doesn't show you properties you like—in other words, if you are getting poor service—you should try out a new agent (assuming you don't have a contract that prohibits this).

One word of caution, however: Be loyal to the agent with whom you're working. At least give that person a chance. Typically, you sign a contract when you hire a buyer's agent, and it generally runs for at least 30 days, and sometimes as long as 90 days. It can get terribly confusing if you're out with one agent on Friday, another on Saturday, and two more on Sunday morning and afternoon. What if two agents show you the same house? That gets a bit sticky. The last thing you want is to have the agents fighting among themselves instead of working diligently for you.

Just as you become loyal to an agent with whom you work, the agent will develop a loyalty to you, and when the time comes to make offers and counteroffers, that could be an important consideration. Certainly, if you don't like an agent, or if you feel neglected or not properly serviced, move on. But it's to your benefit to give each agent with whom you work a chance to at least show his mettle.

▶ Hitting the Road: How to Look at Houses

There is a certain art to finding your dream home, and it all of it starts with preparation.

1. Explore the neighborhood. If possible, a couple of days before you go on a house-hunting expedition, get a list of properties you will be touring. If you can, predrive the neighborhoods. Don't stop at any of the target houses (no matter how friendly you are, you are still a stranger to the seller and you want to keep it that way for a while), but feel free to observe the home from the outside and the neighborhood around it. Take notes on anything that strikes you as interesting or unusual.

2. Wear comfortable clothes, especially comfortable shoes. You are going to be walking through basements and garages. You will be walking through the yards—even if it's a rainy day. Be prepared, because you are buying both the inside and the outside of the house, and you do not want your investigation interrupted just because of bad weather.

3. Bring your list of preferences and a pad. If you plan to visit many sites in a single day, by the end of the day you are going to have a hard time remembering which features went with which house. Identify each house and list some key information to help you remember it. Some people even take instant or digital cameras so they have a photo to remind them.

4. Don't bring your checkbook. Buying a house is an emotional purchase. If you are a first-time homebuyer, you want to sleep on it before making a decision.

5. Bring all decision makers. If someone other than you is going to have a say in the purchase of the house, that person should be in the car to see the houses and have an opportunity to ask questions. Make sure you tell your agent who will be joining you on the house hunt so they can provide enough copies of the listing sheets, maps of the area, etc. Note: If there are youngsters coming, you may not be able to see as many houses in a day.

6. Be talkative. When you're in the car, tell your agent what you've been up to—whether you had a chance to look at the houses on the list and what you thought of them. Let him know if you've seen other houses you'd like to add to the list. Conversation brings about awareness. The more the agent knows about you, your likes, and your dislikes, the faster you

are going to be able to close in on the house you want. What will also come out over time is whether the agent is interested in "selling you" or "servicing you." You want service.

7. Pay attention as you drive into the neighborhood. The agent should be pointing out landmarks and highlights (churches, schools, shopping centers, etc.) as you enter a neighborhood. If the agent is familiar with the neighborhood, they would discuss traffic during rush hour or zoning that could have an impact. If you've come on a Saturday, the agent may suggest coming back on a weekday.

If your agent is a buyer's agent (which we recommend), they should be pointing out things as you approach the target house. Are there burglar bars on the windows of other homes? Are there cars parked along the street making it seem crowded? Are the yards kept up? Are the other homes well maintained? A buyer's agent will point out the negatives as well as the positives about a neighborhood.

1. Be aware of everything around you. As you get out of the car, listen for traffic or other noises on the street. Be sure to notice the houses beside and in front of the target house. Look at how well they are kept up, as well as how well the target house is kept up.

2. Focus on what you're doing. If you've been talking about the stock market or the latest disaster on the other side of the world, end that conversation and focus on the task at hand. Your agent should be pointing out things to you that—should you decide this house is a keeper—you may want to have investigated. Are there dirt tunnels on the foundation? Could be termites. Are there wet places in the yard? Could be drainage issues.

Ask the agent for data on each property, and take it back with you. To concentrate fully on the house, take notes when you have finished, possibly when you are back in the car. Jot down your impressions of the things you liked and disliked right on the computer printouts, builder brochures, or copies of the listing sheets for the houses you inspect. Roadmap 4.3 is a sample worksheet with space for rating various features of a home from 1 to 10. A rating of 1 is the lowest. You may want to mark up a street map of the area, locating the houses you view and also noting schools, religious institutions, shopping areas, approximate commute times, parks, and other important items.

Comparing Houses

Address	Price	Lot Size	Construction	Roof	Driveway	Landscaping	Square Feet	No. Bedrooms	No. Baths
275 Isabell	110,000	School Near — 6	2-story Wood — 5	New shingle — 8	Gravel — 2	Big Trees — 4	1,550	3 1-small — 4	1½ — 4
27W245 Patricia Ln. Winfield	125,900	Nice Open High — 9	Ranch Brick — 9	10 yrs. old shingle — 5	B.T. — 6	Good — 8	1,900	3 — 6	3 — 8
135 Marian Pl. Carol Stream	129,900	Sloping Lot — 5	Ranch Wood — 4	9 yrs. old shingle — 6	B.T. — 6	Fair — 5	2,000	3 — 6	2 — 6

Dining Room / Dining/Living	Kitchen	Deck, Patio	Garage	Heat, AC	Fireplace	Basement	Plumbing Electricity	Water	General Appeal	Total Rating
Yes	Old cabinets	Breezeway	1-car	Window AC Gas	None	Dry unfinished	OK	City	Older home in fair shape	
4	5	6	3	5	1	4	6	6		71
Yes	Small D.W.	Yes	2-car	Central AC Gas	In L.R. Wood Stove	Finished	OK	OK City	Nice house, good view	
5	5	8	6	6	9	8	6	6		110
Yes	Good D.W.	Screened porch	2-car	Central AC Gas	None	Finished	OK	City	Very pleasant house	
5	6	8	6	6	1	7	6	6		89

Tour the Inside of the House

Ideally, when you are touring the house, the owner is out and the only other person present is the listing agent. As a rule, the listing agent leads the tour of the house. That agent is the one who knows the features and the amenities. Let them emphasize the strong assets of the house. Meanwhile, however, your agent should also be taking the tour, noticing things the listing agent isn't pointing out. After the tour, discuss what each of you has seen.

How Long Will You Be in a House? Depends on how attracted you are to it. If it feels wrong from the time you get out of the car, two minutes may be generous. If the house has possibilities, you might spend 10 to 15 minutes in it. If it has very good possibilities, you may want to spend as much as half an hour doing a thorough combing of rooms, cabinets, closets, etc. As you leave the house with your agent, ask questions. The agent's job is to see the things you don't. Don't be reluctant to ask your agent if the property is worth the money. (If you have a buyer's agent, you're more likely to get an honest answer.)

What If the Seller Is There? This becomes awkward. The seller wants to draw your attention to the high points, of course, and will try to steer you away from low points. You should be friendly but direct your own tour and be sure to see what you want to see. You can ask the seller all the questions you'd like, but don't expect your agent to join in. Usually, principals can deal with principals (you and the seller are the principals) but agents should only deal with other agents. It's a matter of professional courtesy. Also, a good buyer's agent isn't going to believe much of what a seller says. They'd want to get it verified in writing in the seller disclosure statement.

After You Leave, Review. Start ranking the homes you see. Be sure to write down the order in which you saw them and a few notes about the positives and negatives of each one. Prioritize out loud so your agent can hear you to get a feel for what you liked and didn't like.

How Many Homes Should You See? If you are a local resident planning to make an in-town move, you can plan on seeing five to 10 houses. It is better to limit your viewing to three or four hours—about a half a day. You want to leave yourself plenty of time to think about what you've seen. If you like one and feel inclined toward it, you may want to drive through the neighborhood later in the day. You may even want to stop and walk around a bit, talking to neighbors if you see any. Ask about noise and what's happening in the community. Don't be too specific about the house you're looking at, but feel free to generally acknowledge that the area is on your list.

Reexamine Your Preferences. Go back over your notes and preferences and priorities. Compare them to the reality of the homes you've seen. If you are like most people, your priorities will start changing. You will have seen things you liked and will add them to your list, and you will even knock some things off. Be sure to discuss your new preferences with your agent, who will not be surprised that you've changed your mind on some things.

New Home Construction. One of the most fun parts of house hunting can be going to look at new homes. But there also are some additional issues you need to keep in mind as you visit them.

First, by all means take your agent with you or let your agent know you plan to visit a new homes development. Reputable builders will work with buyer's agents just like listing agents do. Second, apart from the normal things you would look at on an existing home, when you walk through a new home model there are some additional questions to consider.

▶ How many homes are being built in the development?
▶ How long will it take to complete them all? (If the developer won't finish for a couple of years, that's how long you are going to have to live with big trucks going up and down your street.)
▶ If you decide to buy, how soon can the builder break ground and how soon will they finish? What performance guarantees is the builder prepared to make?
▶ How much money is going to be needed upfront and how much will be drawn out—and at what intervals—as construction continues?
▶ What kind of appliances are standard, what upgrades are available, and how much will upgrades cost? What about cabinet finishes and carpet quality?

Evaluating the Sights: Dream Home or Mirage

Here are just a couple of the tricks home shoppers might expect as they visit potential homes:

▶ Bread is baking; spices simmering. This is almost a cliché among real estate agents (and certainly among real estate writers).

▶ The table will be set for a formal dinner party. As an astute buyer, however, you'll note a couple of things. If the table actually seats eight, it will be set for six. If it could seat six, it will be set for four. The seller is trying to create an impression of roominess—an impression they'll try to create throughout the house.

▶ The kitchen is clean. There will be almost nothing on the countertops. Nothing kills a good impression faster than the slightest hint of a crowded kitchen. Some agents even suggest that sellers clear off shelves and get the clutter off the premises entirely.

▶ The children's rooms will be clean, orderly, and bright.

▶ There may be flowers everywhere.

▶ All the lights will be on, and expect all the curtains to be open and light to be streaming in. This, too, is to create an impression of roominess. The agent wants the house to "show big."

▶ The furniture will be perfectly placed. All homes show better with furniture in them. Sometimes some furniture has been removed with the idea of making the rooms look more spacious. Look for carpet dents where furniture was once placed, or go into the basement to see where all the stuff that was removed is stashed.

▶ Look for planned nonchalance. A copy of *House Beautiful* or that day's *Wall Street Journal*. Golf clubs, tennis rackets, etc. convey a lifestyle that comes with the house.

▶ The lawn is manicured, the bushes well-trimmed, and the house-front clean.

All of this effort in the hope you'll be attracted enough to take a second look. And, one day you will, and it won't be a mirage. But now it's now time to enter the perilous waters: negotiating the price you want to pay for your dream home.

Learn the Language

Key Terms to Know When Buying a Home

Agency relationship A legal relationship an agent has with clients and customers, including fiduciary duties, to a client.

Agent A licensed representative of a consumer—buyer or seller—in a real estate deal.

Appraisal A report from an independent person estimating the value of real estate.

Binder (escrow deposit) A small percentage of the purchase price put down by the buyer to demonstrate good faith in going forward with a transaction.

Broker An experienced agent, who has passed a more extensive state-required qualifying exam; only a broker can open and maintain a real estate office and act as a supervisor over sales agents.

Broker's open An open house that is restricted only to real estate agents; allows agents to preview a home to determine whether it is right for clients.

Buyer's agent A person who is legally obligated to represent the best interests of the client, the buyer.

Client A home buyer or seller who usually has signed a contract agreeing to work with a specific real estate agent and has agreed to terms of compensation provided in the contract.

Commission The percentage of a sales contract that goes to a real estate brokerage for selling a home; *split commission:* fee split between the listing brokerage company and the real estate company whose agent brings the buyer; in addition, the agents who actually worked with the buyer and the seller each receive a portion of the money their company received.

Customer A person a real estate sales associate works with, usually without a contract.

Exclusive buyer's agent A person who works only with homebuyers and does not list homes at any time.

Facilitator A real estate license holder who does not legally represent the interests of either the buyer or seller, but whose duty it is to help the transaction come together by making sure forms are signed and filled where appropriate.

Fee for service A concept that an agent should be paid regardless of whether a deal closes.

Foreclosure The right of a lender to take real estate secured by its mortgage and sell it to satisfy the underlying debt.

For sale by owner (FSBO) Properties whose owners are attempting to sell them without assistance from a real estate professional.

Home owner Someone who has title to a property and is legally entitled to sell it.

Independent contractor   Most sales associates in real estate are considered independent contractors, meaning they are free to develop their business and work habits inside the framework of their company.

In-house listings   A term used when referring to a property listed by one sales associate in a company that another sales associate in the same company may have a buyer for; sometimes agents get a bonus if consumers buy in-house listings.

License   A state-granted permit given to real estate sales associates and brokers to participate in the purchase and sale of real estate for compensation.

Listing   A house for sale by a real estate agent; owner of the home signs a "listing agreement," which is a contract that outlines how the agent will market the house and what compensation, usually a commission, will be received in return.

Listing agent   An agent who has a signed agreement with the person selling the house.

Lot   Any portion of real property; usually a portion of a subdivision.

Marketable title   A title which a reasonable purchaser would be willing to accept.

Market value   The average of the highest price that a buyer, willing but not compelled to buy, would pay and the lowest price a seller, willing but not compelled to sell, would accept.

Model home   One of the first homes a builder will construct in a new housing development; used to show buyers basic floor plans and typical features of homes in the development.

Multiple Listing Service   A central database of most, if not all, of the homes listed for sale by MLS members within a certain geographical area.

National Association of Realtors (NAR)   A trade association of some 900,000 members. Membership is voluntary, but most real estate companies belong. NAR owns the word Realtor and prohibits its use by real estate licensees who are not members of the trade association.

Net home price   The selling price of a home after subtracting any sales commissions.

Open house   A home for sale held open for public visitation by either the listing agent or an assistant for a specific number of hours on a specific day.

Option   The right to buy, sell, or lease land at a fixed price within a specified time.

Realtor A member of the National Association of Realtors.

Referral fee The money either paid or received in the transfer of business from one brokerage to another.

Salesperson An entry level position in real estate.

Selling agent The agent who brings the buyer to the deal.

Transactional broker A person who represents the transaction only, safeguarding the legal transfer of property from buyer to seller, but without giving negotiating advice to either side.

Navigating the Waters

Buying Your First Home

► Who's Going with You? Lawyers, Escrow, and Title Companies

Customs in real estate vary tremendously from one area to another. In some states, you may be told that no one uses lawyers for real estate transactions except when something goes wrong or you just want to seek legal advice about your purchase. In the states located mostly in the West, Midwest, and South, escrow companies act as neutral third parties, assisting both buyers and sellers in residential real estate transactions. Title companies (sometimes combined with escrow firms) in these states make sure you have clear title to the property and that the deed is recorded so that the property is legally in your name. In other states, attorneys are used for handling the paperwork and the closing on your house. The law does not require that you have legal counsel in these states, but it is wise to proceed with professional legal help on your side. Even in states where they are not required for general real estate functions, lawyers are useful not so much for getting you out of trouble as for heading off trouble before it starts.

Travel Insurer 1: What Your Lawyer Does

An attorney can make sure that the sales contract protects your interests, intervene if problems arise before closing, and review documents so that you get proper credit at closing (in some states called settlement) time. If you don't have an attorney, you can find a real estate attorney by asking the broker to suggest two or three names, check out some large law firms and ask who specializes in real estate law, or search the Internet for sources.

In states where attorneys are used for real estate purchases, contact the attorney you have chosen early on and explain that you're starting to house hunt, and inquire about the fees for handling an eventual purchase. They will probably suggest at what point to touch base once again, unless you have some legal matters to clear up before going ahead with the purchase of a home.

One of the best set of eyes to help you look before you leap is the one belonging to your attorney. You want a lawyer who will give an honest opinion, look out for your interests, and act as a facilitator rather than a deal breaker.

Most problems, if they occur, will most likely surface during the attorney approval period. This is a set timeframe, usually a number of days, specified in the contract that allows your attorney time to review the contract. It's a standard and important part of any good contract. The law, the boilerplate, and the legalese are almost impossible for most buyers to comprehend. Small changes in a word or phrase can have incredible consequences after the document is signed. That's why you need a lawyer—that is, a watchdog.

Your attorney should know that you want to buy the property but that you don't want to buy any unnecessary problems as part of the deal. The attorney may recommend certain contract modifications in your favor. These generally have nothing to do with the price, closing date, or contingency dates and can be easily negotiated with the seller.

Always remember that you are the client. You are paying the legal fees and you are the individual in charge. If you have a question about your attorney's recommendations, ask. If something doesn't feel right, find out why. Take command of the situation. Ask why a particular change is being recommended in the contract language.

Remember, most real estate transactions do not provide for recourse after the closing. The cost of hiring an attorney to pursue damages after the fact can be financially painful, win or lose. That's the value of finding and working with a good attorney who has your best interests at heart.

If you are buying new construction, there are special concerns. Warranties are good protection against things that will go wrong, but—as always —there is nothing more important than a skilled professional on your side to help negotiate the deal at the beginning. Your agent and your lawyer need to check for probuilder clauses in the "standard" builder contract. (There is no such thing as a standard contract. If a builder says you have to sign the standard contract, have your lawyer and buyer's agent work up a list of "standard" addendums that make it more favorable to you.)

Every year, hundreds of thousands of people buy new homes and are thoroughly satisfied. But without fail, every year thousands of buyers of new homes end up in lawsuits against builders who suddenly go out of business, fail to deliver what they promise, or do such shoddy work that the homes are unlivable. Keep your own professional at your side, always. And yes, have the home inspected before you take possession, just as you would any other home. Even brand-new homes have leaky roofs and faulty foundations.

Travel Insurer 2: Escrow and Title Companies

Where escrow companies handle buyer and seller paperwork, most escrows (the period following the initial contract and before the closing or settlement takes place) can be opened or started up by a simple phone call or by having an agent deliver the signed contract to their offices. Escrow and title firm selection, as with every other aspect of real estate, is negotiable, but just to make things simple, most buyers try to use the same firms for both buyer and seller. New home builders may use the same companies for all their new home subdivisions, taking advantage of reduced fees due to the volume of escrows they handle. These discounted fees are usually attractive to their buyers as well. Ask your real estate agent how real estate purchases are handled in your state in this regard.

Holding Proceeds in Escrow. It's extremely important to have problems cleared up before you hand over your check or the lender's. Once the transfer of title has taken place, many matters are merged into the closing—you have bought the problems along with the property. Don't rely, then, on promises that something will be taken care of "in the next few days." If it is impractical to solve the problem immediately, ask that part of the purchase price be held in escrow, to be turned over to the seller only after the matter is attended to.

In new home purchases, an escrow holdback of mortgage funds can occur if there is work to be done after the close. In other cases, there may have been work that was not permitted on the builder's land before the property became yours. A swimming pool is one such example, because a homebuilder may not have wanted to permit a huge hole to be dug in the backyard until after the property was passed to you. If the seller is to remain in occupancy after closing, be sure that there is plenty of financial motivation to move out as promised; otherwise, you could find yourself stuck with a lengthy and expensive eviction. Daily rental should be set at a high figure, with the provision that it will be deducted from that part of the purchase price held in escrow until the seller leaves as agreed.

Escrow Documents. The escrow holder, whether it is an attorney or an escrow company, will ask you to sign "escrow instructions." These reiterate everything on the sales agreement and instruct the escrow holder to gather all the documents, signatures, and money necessary to close the deal. This is usually a long form. Read it carefully with your attorney, making sure it accurately reflects what is in the sales agreement. Once you and the seller sign the escrow instructions, they are as binding, if not more so, than the sales agreement. If there is anything that's different, point it out and get it made right. Don't sign until it's right. The escrow holder may also ask for a variety of other documents.

Protecting Your Trip: Title Insurance

You want title insurance because it guarantees that your title to the property is good. Title insurance protects you in case someone later challenges the seller's right to sell the property in the first place. If the title is unclear, the home cannot be sold easily.

To get it, however, you have to pay for it. In most areas, buyers pay for title insurance. In some parts of the country, however, sellers traditionally pay or the fees are split. You'll be told what's common for your area.

The title insuring company will record the deed either last thing at night or first thing in the morning at the county hall of records. (The reason it's done first or last thing in the day is to ensure a sneaky seller doesn't first dash down there and sell the property a second time to someone else! Of course it's highly unlikely, but when lots of money and insurance are involved, all the precautions have to be taken.)

▶ Safeguarding Your Investment: Homeowner's and Liability Insurance

The lender will require that you keep *hazard insurance* (fire and similar risks) on the property in an amount sufficient to cover the loan, and in areas where it may be required, flood insurance as well. As a prudent homeowner, you will want wider coverage, and for a larger amount. Rebuilding after a fire, even partially, can sometimes cost more than your original purchase price. And you need personal protection for risks that don't concern your lender —liability for a guest who is hurt on your property, for example.

The process of buying insurance to protect your home and its contents is similar in many ways to buying auto, disability, and health insurance. The clauses in the policies are filled with unfamiliar jargon, and it can be quite difficult to determine how much coverage you really need. Nevertheless, you should wade through this morass because you need to protect yourself against all forms of disaster that might afflict your home and your possessions.

Property Damage. The primary reason that you buy homeowner's insurance is to compensate yourself for property damage or loss. There are two sources of damage: natural occurrences and man- or equipment-made disasters. Some of the more common natural causes include earthquakes, fire, floods, hurricanes, mudslides, storms, tornados, volcanos, wind, hail, and weight of snow. Losses caused by people or the malfunctioning of equipment include arson, burglary, electrical fires, explosions, riots, theft, vandalism, and water pipe breaks.

Insurers offer two policies to cover these risks: named peril insurance and the all-risk insurance. Named peril coverage protects you against only the specific dangers spelled out in the insurance contract. The perils usually named are fire, wind, hail, riots, smoke, vandalism, and theft, among others. Under this policy, if you have a claim, you must show that the loss or damage was caused by one of the named perils. All-risk insurance, on the other hand, covers almost every possible source of loss or damage except those specifically named, such as floods, earthquake, nuclear war, dry rot, termites and insect damage, and wear and tear. You will need special insurance—for example, from the National Flood Insurance program—to cover those risks. Because the all-risk policy is more comprehensive, its premiums are usually higher than those on a named peril policy covering the same property.

There are six basic types of homeowner's policies, each offering protection against certain losses on both your home's structure and its contents. They are all labeled HO (which stands for homeowners), followed by a number. The most basic plan is HO-2. The most comprehensive plan, HO-3, is an all-risk policy that also provides special coverage. Policies for condominium owners are called HO-6. If you own an older home, you will need an HO-8 policy.

Both the basic HO-2 policy and the HO-8 policy for older homes protect you against the following specific perils:

► Fire or lightning
► Windstorm or hail
► Explosion
► Riot or civil disturbance
► Damage from an aircraft
► Damage from a vehicle
► Smoke damage
► Vandalism or malicious mischief
► Theft
► Breakage of glass that is part of a building
► Volcanic eruption

The HO-2, or broad coverage, policy covers all of the perils of an HO-1, as well as the following:

► Falling object
► Weight of ice, snow, or sleet
► Freezing of a plumbing, a heating, or an air-conditioning system, of an automatic fire protective sprinkler system, or of a household appliance
► Accidental discharge or overflow of water or steam from a plumbing, a heating, or an air-conditioning system
► Sudden and accidental discharge from an artificially generated electric current
► Sudden and accidental tearing apart, cracking, burning, or bulging of a heating, an air-conditioning, or a protective sprinkler system, or an appliance for heating water

The HO-4 for renters and the HO-6 for condo owners cover the same perils as the HO-2. In addition, these policies cover contents and some structural aspects of an apartment or condominium, such as a wall that is not shared with another unit or separate balcony.

The special homeowners HO-3 policy covers a house for all perils except those explicitly excluded from the contract, such as flood, earthquake, war, nuclear accidents, wear and tear, dry rot, or termite or insect damage. Clearly, because the HO-3 offers the most protection, it costs more than the HO-2 and HO-8, and the condo owner's HO-6.

Replacement versus Depreciated Value. The purpose of homeowner's insurance is to replace what has been lost or damaged. In determining how much coverage to buy, follow the most important rule of homeowner's insurance: Buy enough to replace most or all property at risk. Frequently, homeowners insure their homes and the contents of their homes for what they paid for them, perhaps years ago. When these homeowners suffer a loss, they find —to their dismay—that they are reimbursed only for the present market value of the objects, which is usually far less than it cost to replace them. Unless your homeowner's policy specifically stipulates that it pays replacement cost, the insurer covers only the actual, depreciated value of the goods. Though you will pay premiums that are 10 or 20 percent higher for replacement cost insurance, the coverage is worth the extra money. If you cannot afford the premiums on full replacement cost insurance, the least you should settle for is 80 percent replacement cost. Cutting back from 100 percent to 80 percent will slash your premiums by as much as a quarter. However, if you settle for less than 80 percent, you expose yourself to too much financial risk. Whether you opt for 100 percent or the 80 percent, always insist on a clause that indexes your coverage to changes in inflation.

In addition to your regular homeowner's coverage, you might want to purchase special insurance, known as a rider or a floater, for particularly valuable artwork, collectibles, silver, furs, jewelry, or other items. Without these riders, if such precious objects were damaged or stolen you would collect nowhere near their true value.

Home-Based Businesses. If you run a home-based business, you probably need extra insurance protection for all your equipment. Most homeowner's policies provide only $2,500 in coverage for property used for business purposes. Therefore, acquire an endorsement, or an additional clause that specifies particular items, to cover your computers, fax machines, office furniture, copiers, file cabinets, and other equipment.

Many insurance companies offer special-rate policies tailored to cover small businesses. Usually, homeowner's policies do not cover liabilities arising out of business activities.

For example, you would not be covered against a suit filed by a delivery person who falls on your property while delivering a package for your business. A small business specialty policy insures against such an event. You might also investigate business interruption insurance, which pays for your temporary relocation to other quarters while your office is being repaired due to fire or another disaster.

Condo Owners. Insurance for condominium owners is similar to coverage available for renters. The condominium association buys insurance that protects the buildings, grounds, and common areas, while each owner must obtain special condominium coverage for the contents of their apartments, walls that are not shared with other apartments, and other things that are not commonly owned, as well as liability claims.

Taking Inventory. Keeping those general guidelines in mind, determine how much homeowner's insurance you need. First, take a household inventory to see what actually needs insuring. Walk around your home and list on an inventory sheet each item you own, what you paid for it, and how much it might cost to replace. Also note model and serial numbers. If you have no idea what things cost today, you might consider bringing in an appraiser to help you. The worksheet in Roadmap 5.1, divided by rooms in your house, will help you inventory the contents of your home.

In addition to listing your household possessions, photograph or videotape each room. If you videotape, talk about the objects you are taping and estimate how much they cost. Keep the pictures or tape somewhere other than your home, such as at work so you will have access to it if your house is destroyed or damaged. These physical records can be invaluable if you ever must file a claim and convince an adjuster that you owned a particular item or what an item is worth.

Liability Coverage. In addition to reimbursing you for lost or damaged property, homeowner's insurance protects you and members of your household against claims and lawsuits for injuries or property damage that you or your family members may have caused accidentally. For example, if your son throws a baseball through your neighbor's window, your neighbor can sue you to pay for the damage. If your dog bites the mail carrier, your liability

Roadmap 5.1

Household Inventory Worksheet

Article and Description	Purchase Price	Replacement Cost	Total Purchase Cost	Total Replacement Cost
Bathrooms				
Carpets/Rugs	$ _____	$ _____		
Clothes Hampers	_____	_____		
Curtains	_____	_____		
Dressing Tables	_____	_____		
Electrical Appliances	_____	_____		
Lighting Fixtures	_____	_____		
Linens	_____	_____		
Scales	_____	_____		
Shower Curtains	_____	_____		
Other	_____	_____		
Total for Bathrooms			$ _____	$ _____
Bedrooms				
Beds/Mattresses	$ _____	$ _____		
Books/Bookcases	_____	_____		
Carpets/Rugs	_____	_____		
Chairs	_____	_____		
Clocks	_____	_____		
Clothing	_____	_____		
Curtains/Drapes	_____	_____		
Desks	_____	_____		
Dressers	_____	_____		
Lamps	_____	_____		
Mirrors	_____	_____		
Plants	_____	_____		
Records/Tapes/CDs	_____	_____		
Stereos/Radios	_____	_____		
Tables	_____	_____		
Televisions	_____	_____		
Wall Hangings/Pictures	_____	_____		
Wall Units	_____	_____		
Other	_____	_____		
Total for Bedrooms			$ _____	$ _____
Dining Room				
Buffets	$ _____	$ _____		
Carpets/Rugs	_____	_____		
Chairs	_____	_____		

Article and Description	Purchase Price	Replacement Cost	Total Purchase Cost	Total Replacement Cost
Dining Room (cont'd)				
China	_____	_____		
Clocks	_____	_____		
Curtains/Drapes	_____	_____		
Glassware	_____	_____		
Lamps/Fixtures	_____	_____		
Silverware	_____	_____		
Tables	_____	_____		
Wall Hangings/Pictures	_____	_____		
Other	_____	_____		
Total for Dining Room			$_____	$_____
Garage/Basement/Attic				
Furniture	$_____	$_____		
Ladders	_____	_____		
Lawn Mowers	_____	_____		
Luggage	_____	_____		
Shovels	_____	_____		
Snowblowers	_____	_____		
Sports Equipment	_____	_____		
Sprinklers/Hoses	_____	_____		
Tools/Supplies	_____	_____		
Toys	_____	_____		
Washer/Dryer	_____	_____		
Wheelbarrows	_____	_____		
Work Benches	_____	_____		
Other	_____	_____		
Total for Garage/ Basement/Attic			$_____	$_____
Kitchen				
Buffets	$_____	$_____		
Cabinets	_____	_____		
Chairs	_____	_____		
Clocks	_____	_____		
Curtains	_____	_____		
Dishes	_____	_____		
Dishwasher	_____	_____		
Disposal/Trash Compactor	_____	_____		
Food/Supplies	_____	_____		
Freezer	_____	_____		
Glassware	_____	_____		
Lighting Fixtures	_____	_____		
Refrigerator	_____	_____		

Article and Description	Purchase Price	Replacement Cost	Total Purchase Cost	Total Replacement Cost
Kitchen (*cont'd*)				
Pots/Pans	_____	_____		
Radio/Television	_____	_____		
Small Appliances	_____	_____		
Stove	_____	_____		
Tables	_____	_____		
Washer/Dryer	_____	_____		
Other	_____	_____		
Total for Kitchen			$_____	$_____
Living Room				
Books/Bookcases	$_____	$_____		
Carpets/Rugs	_____	_____		
Chairs	_____	_____		
Clocks	_____	_____		
Curtains/Drapes	_____	_____		
Desks	_____	_____		
Lamps	_____	_____		
Mirrors	_____	_____		
Musical Instruments	_____	_____		
Plants	_____	_____		
Records/Tapes/CDs	_____	_____		
Sofas	_____	_____		
Stereo/Radio	_____	_____		
Tables	_____	_____		
Television	_____	_____		
Wall Hangings/Pictures	_____	_____		
Wall Units	_____	_____		
Other	_____	_____		
Total for Living Room			$_____	$_____
Porch/Patio				
Carpets/Rugs	$_____	$_____		
Chairs	_____	_____		
Lamps	_____	_____		
Outdoor Cooking Equipment	_____	_____		
Outdoor Furniture	_____	_____		
Plants/Planters	_____	_____		
Tables	_____	_____		
Other	_____	_____		
Total for Porch/Patio			$_____	$_____
TOTAL HOUSEHOLD			$_____	$_____

insurance would cover the medical expenses. Someone who slips on ice on your sidewalk may also sue you for negligence. This general liability coverage does not apply to any damage you do in your car, which is covered by your auto liability insurance.

If you think the chances of being sued are remote, think again. The courts are clogged with thousands of seemingly frivolous liability suits. Such a lawsuit can cost thousands of dollars and waste days of your time—even if you end up winning. If you are unfortunate enough to get sued, your insurance carrier will pay for your legal defense, as well as any settlement or jury verdict against you, up to the liability limits of your policy.

To protect against a huge jury award, purchase extra liability coverage as part of your regular policy. This is generally known as umbrella coverage and it usually extends your liability insurance to $1 million or more.

Living Expenses. If your home sustains so much damage that you are not able to live there while it is being repaired, your homeowner's insurance will pay for your living expenses until you can move back home. This might include the cost of hotels and restaurant meals. Don't expect to take on a luxury lifestyle. These policies impose strict limits on how much they will pay for living expenses, both on a daily basis and in total.

Minimizing Your Premium. The best way to qualify for the lowest insurance rates is to guard against accidents, thefts, and losses. Some of the more obvious precautions you can take, which often qualify for direct discounts, include the following:

1. Install deadbolt locks on doors and key locks on windows. If your home or apartment is at street level, add grates or grills to protect windows.
2. Install a burglar alarm system that attaches to doors and windows, that rings loudly if activated, and that automatically notifies the local police department or alarm company of an intruder.
3. Keep wiring in top condition.
4. Maintain stairs, railings, carpets, and flooring to minimize the possibility of slips or falls.
5. Keep fresh batteries in smoke detectors, and install a sprinkler system and fire alarm that automatically alerts the fire department when it senses smoke.
6. Install exterior lights to make it difficult for a burglar to work in secrecy.

7. Stop smoking cigarettes because nonsmokers are less likely to start fires than smokers.

Most companies also shave your premiums if you are a long-time customer who has never filed a claim or if you have policies for auto or life insurance with the same company. Rates on homeowner's policies are also based on the neighborhood in which your home is located. Obviously, owners of homes in crime-infested areas will pay higher premiums than those whose neighborhoods boast tight security and few crimes. Also, the closer your home is to fire and police protection, the lower your premiums. In general, newer homes qualify for lower rates than older homes because more can go wrong in older buildings as wiring, plumbing, and heating systems deteriorate over time.

Another way to cut your premiums is to accept higher deductibles. If you increase the amount of loss you cover out of your own pocket from $100 to $500 or more, your premium cost plummets. Even when you agree to a substantial deductible, you gain protection against the enormous losses that homeowner's insurance is designed to cover.

Keeping Your Policy Up-to-Date. Once you purchase a homeowners policy, keep it up-to-date as your home and lifestyle change. For example, tell your insurance agent if you build an addition on the house or remodel the kitchen. It might be worth increasing your coverage to protect the enhanced value of your property. The same holds true if you add several valuable possessions, such as artwork, computers, or electronic gear. Reassess your policy to determine whether you have enough insurance to cover the new valuables or whether you need to add any riders.

Caveat Emptor. There are several things to note about homeowner's insurance.

1. This is not flood insurance. Flood insurance comes from the federal government and is only required in high-flood-risk areas. Your lender will tell you if you need it.
2. This also is not a home warranty (see below). Home warranties, which you can buy for new or existing homes, protect you against things like appliances breaking down, pipes bursting, or the air-conditioning system expiring. Talk to your real estate agent.

3. This also is not title insurance, which covers you in case someone makes a claim that you've bought a house from someone who didn't have the right to sell it.

4. In some parts of the country, the lender will also require special coverage for things like earthquakes, mud slides, etc.

What has become troublesome about homeowner's insurance, however, is that insurance companies are becoming increasingly reluctant to cover people and properties with claims histories. In recent years, insurers have paid out huge, multimillion-dollar claims over things like mold, radon, lead-based paint, and other hazards that no one really thought much about when the policies were first purchased. As a result, all premiums have gone up and, in some cases, companies are refusing to write policies in some areas.

To make sure you can get coverage for your home, you need to start shopping for homeowner's insurance at the same time you start shopping for money—both of which take place before you actually start shopping for the house.

As always, if you can talk on the phone or sit across a desk from a human being, you will be a much happier person in the end. If you've had a homeowner's insurance claim in the past, don't hide the fact, but explain it.

That first conversation is just to get acquainted and get a name of an insurance agent. The company will not be able to write the policy until it knows the location of the home, its age, the quality of the plumbing and electrical systems, its proximity to fire hydrants and fire stations, etc.

A fairly new wrinkle in obtaining homeowner's insurance is something called a CLUE report—which stands for Comprehensive Loss Underwriting Exchange. A CLUE report is pulled out of a huge computer database that not only likely has your name on file but also the address of the home you want to buy and the name of the sellers of that home.

Before an insurance company provides you with coverage, it would want to know whether your target home has been the subject of claims in the past and whether you have made claims on other homes yourself. Based on that history and depending on its underwriting criteria, you could be denied coverage, or offered a more expensive package. Sometimes companies will write coverage for you in good faith that there aren't any problems with you or the house, and cancel your insurance several months later when it checks the CLUE report.

The next phone call you'd get would be from your bank, wanting to know what you are going to do about it. (Remember, insurance is required to keep the bank happy.) When you settle on a house you want to buy, you may give serious consideration to asking the seller for a CLUE report. (You cannot get the report yourself. It can only be provided to the owner of the house.) If the report is filled with red flags, you can bet your insurance company will want to discuss your coverage. The good news is that the records only go back seven years.

A final thought about insurance: As you talk to insurers, ask if they will provide coverage of your goods while they are being moved. When you start meeting with moving companies, you'll discover that they have a variety of different insurance options to offer you in case your goods are lost, stolen, or broken. The basic coverage, however, is only 60 cents per pound. Under this coverage, if you have a really nice, multithousand-dollar television that weighs 75 pounds, the extent of the movers' liability is only $45 if the TV is damaged. Needless to say, they'll offer you other forms of coverage up to the full replacement cost but it will cost extra. It's worth discussing moving coverage with your insurance company.

Home Warranties. Another way to protect your investment is through a home warranty. Many builders of new homes participate in the HOW (Home Owners Warranty) program, which insures a home against major system and structural defects for up to 10 years. You can learn more about the program by contacting

HOW
P.O. Box 901021
Fort Worth, TX 76101-2021
800-834-0577
http://www.howcorp.com

Warranties also exist for occupied homes. If you have your home examined by a warranty inspector, you can get a policy to cover your major systems for several years. Policies issued without inspections restrict coverage greatly and usually are not worthwhile.

▶ Negotiating the Package: Making the Offer to Buy

Although local customs vary, in most areas the broker will present your offer to the seller. You'll be advised to go home and wait by the phone. The agent, meanwhile, may contact the listing broker and the seller to arrange for presentation of the offer as soon as possible. Prompt forwarding of all offers is one of the broker's primary legal responsibilities. No broker has the right to refuse to convey a written offer, no matter how small.

Pricing the Trip: How Much Should You Offer?

Sellers frequently price their homes a bit high, expecting a lower than full-price offer. Thus, most are prepared to come down in price, by at least a small amount. You may even get them to come down by a large amount, depending on how well you negotiate. Statistically, most buyers initially offer around 5 percent lower than the asking price for the home. This does not mean they get that much off the price. The seller may counteroffer. But as a general rule of thumb, 5 percent is a place to start. In a depressed market, you would, of course, probably offer less. In a hot market, you may want to offer close to full price. A good agent should be able to help you out in determining just what is a reasonably good offer. Remember, the agent may represent the seller. But if the agent represents you, you could get some excellent advice.

One excellent tool to help you determine not only how much you should offer, but also how much the home is worth, is a list of comparable past sales that your agent can print out. Because almost all agents today are linked by computer, this should only take a few minutes. You'll be able to see what similar homes in the neighborhood sold for going back at least six months. You should also get a list of the prices of similar homes currently on the market. Very quickly you'll be able to get a good idea of what a realistic price is. You'll also know if you are offering a good price or a bad one from the seller's perspective.

Bargaining for Extras: What Else Is Included in the Offer?

After price, what else should you put into the offer? Actually, there are a number of contingencies that you and your agent want to make sure are included.

A contingency in real estate means: "I'll buy your house if . . ."; in essence subject to certain things happening. The contingencies could include

1. I can have it professionally inspected first and review my offer depending upon what's found.

2. The appraisal and title reports are satisfactory and I can finalize my financing (mortgage contingency). If you are going to assume a present loan or place your mortgage with the sellers themselves, these terms are detailed. You'll stipulate that the mortgage you are taking over must be current (paid up to date) at the time of transfer. If you must obtain financing, the details of your proposed mortgage are spelled out, along with a statement that the contract is "contingent upon" or "subject to" obtaining the loan. If you cannot find financing at the specific interest rate you have stipulated in the offer, you cannot be required to go through with the purchase. The contract should state that in such a case your deposit is to be returned. This is usually spelled out in a part of the contract called (in most states) *liquidated damages*. Ask your agent or attorney to explain this vital part of your purchase offer.

3. You will make available to me a CLUE (comprehensive loss underwriting) report on the property and I can get homeowner's insurance. (Getting the CLUE report is becoming incredibly important.)

4. My buyer's agent is paid from the proceeds of the transaction (or whatever compensation plan you decided upon when you hired your agent).

You may also need to include other sorts of things like repairs. Some may be mandatory, others may provide wiggle room—things that are worth talking about that you may or may not get or that you may have to trade off for other considerations.

Do not, however, trade off any of these first three things. You want an inspection, you need financing, and you need a CLUE report. The fourth, your agent's compensation, also is important. (When you are done discussing the price and the contingencies, you and your agent will discuss your earnest money deposit that you will use to show the other side that you are negotiating in good faith. Be prepared to write a check.)

There are other things that you and your agent also need to talk about as you draw up your purchase offer—namely, when you want to close on the deal. When you write your first purchase offer, you are in fact creating a path to a smooth close some two, three, or four weeks from now. The criteria you set forth in the agreement now will become the legal framework of your closing later.

If you are currently renting a property, you need to make sure you can move into your house on the same day you have to leave your apartment. Keep in mind the sellers may have some pressure as well, in terms of when they can move out. They may need for this deal to close before they can close on the house they are trying to buy. Moving dates can become a sticky subject and have to be talked out, but they rarely break the deal.

The last thing you will put in your purchase offer is an expiration time on the offer. The common time period is 48 hours, but tailor it to your circumstances (for instance, the seller may be out of town for three more days so you'll need to extend the period). Your agent can give you some guidance.

There may be other contingencies (conditions of the sale that must be satisfied before the purchase is complete). You may need to sell your present home in order to have the necessary down payment money. You may make the deal contingent on landing the job you came to town to interview for, or you may not feel comfortable with proceeding fully until an inspector's report is acceptable to you. These conditions are inserted into the contract. Sellers will be nervous about contingent offers. They will be taking their house off the market on your behalf, without any guarantee that the sale will go through. So it's customary to set a time limit on contingencies. For longer contingencies, particularly those involving the sale of your present house, the sellers may envision waiting around forever. Instead of worrying about the sale of their home, they must now worry about yours, an element over which they have even less control. So it's only fair for sellers to insert an escape clause, or kickout. The wording may differ according to local practice, but the escape clause usually gives the seller the right to continue to show and market the house. If another good offer comes in, you may be required to remove the contingency and make your offer firm or else drop out.

If your contingency is called, you don't have to meet anyone else's offering price; your deal has been nailed down. But you would have to agree, for example, to buy the property whether or not you sell your present home if you wish to proceed further.

In a new home purchase, buyers can also request that contingencies be written into their purchase agreements, even though builders don't particularly like them. Making a new home purchase contingent upon the sale of an existing unsold home can be setting yourself up for heartbreak in a good estate market, because the builder can continue to look for solid buyers without contingencies, guaranteeing them a sale. You may lose the home site for which you had heart palpitations and have to start all over again.

If your present home already has a sales contract, however, making the deal contingent upon the close is usually a no-brainer for the builder. New home purchasers are wise to list other types of contingencies, such as seeing the floor plan they are about to buy at drywall stage (for their approval) if there is no model home to use as an example.

The Offer. The broker almost never reveals terms or price over the phone. The seller cannot accept over the phone and deserves the right to look over all the details of your proposal at leisure. Faxes for these purposes have become almost universally acceptable. The next move is the seller's. The response can be yes (acceptance), no (rejection), or maybe (counteroffer). If it's yes, the seller accepts all your terms, and you have a binding contract. It's very seldom (usually only in a very hot market) that the buyer will agree to pay full price and give the seller just the terms they are asking for. If there is no response when the time limit has expired, the deal is usually dead. If it's no, the homeowners cannot later change their minds and get your offer back (unless you agree).

The Deposit. It is customary, though not always necessary, to accompany your offer with some money, variously known as *binder or earnest money*. This sum serves several purposes. It proves to the sellers that you mean business. They are, after all, going to take the place off the market on your behalf. It also serves as a source of damages if you back out for no good reason a month down the line.

The deposit is usually placed with a broker or attorney who puts it into a separate escrow, or trust, account. Avoid giving the deposit directly to the seller, especially in a FSBO situation. In this case, you and the seller are pretty much on your own to figure out how to keep these funds in a neutral, third party account if no agents are involved.

How much is up to you, but it should be enough to show that you are serious about buying the property. Keep in mind that it is at least theoretically possible that if the seller accepts your offer and you don't go through with the deal, you could lose your deposit! You may be told that 6 percent or 10 percent of the purchase price is necessary. If this is inconvenient, insist that you can come up with only a smaller amount. Remember, though, that the sellers are weighing your offer to see if it will result in a successful sale. Without much earnest money, it may not look convincing.

This earnest money, of course, counts toward the sum you'll need at closing. Your full deposit is credited toward the down payment or other settlement costs. The contract should clearly state under what circumstances it may be returned.

It's also a good idea to make the deposit check payable to an escrow company rather than to the seller. If you make the check payable to the seller (or their agent), the seller can cash the check, and later if the deal doesn't go through (without any fault of yours), you might have a lot of trouble getting the deposit back.

The Seller's Counteroffer. Then there's maybe. Rather than a rejection, a good negotiator will bring you a counteroffer. That means that they've rejected your offer and are now making an offer to you. Keep in mind that the original offer and the counter are separate. The sellers can't both accept and counter. It's either one or the other. You're under no obligation to accept a counteroffer from the sellers.

Typically, sellers will counter at below their asking price (although they may insist on the asking price and counter by insisting on different terms than what you offered). Now the ball is back in your court. For many first-time buyers, this is a time of soul-searching and hand-wringing. Usually the counter is better (for you) than the original asking price and terms, but not as good as you offered. Should you accept it? Or should you reject it?

Your agent may be able to give you good advice. Just keep in mind, however, that you can't both accept the counteroffer and change it. Either you accept it exactly as it is written or you reject it. If you reject it, you can counter the offer.

The seller is now bound by the counteroffer, which probably contains a time limit, while you are free to consider its terms. You may want to counter the counteroffer, perhaps split the difference. Too many volleys, though, result in hard feelings and often kill the deal. They concentrate on winning and lose sight of their original goals.

Before you start, make up your mind that you will not lose the house you really want over the last thousand dollars. When you cannot make any further concessions on price, try to include some face-saving gesture, such as moving the closing date for their convenience. Make your first offer, certainly your second one, close to the top price you'd really pay. The idea is to tempt the sellers to wrap up the deal, even if it isn't quite what they had in mind.

At each stage, the person who made the last proposal is bound by it until it's withdrawn or answered. The negotiation ends when one side accepts unconditionally the other's last offer. Remember that if your proposal is accepted, you will have a binding legal contract. Don't fool around with a purchase offer unless you really want to buy the property. It should be a thrill when you finally receive the notification of acceptance that is the final legal requirement to make a contract binding and your broker says, "Congratulations! Your offer is accepted!"

Buyer's Remorse. It's not at all unusual to experience a malady known as buyer's remorse within 24 hours to two weeks after your purchase offer was accepted. Rather than lose any sleep, call the real estate broker and ask if you can see the house again, preferably with the sellers absent. "Measuring for curtains" is a logical request, and won't cause alarm. You may even bring your video camera along, so you can see the house over and over again while you are in escrow, waiting for occupancy.

You will probably find that all that hard work, the research, the exhausting house hunting did pay off; this was clearly the right choice for you. If it happens that you are more depressed than ever after your return visit, it's time for a conference with your broker or attorney to determine your legal position if you back out now, and how much money you might forfeit.

Green Light: The Sales Contract

The document with which you make your offer (and usually with which you counter) is called the sales agreement. Until both you and the seller sign the exact same agreement for the exact same price and terms, it's simply an offer.

Once both parties sign off, the sales agreement becomes a binding contract. For that reason, you should read it over carefully before you sign it and have your attorney check it as well.

Many people read only the parts of an agreement that are filled in by the agent, the seller, or the buyer at the time of the offer. The preprinted material (called the "boilerplate") is often overlooked, but virtually all of the important information is in preprinted form. Very little is actually handwritten in. Read the boilerplate carefully. Have your agent and an attorney carefully explain anything you aren't sure about. Make sure it specifies what the seller has included and what the sellers are taking with them. These terms should include the following:

- ▶ Sales price
- ▶ Address and legal description of the property
- ▶ Amount of your earnest money deposit, which reserves the house for you while the contract is prepared and executed
- ▶ Amount of the down payment—perhaps 5 percent or 10 percent of the sales price—which holds the house for you while you apply for a mortgage (also known as an escrow deposit)
- ▶ Terms of your mortgage, allowing you to withdraw from the sales contract if you cannot qualify for a mortgage or if interest rates rise so much that you can no longer afford to buy the home
- ▶ Terms of assuming the seller's mortgage, if applicable, which may allow you to obtain a lower rate than is currently available in the market
- ▶ Details of owner financing, if applicable, which should include repayment terms, interest rates, and down payments. (The contract should not impose a prepayment penalty.)
- ▶ Closing details, such as when and where the closing will take place
- ▶ Date of occupancy, so that it is clear when you can move into your new home
- ▶ Type of deed required to be transferred from the seller to the buyer at closing
- ▶ Personal property and fixtures included with the house, such as appliances, carpeting, draperies, and lighting fixtures. (The contract can define something as a fixture or as personal property, which thus establishes what goes with the property and what does not.)
- ▶ Repairs the seller agrees to make, including necessary inspections for such problems as termites. (This list should also include any required inspections by the city or county to ensure that the building has no code violations and has a valid certificate of occupancy.)
- ▶ Explanation of easement rights, which give someone else—such as a utility—the legal right to use your land
- ▶ Amount of the real estate broker's fee, if any, and who will pay it (usually the seller, but this should be spelled out in the contract)
- ▶ Account where your earnest money and down payment will be kept, usually in escrow in a special bank account. (Another clause should explain the conditions under which you can receive a refund.)

▶ Proration of home ownership costs, specifying how property taxes, utility bills, and rent from tenants will be split during the period between the signing of the contract and the time you take possession of the home

▶ Provisions about title insurance, specifying which title insurance company will issue a policy (see Chapter 6)

▶ Warranty against liens, stating that all renovation or repair bills and taxes have been paid. (You don't want to take possession, then have to deal with a contractor trying to collect an unpaid bill dated several months or years ago.)

▶ Financing arrangements, specifying that you will apply for a mortgage loan. (The entire sale will usually be contingent on your obtaining financing. There should be a clause in the contract stating that if you can't get a mortgage, the contract is void. If the seller provides financing, the terms should be included in the sales contract. The seller has the right to run a credit check on you to ensure that you are creditworthy.)

▶ Lead Paint Addendum: If the house was built before 1978, the EPA requires that you be given 10 days in which to conduct an inspection for lead paint hazards before any contract can become binding.

A final walk-through or buyer inspection is usually written into purchase agreements. In a resale purchase, you'll usually re-inspect the premises within 24 hours before closing. In a new home purchase, the builder may cushion completion and buyer possession by a few days or a week to fine-tune and touch up the home after you tour it with the building superintendent. You will want to make sure that everything you and the seller agreed to include or remove has been tended to, and that the owner hasn't left the house in disarray or the builder has not left building materials there.

Clean is a matter of interpretation. You know that no two people view cleanliness identically, so be fair and broad-minded here. Most buyers re-clean homes to their own tastes no matter how hard the previous owners may have worked to get ready for them.

Also necessary in the contract are a target date and place for transfer of title. Choose a date that allows for processing of your mortgage application; the agent will have suggestions. What if that date comes and goes? You still have a binding contract. "Time is of the essence," included in some real estate agreements, can have stronger legal meanings in some states than others. Consult your own attorney if you want to take the risk of setting up a powerful legal deadline. In a new home purchase, many builders stipulate that buyers must close within five days of the certificate of completion of the home, so that they no longer have to carry the unit. In a resale purchase, however, factors on both sides figure into this equation.

Experience has taught agents and lawyers to provide for all sorts of complications that may not have occurred to you. Homebuilders have become masters at disclosing everything that has the potential to come back and bite them. What if the place burns down before closing? If the appraiser thinks it isn't worth the price you're paying? What if taxes weren't paid last year? If the sellers can't prove they have clear title (ownership)? Will you receive occupancy on the day you become the owners? What constitutes closing escrow or settlement in your state? In some states, signing and physical acceptance of the deed transfers ownership. In others, closing takes place when a confirmation call is received by an agent, builder, or buyer by the escrow or title company that the new deed is on record at the county recorder's office; then (and only then) can buyers receive keys. In a few areas, sellers are allowed to remain for up to a month; the contract should stipulate exactly to what you agree. If you need, for some reason, to move in before closing, be prepared for some resistance on the part of the sellers, their attorney, and their agent.

Lawyers, builders, and sellers' agents know that it is a risky arrangement, and a good one will write a contract nailing down all possible problems. It is difficult for anyone to be evicted from a house once they have taken occupancy. The liability involved could curl your hair. Sometimes an agreement can be reached in an emergency situation, such a garage rental, where the seller agrees to store your items in the home's locked garage until escrow officially closes. You would probably pay a daily rental fee and need to arrange for a binder to your homeowners insurance policy. Your offer should have a time limit, and it should be a short one. A day or two is enough time for the sellers to consider your proposal. If you give them more time, they may be tempted to stall until after they see what next Sunday's open house might bring. They might also use your offer as an auction goad to bid up another prospective buyer. If the sellers are out of town, they should be available by phone, and could answer your offer by fax with a confirming letter to follow.

Final Jitters. If this is your first homebuying experience, you will feel shaky when the time comes to sign the offer. You should receive an immediate duplicate of everything you sign; if it isn't offered, ask for it. You need not walk out wondering what you've just committed yourself to. It's reassuring to take the contract to your lawyer or review it with a third party before you sign it. Many sales, though, are made after office hours and on weekends, and you may risk losing the right house by delay. You can write above your signature "subject to the approval of my attorney." This means that you can go ahead and make your offer, while reserving for your lawyer or someone else you trust the right to object later to any wording or provisions that don't protect your interests.

Personal Property vs. Real Estate. It is essential to spell out all the gray-area items (unattached carpeting, fireplace equipment, chandeliers, drapes, workshop, pool equipment, etc.) about which there may be disputes as to whether they stay with the property.

In general, personal property is that which can be picked up and moved by the seller without leaving any nail or screw holes. By contrast, real estate is the land and anything permanently attached (affixed) to it. The rules are complicated, though, and it's best to stipulate in the contract that "Stove and refrigerator are to remain" or "Seller may remove dining room chandelier." Items like custom-sized area carpeting, wood stoves, play equipment, and satellite dishes are subject to occasional differences of opinion; head off trouble by detailing them in the written offer. If the listing agent did a proper job, the sellers would have indicated which items they are taking and which ones they are leaving behind. Ask the broker to do some delicate investigating about the sellers' plans for the aboveground pool or the tool shed. Garage cabinetry may or may not be bolted to the floors or walls, and your dreams of stashing your holiday decorations and kids' toys there can go up in smoke if you don't address the inclusion of them upfront, in writing.

Don't get bogged down over small items. Just make sure that your offer specifies what you expect to remain.

▶ Almost Home: After the Sales Agreement

After the sales agreement is finalized and you and the seller have signed, you have a deal. But you don't yet have a home. There's a long way to go between signing the sales agreement and getting the key. But normally, there is a time limit. For example, one of the clauses in that sales agreement will usually say that you have only so many weeks to come up with financing and remove all contingencies in order to complete the purchase, typically four to eight weeks. No mortgage, no home. During the next few weeks both you and the seller will have a lot of work to do to ensure that the sale is consummated. In the next chapters, we'll take a look at the process of concluding the purchase transaction.

Paying for the Voyage: Completing the Financing

If you require a new mortgage to finance your purchase, the sales contract probably contains your promise to apply promptly at a lending institution. Your real estate broker can often suggest the lender most favorable to your situation and the seller's. Perhaps, as we suggested, you have already checked out several and have a comfort level with a lender who has prequalified, or better yet, preapproved you for a certain loan amount.

After the Application. While the lending institution completes all the paperwork (assembling the loan package), the real estate agent should keep in touch in case any hitches develop. You might check yourself from time to time to see if things are going smoothly. Usually, however, no news is good news.

Within three days of your application, the lending institution must send you a *good faith estimate* of your closing costs, and notification of your APR, the adjusted percentage rate. If you paid for the appraisal, you are entitled to receive a copy; if it isn't offered, request it in writing.

Keep the broker or your lawyer informed of any communication you receive from the lending institution, local government, or FHA. Above all, don't go out and put a major purchase on credit. This is not the time to incur additional debt or deplete your cash.

After the loan package has been assembled, your loan consultant will submit the package to the mortgage-underwriting department for review. This is now done electronically with most lenders, a process called *desktop underwriting.* The lender may then issue its findings either in the form of a commitment letter or a conditional commitment dependent, for example, on certain repairs to the property before closing or on your clearing up an outstanding judgment, or even a final appraisal, if the house is brand new. In any event, be sure to contact the broker, your lawyer, or closing agent as soon as you hear from the lender.

While all of this is going on, you will have arranged for an inspection and completed any final negotiations (see Chapter 6). Then, once you have the commitment safely in hand, nothing remains but to find a time (within the number of days stipulated in the commitment letter) that suits everyone for arranging your walk-through and transferring the property. You are ready for closing.

Learn the Language

Key Terms to Know When Buying a Home

Agreement A legally binding contract made between two or more persons.

Binder (title commitment) A document issued by a title insurance company that states the conditions under which a title insurance policy will be issued.

Contract for deed (installment sales and land sales contract) A document used to secure real property when it is seller-financed; contains the full agreement between the parties, including purchase price, terms of payment, and any additional agreements.

Contract of sale An agreement by one party to buy and another party to sell a piece of property for a specific price.

Escrow An impartial holding of documents pertinent to the sale and transfer of real estate; also the term used to describe the long-term holding of documents, such as with seller financing, called a long-term escrow or escrow collection; *escrow holder:* an impartial third party who holds the documents pertinent to the transfer and sale of real estate.

Exception The provision in a title insurance policy that excludes liability for a specific title defect.

Exclusion General matters affecting title to real property excluded from coverage of a title insurance policy.

Fixtures Personal property that is attached to real property, such as chandeliers, window blinds, and medicine cabinets.

Home insurance The amount you pay based on a percent of the value of your home.

Homeowner's insurance The real estate insurance protecting against loss caused by fire, some natural causes, vandalism, etc., depending on the terms of the policy; also includes coverage such as personal liability and theft away from home.

Insurable title A land title that a title insurance company is willing to insure.

Lawyer, real estate Not all lawyers are the same; it is best to have real estate attorneys review real estate contracts.

Lease purchase A type of delayed closing; agreement is drafted on a purchase and sales contract, stating the terms of the purchase, as well as a date for closing the sale. Should the buyer default, the seller has all the remedies available under the sales contract.

Loan policy (mortgage policy) A title insurance policy insuring a mortgagee or beneficiary under a deed of trust against loss caused by invalidity or unenforceability of a lien.

Power of attorney A written document that authorizes one person to act on behalf of another in the specific actions described in the instrument.

Premium The amount payable for an insurance policy.

Real estate The land and anything permanently affixed to the land, such as buildings, fences, and those things attached to the buildings, such as plumbing and heating fixtures or other such items that would be personal property if not attached.

Standard coverage policy A form of title insurance which contains certain standard printed exceptions; used primarily in some of the Western states.

Title covenants Covenants ordinarily inserted in conveyances for the purpose of giving protection to the purchaser against possible insufficiency of the title received.

Title defect Any possible defect in a chain of title that is adverse to the claim of ownership; any material irregularity in the execution or effect of an instrument in the chain of title.

Title insurance A guarantee that the property is free of claims from unknown third parties, such as former spouses or contractors; required by most lenders before a mortgage can be approved.

Underwriter An insurance company that issues insurance policies to the public or to another insurer.

Waiver A voluntary and intentional relinquishment of a known right, claim, or privilege.

Warranty The provisions in a deed, lease, or other instrument transferring real estate under which the seller becomes liable to the purchaser for defects in or encumbrances on the title.

Know Before You Go

The All-Important Inspection

▶ Don't Pack Yet: Learning from Disclosures and a Home Inspection

Of course, you've looked at your new property, but now you need to have a far more in-depth look. Well, you have the right to do so. Your contract gives you the right to have a professional inspection of the property to make sure that it is as sound as you have been led to believe. The contract will state a timeframe within which you must make your inspections. The actual amount of time may vary according to your agent's suggestions or your own timeframe, but generally the mortgage contingency runs 45 days, attorney approval requires five business days, and the inspections occur within five to 10 business days after acceptance of the contract.

Even before a seller accepts your offer on a home, the subject of disclosure and inspection is sure to come up. The seller's agent may offer you a set of disclosures or will tell you when to expect them. Your agent, if a good one, will insist that you have the right to inspect the property and approve the disclosures, in which case a clause to that effect will be inserted into the sales agreement/offer.

What are disclosures and why do you get them? What is an inspection and do you really need one?

Amber Light: The Fine Print—Disclosures

Over the past decade, largely because of increased litigation (mainly by buyers who sued sellers over undisclosed defects and won), sellers increasingly offer buyers a disclosure statement that details known problems with the property. In fact, in nearly half the states today, a disclosure statement is *required* from the seller as part of the standard real estate transaction.

The disclosure statement can be either very helpful or virtually useless, depending on how dutiful the sellers are in filling it out. Ideally, it is something that buyers can effectively use to determine what, if anything, is wrong with a property. Disclosure gives you a powerful legal tool and can help you leverage a better deal. If the sellers leave something off the statement and you later find out that they knew about the problem (or should have known) and failed to disclose it, and if the defect causes you a loss (either of the cost of having something fixed or in the value of the property), you can use the failure to disclose as part of a lawsuit. If you win, the sellers can be forced to repay you for your loss.

In some cases where the problem is extreme, you might actually have the sale rescinded. In other words, the sellers might have to take the property back and return your money to you. But this very rarely happens. In addition, if the disclosures are given to you after you conclude a purchase agreement (as they usually are), and if they disclose something significantly wrong with the property, you normally can reopen negotiations and insist on a lower price, better terms, or correction of the problem by the sellers before the sale is concluded.

The disclosure statement is a real boon for the sellers, too, if it is handled properly. By disclosing everything that's wrong with the home on the statement, the sellers put you on notice about the problems the property has. If you accept these problems, you have very little to come back and complain about later on. Nevertheless, there is a great danger that the sellers will be tempted to lie or at least fudge on the disclosure statement. The possibility that the disclosures are incomplete is a good reason to have a home inspection.

Sightseeing: What to Look For

If possible, read the disclosure statement before you commit to buying the property. You should definitely read it before the home inspection, and you should take it to the inspection. There is usually a specific time during which you can reject the property because of the disclosures. That is when you should make any objections or reopen negotiations.

The disclosure statement can take a wide variety of forms. Roadmap 6.1 is a typical example. It goes without saying, however, that you should carefully scan the statement, noting any check marks that indicate a problem. For example, in our sample statement, the first two items indicate leaks. (Make a copy of your disclosure so you can make notes and highlight key issues. Take it to the inspection, and as you and the inspector investigate the problems, check them off or make additional notes.)

Now, let's review the sample statement to give you an idea of what to look for and how to read between the lines.

Leakage Problems. Because the owner has indicated that there are leaks and that they were not fully corrected, you would

- ask when and where the leaks occurred,
- ask to see them (see also the last area on this sample form), and note their current condition,
- have a competent roofer check the condition of the roof, and
- check for damage to ceilings or walls and for dry rot.

It's a good idea to assume that leaks are worse than disclosed.

Plumbing Problems. There is only one suggestion of a plumbing problem —low water pressure in the master bathroom. Why in only one room? Are there galvanized pipes in the home that are corroded and blocked? Is the plumbing in that bathroom not up to code? Could there be a leak in the line? You may want to have a plumbing contractor check out the property.

Title Problems. "Encroachments or easements" have been checked affirmatively. This could be simple or serious. Much of this should be disclosed by the title insurance company, but you should also get an expanded explanation (in writing) from the owner.

Another potential title problem has to do with the fact that the property is part of a homeowners' association (HOA) that is involved in a lawsuit.

Roadmap 6.1

Seller's Disclosure Statement

The following statement is intended as an example. Do not use it without first taking it to your attorney and asking them to make it appropriate for your state and locale and for your specific transaction.

(To be filled out by the seller and given to buyer. Seller, use a separate page to explain any defects or problems with property.)

Water

1. Any leaks (now or before) in roof?   Yes _X_ No ____
   Around a skylight; at a chimney, door or window; or elsewhere?   Yes ____ No _X_
2. Was problem corrected? _Mostly_
3. How? _Caulking_
4. By whom? _Owner_
5. When? _'94_ By permit? _No_ Final inspection when? ____
6. Does home have gutters?   Yes ____ No _X_
7.   Condition? ____
8. Does home have downspouts?   Yes ____ No _X_
9.   Condition? ____
10. Any drainage problems?   Yes ____ No _X_
11.   Explain _Uses sump pump_
12.   How corrected? ____
13.   When corrected? ____
14. Is water directed away from home?   Yes _X_ No ____
15. Any flooding or grading problems?   Yes ____ No _X_
16. Any settling, slipping, sliding or other kinds of soil problems?   Yes ____ No _X_
17. Any leaks at sinks, toilets, tubs, showers or elsewhere in home?   Yes ____ No _X_
18. Public water? _X_ Or well? ____
19.   Date well pump installed? ____
20. Low water pressure?   Yes _X_ No ____
    Where? _In master bath only_

Title

21. Are you involved in a bankruptcy?   Yes ____ No _X_
22. Are you in default on any mortgage?   Yes ____ No _X_

23. Do you currently occupy the property? Yes _X_ No ____

24. Have you given anyone else an option, a lease or a right of first refusal on the property? Yes ____ No _X_

25. Does the property have any bond liens? Yes ____ No _X_

26. Can they be paid off without penalty? Yes _X_ No ____

27. Any boundary disputes? Yes ____ No _X_

28. Any encroachments or easements? Yes _X_ No ____

29. Any shared walls, fences or other such areas? Yes _X_ No ____

30. Any areas held in common, such as pools, tennis courts, walkways, green belts or other areas? Yes ____ No _X_

31. Any notices of abatement filed? Yes ____ No _X_

32. Any lawsuits against seller that will affect title? Yes ____ No _X_

33. Do you have a real estate license? Yes ____ No _X_

34. Is there a homeowners' association to which you must belong? Yes _X_ No ____

35. Any current lawsuits involving the homeowners' association? Yes _X_ No ____

36. Any conditions, covenants and restrictions (CC&Rs) in deed affecting the property? Yes _X_ No ____

37. Any easements or rights-of-way over the property to public utilities or others? Yes _X_ No ____

Structure

38. Any cracks in slab? Yes ____ No _X_

39. Any cracks in interior walls? Yes _X_ No ____

40. Any cracks in ceiling? Yes _X_ No ____

41. Any cracks in exterior walls? Yes _X_ No ____

42. Any cracks in foundation? Yes ____ No _X_

43. Any retaining walls? Yes ____ No _X_

44. Cracked? ____ Leaning? ____ Broken? ____

45. Any cracks in driveway? Yes _X_ No ____

46. Any problems with fences? Yes ____ No _X_

47. Is home insulated? Yes _X_ No ____

48. Attic? _X_ Walls? ____ Floor? ____

49. Any double-paned glass windows? Yes ____ No _X_

50. Is there a moisture barrier in areas below ground level? Yes ____ No _X_

51. Is there a sump pump? Yes _X_ No ____

52. Where? _Under patio deck_

53. Why? _Drainage in winter_

54. Is there a septic tank?   Yes ____ No _X_

55.   Active? ____ Abandoned? ____ Filled? ____

56. Connected to sewer?   Yes _X_ No ____

Equipment

57. Is there a central furnace?   Yes _X_ No ____

58.   Forced air? _X_ Radiant/water? ____

59.   Radiant/electric? ____ Other? ____

60. Any room heaters?   Yes ____ No _X_

61.   Type? _____

62.   Location? _____

63. Is there central air-conditioning?   Yes _X_ No ____

64.   Installed date? _____

65. Any room air conditioners?   Yes ____ No _X_

66.   Location? _____

67. Is furnace room vented?   Yes _X_ No ____

68. Is there a temperature relief valve on
water heater?   Yes _X_ No ____

69.   On spa?   Yes ____ No _X_

70.   On pool?   Yes ____ No _X_

71.   Is the pool heated?   Yes _X_ No ____

72.   Any cracks, leaks or other problems
with pool?   Yes _X_ No ____

73.   Explain _____

74.   Other? _____

75. Any aluminum wiring?   Yes _X_ No ____

Hazards and Violations

76. Any asbestos?   Yes ____ No _X_

77. Any environmental hazards, including but not
limited to radon gas, lead-based paint, storage
tanks for diesel or other fuel, contaminants
in soil or water, formaldehyde?   Yes ____ No _X_

78. Is there a landfill on or near property?   Yes ____ No _X_

79. Is property in earthquake zone?   Yes ____ No _X_

80. Is property in flood hazard zone?   Yes ____ No _X_

81. Is property in landslide area?   Yes ____ No _X_

82. Is property in high-fire-hazard area, as
described on a Federal Emergency
Management Agency Flood Insurance Rate
Map or Flood Hazard Boundary Map?   Yes ____ No _X_

83. Is property in any "special study" zone, which indicates a hazard or requires permission to add or alter existing structure?   Yes _____ No _X_

84. Any zoning violations pertaining to property? (Explain separately)   Yes _____ No _X_

85. Any room additions built without appropriate permits? (Explain separately)   Yes _X_ No _____

86. Any work done to electrical, plumbing, gas or other home systems without appropriate permit? (Explain separately)   Yes _____ No _X_

87. Does property have an energy conservation retrofit?   Yes _____ No _X_

88. Any odors caused by gas, toxic waste, agriculture or other sources?   Yes _____ No _X_

89. Were pets kept on property?   Yes _X_ No _____

90. Type? _Cat_ Inside? _Yes_

91. Any pet odor problems?   Yes _____ No _X_

92. Any active springs on property?   Yes _____ No _X_

93. Any sinkholes on property?   Yes _____ No _X_

94. Is property adjacent to or near any existing or planned mining sites, toxic waste sites, or other environmental hazards?   Yes _____ No _X_

95. Any real estate development planned or pending in immediate area, such as commercial, industrial, or residential development, that could affect property values?   Yes _X_ No _____

96. Any abandoned septic tanks?   Yes _____ No _X_

97. Is a home protection plan available to buyer?   Yes _X_ No _____

Reports That Have Been Made

Seller notes that the following reports have been made and are available to buyer:

98. Structural   Yes _____ No _X_

99. Geologic   Yes _X_ No _____

100. Roof   Yes _____ No _X_

101. Soil   Yes _____ No _X_

102. Sewer/septic   Yes _____ No _X_

103. Heating/air-conditioning   Yes _____ No _X_

104. Electrical/plumbing   Yes _____ No _X_

105. Termite   Yes _____ No _X_

106. Pool/spa	Yes _____	No _X_
107. General home inspection	Yes _____	No _X_
108. Energy audit	Yes _____	No _X_
109. Radon test	Yes _____	No _X_
110. City inspection	Yes _____	No _X_

Items That Go with the Property

111. _____	Yes _X_	No _____
112. Window coverings	Yes _X_	No _____
113. Floor coverings	Yes _X_	No _____
114. Range	Yes _X_	No _____
115. Oven	Yes _X_	No _____
116. Microwave	Yes _____	No _X_
117. Dishwasher	Yes _X_	No _____
118. Trash compactor	Yes _X_	No _____
119. Garbage disposal	Yes _X_	No _____
120. Bottled water	Yes _____	No _X_
121. Burglar alarm system	Yes _____	No _X_
122. Gutters	Yes _____	No _X_
123. Fire alarm	Yes _X_	No _____
124. Intercom	Yes _____	No _X_
125. Electric washer/dryer hookups	Yes _X_	No _____
126. Sauna	Yes _____	No _X_
127. Hot tub	Yes _____	No _X_
128. Spa	Yes _____	No _X_
129. Pool	Yes _____	No _X_
130. Central heating	Yes _X_	No _____
131. Central air-conditioning	Yes _X_	No _____
132. Central evaporative cooler	Yes _____	No _X_
133. Water softener	Yes _____	No _X_
134. Space heaters	Yes _____	No _X_
135. Solar heating	Yes _____	No _X_
136. Window air conditioners	Yes _____	No _X_
137. Sprinklers	Yes _X_	No _____
138. Where? _Front and back_		
139. Security gates	Yes _____	No _X_
140. Television antenna	Yes _____	No _X_
141. TV cable connections	Yes _X_	No _____

142. TV satellite dish   Yes _____ No _X_

143. Attached garage   Yes _X_ No _____

144. Detached garage   Yes _____ No _X_

145. Water heater   Yes _X_ No _____

146.   Gas _X_ Electric _____

147. City water supply   Yes _X_ No _____

148. Public utility gas   Yes _X_ No _____

149. Propane gas   Yes _____ No _X_

150. Screens on windows   Yes _X_ No _____

151. Sump pump   Yes _X_ No _____

152. Built-in barbecue   Yes _____ No _X_

153. Garage door opener   Yes _X_ No _____

154.   Number of remote controls _2_

155. Is the property equipped with smoke detectors?   Yes _____ No _X_

Items That Are Specifically Excluded from the Sale

156. Lamps? _X_
       Where? _____

157. Window coverings? _____
       Where? _____

158. Other Items?   Yes _X_ No _____

159.   Explain _____
           _____

160. Seller is aware of the following defects or malfunctions and specifically draws buyer's attention to them:
Some cracks here and there, inside and out.
Nothing seems serious. Occasional heavy rains
produce puddling, sometimes under home.

Buyer is encouraged to make a physical inspection of the property and to employ the services of a competent inspection company to obtain an independent verbal and written report of the property's condition.

Signed by seller and buyer

_____

_____

Many properties these days have common areas, swimming pools and tennis courts, all run by an HOA. And today, as never before, these organizations are embroiled in lawsuits.

Foundation and Slab Problems. The owner has not answered yes to number 38, indicating cracks in the slab, or number 42, disclosing cracks in the foundation, but cracks in interior and exterior walls and ceilings have been noted. It could be that the owner is just being overly cautious (tiny cracks often appear in sheetrock, stucco, and plaster as a building settles over time); on the other hand, bigger cracks are almost always the result of foundation and slab problems. Even though the owner hasn't detected problems, you would definitely be concerned about the slab and foundation.

Drainage. The sump pump outside indicates a drainage problem. Water is getting under the foundation, and the pump has been installed to help move it away from the home. Be sure to investigate the operation of the pump, the reason for it, and whether the ground underneath the home is dry. Also, check for a cracked foundation, which could have occurred because of poor water drainage.

Hazards and Violations. Hazards and violations are important areas of concern because they tell you whether there are any problems exterior to the property, such as zoning violations or the threat of floods or earthquakes. If any of these items is checked, get down to city hall to find out what studies have been done and what regulations are appropriate.

In this case, the owner indicates that a room was added without the benefit of a permit. This could be a serious defect because, at least in theory, the building department might at some future time require that the addition be brought up to code. (In some communities, a building inspection is required upon every sale to detect any such work.)

Pet Problems. The owner notes that a cat was kept indoors. It could be a problem if a proper litter box was not provided. Check for odors and any damage to carpet, hardwood floors, and walls.

External Developments. You need to know future development plans and the seller needs to tell you that it could affect the value of your home. A check in the yes column of number 95 will alert you to any possible problem. However, you might also want to check with the local newspaper for information on the subject, as well as with the office of county records.

Reports. Any reports that have been filed on the property should be given to you, including any completed by a buyer who did not purchase the property. A seller's failure to give you the report could be considered covering up a problem. Check with your agent to see what sorts of reports are usually done. For example, properties in flood zones will usually require a flood report indicating where the property is located in terms of the flood plain and assessing the likelihood of flooding. You may not be able to get financing or insurance without such a report. If appropriate reports have not been completed, you may want to pursue them. The cost may be the buyer's, the seller's or a combination, usually depending on custom in the area, although everything is negotiable.

Items Included. Be very careful here. Be sure that everything you think comes with the home really does. If you want an item included in the sale, be sure it's listed on the disclosure statement and on the sales agreement.

What Else to Examine. A careful reading of the report can offer many clues; here are some:

1. Look for what's not there. The sellers should say something positive about different aspects of the home. If these statements are missing, perhaps there's a reason.
2. Look for items barely mentioned. Sometimes sellers try to minimize a problem so that it's included, but made to sound innocuous.
3. Look for truly minor problems. These days, many sellers realize that to avoid problems later on, it is to their advantage to disclose everything upfront. Therefore, many disclosure statements include items that really may not be serious problems, but that the seller has included to be safe.

Travel Insurance: A Home Warranty Plan

Finally, one last method of protecting yourself is to obtain (usually at the seller's expense) a home warranty insurance plan. These usually cover all appliances, including the furnace and heater, and may cover many structural areas as well. They can often be expanded to cover spas, pools, and other accessories. Home warranty plans normally require that the seller of the property warrant that everything is in good, working condition at the time of the sale. Also, they usually require a minimum payment (deductible) for each service call, typically in the $35 to $50 range.

When a seller hands a buyer a disclosure statement saying that everything is fine, a home warranty plan should be the buyer's next step. Even if there are problems noted on the disclosure statement, a warranty plan can sometimes work as a solution.

Canceling the Trip: Too Many Problems

If the laws of your state do not require an opportunity to reject the property on the basis of disclosures, you should have a clause written into your purchase agreement that specifically allows you to back out of the deal (including getting your deposit back) without penalty. Be sure the clause gives you at least a few days after receiving the disclosures to read them and give approval or to back out, if necessary. Or, if you prefer, you can use your right to back out in your renegotiation with the seller.

▶ The Last Leg of the Journey: Inspection Process

You should insist on an inspection to ensure that all of the home's systems are in good shape. If problems are discovered, you can then negotiate with the seller over what should be done and who should pay for it. When you seek permission to inspect a seller's home, remember that sellers usually want inspections too to avoid problems down the road. As a result, when you ask for a clause in a purchase agreement that allows for a home inspection (usually 5 to 10 days after the sales agreement is signed) that gives them the right to approve the inspection report or back out of the deal, sellers are generally willing to go along. Keep in mind, however, that you, as the buyer, will have to pay for the inspection. This costs around $300–$500 for a typical home. (You should always accompany the inspector so you can follow up on things you noted on the disclosure statement and because you can learn a great deal from what the inspector says as you move through the property.)

There are several problems with home inspections. First, an inspection is cursory by its very nature. Although you and an inspector will have a couple of hours to look things over, there are many areas that you can't really inspect, such as underneath carpets, and inaccessible areas, such as parts of the attic, underneath the house, and inside the walls. In short, you can inspect what you can see. That covers a great deal. But it can also leave a great deal out.

Dear Sis,

You won't believe what's happening! Don and I thought we'd found the perfect home—just what we always wanted—lovely, lakefront property that wasn't too expensive and had just the right view of the mountains.

We couldn't wait to move in. You remember how happy we were when you visited last summer. We thought we were crazy when we began to notice that the lake was disappearing. At first, we thought it was because there had been so little snow the past few years, but that wasn't it.

It turns out, our lake is manmade, and the privately owned, manmade dam that trapped the water on the other end of the lake was condemned by the Army Corps of Engineers. The owner was ordered to drain the lake and remove the dam. Would you believe the battle between the owner and the engineers has been going on for years! No one told us.

We and the other homeowners who bought not knowing this are distraught. We are suing the real estate agent for not telling us the lake was going to vanish. But, even if we win, that won't bring back our idyllic view.

The agent's defense amounts to, "You didn't ask."

Tearfully,
Susan

Second, the quality of home inspectors is not yet uniform throughout the country.

Third, the written report of what the inspector has found is too often simply a printout generated by a home inspection computer program. The inspector fills out a form on the screen, and then the computer spits out the report. Too often these reports fail to draw any concrete conclusions that the buyer will find useful.

On the other hand, an honest and qualified inspector will show you items that you may not know to look for—both good and bad; a good inspector can tell you the lifetime of the heating unit in your new home or that the water heater is an accident waiting to happen. A good inspector can tell you that your water heater is brand new or the rusted bottom means an inevitable flood. In other words, a good inspector is a good investment.

Finally, there's a tendency to sue the home inspector for items that weren't revealed—even if the omission was not the fault of the inspector. Therefore, inspectors often include multiple disclaimers and back away from challenging anything that might lead to an angry buyer or seller. Sometimes this makes the report so wishy-washy that it is virtually useless. Some states, faced with consumer complaints, have begun regulating home inspectors. Soon licensing should become fairly standard. Eventually, home inspectors may be as strictly regulated as real estate agents—but not yet in most areas.

Leading the Tour: Finding a Good Home Inspector

The truth of the matter is that many home inspectors are retired building inspectors, contractors, or engineers. They are competent and strive to do a good job. Work with them, accompany them, ask questions and you should learn a lot. There are two trade associations for home inspectors:

The American Society of Home Inspectors (ASHI)
932 Lee St.
Des Plaines, IL 60016-6546
Telephone: 847-290-1959; 800-743-2744
http://www.ashi.com

National Association of Home Inspectors (NAHI)
303 W. Cypress
San Antonio, TX 78212-0528
Telephone: 800-486-3676
http://www.nahi.org

Both of these promote home inspection and encourage inspectors to improve their performance. ASHI has a set of guidelines for home inspections that is particularly helpful. Your inspector should belong to at least one of these groups.

You should also ask for recommendations. Your agent should be able to recommend a home inspector, but you shouldn't limit yourself to that agent's recommendations. Ask other agents or friends who recently bought a house and had a home inspection. The idea is to use an inspector whose name keeps coming up.

Also, call your local Building and Safety Department. Sometimes home inspectors are retired from local building departments. These are the people who regularly go out and inspect property for the city to be sure it meets the code. They are well versed in what to look for in a home and have had extensive experience with people who try to cover up problems. They also tend to be more candid than others.

You may also want to consider contractors. Sometimes retired contractors become inspectors. Because of their knowledge of home construction, they can be an excellent choice. However, beware of a contractor who wears two hats. If they are both a home inspector and a contractor, they may simply be out scouting for jobs. How will you be able to trust the judgment when the contractor tells you something is wrong and in the next breath gives you an estimate for what it will cost to have it fixed? Remember, it is the contractor who wants to fix it! There's an inevitable conflict of interest. Also, be sure the contractor isn't a specialist. For example, an electrical contractor will presumably know all about wiring, but what will they know about plumbing? Structural and civil engineers also make good inspectors.

If you check these sources and you find the same name popping up over and over again, you may have a winner. Call the inspector and set up an interview.

How to Hire an Inspector. You're paying the bill so you should be the one to hire the inspector. Don't relegate this important job to an agent or anyone else. Do it yourself.

Begin with an interview. At a minimum, ask the inspector for credentials: Did you work in the building department? Are you a licensed contractor? In what area do you have an engineering degree? Are you a member of the ASHI or NAHI? Also ask for the names of at least three people whose homes they have inspected in the past six months. Call each of the named people and find out how their inspections went. Were the customers satisfied? Did something later turn up that the inspector had overlooked?

Once you've hired the inspector, you two will work closely until the report is complete.

Visiting the Site: Making the Inspection

In general, the inspector assesses the structural and mechanical components of the home. Features the inspector will usually not examine include paint, wallpaper, carpeting, household appliances, and draperies. They also will not look for termites, fleas, rodents, or other pests.

The following is a brief rundown of things your inspector should check:

▶ Structural components, including foundations, floors, walls, columns, ceilings, and roofs
▶ Exterior conditions, including wall flashings and trim, doors, windows, chimneys, decks, balconies, stoops, steps, porches, eaves, vegetation, grading, drainage, driveways, patios, and walkways
▶ Plumbing systems, including pipes, drains, and traps, and the operation of showers, toilets, and faucets
▶ Electrical systems, including wiring, grounding equipment, amperage and voltage ratings, circuit breakers, lighting fixtures, and receptacles
▶ Heating systems, including boilers, thermostats, heat pumps, insulation, radiators, and automatic safety controls
▶ Air-conditioning systems, including central controls and distribution systems such as fans, pumps, ducts, and air filters
▶ Interiors, including walls, ceilings, floors, cabinets, doors, windows, and stairs

It is your task to scrutinize the aspects of the home the inspector does not. You should also learn about the state of the local environment. You don't want to pay for damages caused by leakage of toxic or hazardous wastes that have been buried on the land. (This should be noted in the seller's disclosure statement.)

Tools You Will Need. In order to conduct a home inspection (with or without a professional inspector), you'll need certain tools. These aren't expensive, and chances are you already have them around the house. Be sure that before you begin the inspection tour, you have these available:

▶ Wear old clothing (clothes, shoes, and hat that can get dirty). Remember, you'll be crawling under the house and in the attic.
▶ Flashlight with fresh batteries
▶ Long, thin flathead screwdriver

► Large marble
► Short carpenter's level
► Tape measure
► Binoculars (optional)
► Small mirror (for seeing behind things)
► Electrical circuit tester
► Clipboard to hold paperwork

While the written report is an important part of the home inspection, the verbal discussion as the inspection takes place can be far more important. The inspector who accompanies you should be able to point out different things to you. Along the way you can ask questions and receive explanations.

One way to judge whether you have a good inspector is to watch how they conduct themselves. Is the dress appropriate for the inspection? Did the inspector bother to bring along a flashlight and tools for probing and checking? Were your questions answered logically and clearly? A good inspector should inspire confidence.

Souvenir of the Visit: The Inspection Report

You will want a written report of the inspection. You can use this report to point out problems to the seller and, perhaps, get an adjustment on the price. Ask for a report in the inspector's own words. With computer-generated reports, it's too easy for the inspector to simply input standard information and then print out a standard report. One computer-generated report will look much like another. If you're paying several hundred dollars, you want a report with specific comments about the house you are buying, and you want it in the inspector's own words.

If the inspector wants to use a computer program, that's OK, but make sure there are plenty of specific comments. That way you'll be more likely to understand what the inspector really thinks.

When you get the report, review it carefully. If you're not certain about something, ask for an additional inspection. If the inspector notes, for example, that the roof has a problem, have a roofer come in and tell you what's wrong and how much it will cost to repair. Don't be intimidated into approving a bad report. If the inspector finds something wrong, you can back out of the deal, persuade the seller to pay for repairs, or get a price reduction.

Inspector's Warranties and Liabilities. What if the inspector overlooks something? What if a part of the home is left out? Inspectors are liable for their errors, omissions, and outright mistakes. To protect themselves they will often hedge on their answers. As a result, as noted earlier, what you will often get on an inspection report are generalizations and superficial comments about items and conditions that you could have seen for yourself. On the other hand, if there really is a bad condition that's obvious, most inspectors will note it as such.

Inspectors will only warrant the home at the time of the inspection. They will write something like, "This report indicates the condition of the house as I found it," and will include many paragraphs of disclaimers. In short, even though the inspector is presumably responsible, unless there was some sort of gross problem, holding them liable for something that was missed during an inspection is pretty hard to do.

At the Crossroads: After the Inspection

Upon completion of a home inspection, the inspector reviews and explains all of the conditions and defects that were discovered. Buyers, at this point, are often uncertain what to do with the lengthy list of newly disclosed information and commonly ask: "Which items are the sellers required to repair?" and "What if the sellers won't address these problems?"

Home inspectors can provide guidelines and perspectives in answer to these questions, but most essential at this stage of the transaction is representation by an agent or broker with strong negotiating skills and a sense of commitment to the buyers' best interests. How matters are handled at this juncture can determine the degree of benefit buyers attain from the inspection and the level of satisfaction to be enjoyed when the sale is completed. Failure to properly apply the new disclosures can negate the purpose of the inspection.

The first thing you must understand is that home inspection reports are not repair lists for sellers. The one exception to this rule applies to brand-new homes, where the builder or contractor must provide a finished product free of defects. With used homes, inspection reports provide information for buyers rather than directives for sellers. This does not mean that buyers can not submit repair requests to sellers, but most such requests are negotiable, not legally binding upon the sellers. Repair requests can and should be made, but with the understanding that most sellers have the rights of refusal.

With this ground rule in place, you should divide the inspection findings into four distinct categories:

1. *Legally mandated repairs:* Some conditions require repairs in accordance with state laws or local ordinances or by governmental lenders such as the FHA and the VA. Requirements to provide water-conserving toilets and showerheads, to upgrade smoke detector placement, to strap water heaters in areas prone to earthquakes, or to comply with various building and safety standards are common in many areas. Such items are obviously nonnegotiable and must be addressed by the sellers.

2. *Contractually mandated repairs:* Some conditions are specified for repair in the real estate purchase contract. Typical among these are stipulations that all building components be in working condition, that broken windows be replaced, that plumbing leaks be repaired, or that the roof be certified by a licensed roofing contractor. Contractual agreements of this kind are binding upon sellers.

3. *Negotiable repairs:* All property defects not included in items 1 and 2 above are negotiable, and buyers should carefully divide these according to importance. Vital repairs, such as structural problems or safety violations, although not incumbent upon sellers, are generally regarded as reasonable repair requests. Even though sellers are not obligated for such corrective work, most reasonable sellers agree to address conditions of this kind, either by making repairs or by adjusting the sales price of the property. Examples of such conditions include faulty foundations, a nonpermitted addition, a defective furnace, a substandard chimney, and faulty electrical wiring. Although sellers are not required to make these repairs, buyers should feel comfortable requesting that such corrections be completed.

4. *Conditions of minor concern:* Finally, there are those common property defects that should be regarded for disclosure purposes only and that buyers should accept as conditions to be repaired after the sale. Examples are numerous and include rotted fence posts, peeling paint, rubbing doors, cracked pavement, worn carpet, obsolete appliances, and the like.

Before you make any demands of the seller, try to evaluate the inspection report with an eye toward problems of greatest significance. Look for conditions that compromise health and safety or involve active leakage. Most sellers will address problems affecting sensitive areas such as the roof, fireplace, gas-burning fixtures, or electrical wiring. Routine maintenance items warrant a lesser degree of concern and should not be pressed upon the seller. If the house is not brand-new, it is unreasonable to insist boldly upon correction of all defects. Such demands can alienate the seller and kill the deal. Your willingness to accept minor problems may persuade a seller to correct conditions of greater substance.

The purpose of a home inspection is not to corner the seller with a repair list. The primary objective is to know what you are buying before you buy it. All homes have defects; it's not possible to acquire one that is perfect. What you want is a working knowledge of significant defects before you take possession.

How to Negotiate After the Home Inspection. When you receive a home inspection report, deciding what to do next can be perplexing and challenging. It is probably the touchiest transitional phase in the entire purchase process. The original haggling was hard enough: An agreement was made on the price and terms of the deal, and you thought everything was set. Now, suddenly, with new revelations posed by the home inspector, negotiations are reopened and nothing is certain. The question, at this point, is: "What repair requests are appropriate?" As a rule in most transactions, your negotiating position will depend upon the answers to the following five questions:

1. What repairs are mandated by law?
2. What repairs (if any) are specified in the purchase contract? In some contracts, special provisions are made for repairing particular problems; in those cases, sellers are required to address specific issues revealed by the inspector. Other contracts have no such provisions.
3. How motivated and negotiable is the seller? Market conditions and personal circumstances can make a big difference when determining requests and demands to present to a seller. In a "hot" real estate market, an as-is approach might be the best way to secure the deal. When the economy is slow, a seller might be willing to jump through hoops to complete the sale.
4. How capable a negotiator is your agent?
5. Are you willing to walk away from the deal if you don't get what you want? This does not mean that one should be so obstinate as to demand every preference with an "or else" approach. But where critical issues

are at stake, emotional detachment is a valuable tool when discussing the terms of a sale.

These standards should be applied when reviewing the inspection report, as a means of separating repairs to be requested from conditions to be accepted.

At this point, the buyers and their agent typically formulate a letter of request for the sellers. A wise approach for structuring this letter is to state that some defects will be accepted in as-is condition. Listing the items to be accepted is a good strategy for negotiation because enumerating the accepted defects demonstrates a willingness to be reasonable rather than demanding. The letter should then list the items for which repairs are requested, beginning with conditions required by law or by contract and concluding with the items that are subject to the sellers' approval. When submitting this letter to the sellers, it should include a copy of the home inspection report if the seller has not already received a copy.

Seller responses to repair requests vary widely according to circumstances and personalities, and buyers should not automatically expect carte blanche acceptance of their wish list. Most sellers will agree to fix portions of the buyers' listed concerns, a few will refuse to fix anything, and a small, but delightful, group of others will agree to fix everything.

The following are the three most common reasons for seller refusals:

1. The majority of sellers seek to obtain maximum financial advantage when selling a home. Thus, their willingness to address needed repairs will be counterbalanced by monetary concerns.
2. Some sellers, although willing to make repairs, are financially unable to do so.
3. The most difficult group, those who precipitate the most canceled sales, are sellers who are unwilling to make repairs for strictly personal and emotional reasons.

When sellers flatly refuse to make specified repairs, buyers are faced with a critical choice: whether to cancel the transaction or accept the unrepaired defects as they are. Decisions of this kind hinge upon many factors: individual temperaments, personal circumstances, various contingencies of the sale, and, mainly, the financial implications of the problems needing repair.

When negotiations become deadlocked, a useful way of leveraging the conversation is to obtain repair bids from licensed contractors. Genuine numbers, particularly those that begin with dollar signs, add a dimension of reality to any discussion. Suddenly, the issue boils down to basic arithmetic. The buyer simply adds the appraised value of the property to the estimated repair costs. If the total does not exceed the sales price, then the purchase may still be acceptable. If the total does exceed the sales price, the seller's negotiating position is weakened.

A variation of this approach is to provide copies of the home inspection report and the contractor's repair bid to the real estate appraiser—the person who determines the official value of the property. This could prompt the appraiser to adjust the appraisal, thereby inducing the seller to adjust the sales price accordingly.

Dealing with Repairs. In the majority of residential sales, repairs are performed as a result of the home inspection. This fact affects real estate sales procedures by making the complicated repair phase an expected element of the routine. The demanding process of arranging and orchestrating repairs can be complicated and time consuming and has become the de facto responsibility of agents for the buyers and sellers. Contractors and handymen must be contacted and scheduled in a timeframe that coincides with the specified closing date for the sale. Scheduling must be coordinated with the daily routines of sellers, and all parties must agree that completed repairs were performed in an acceptable manner.

▶ What's This Trip Worth: The Appraisal

If the home passes both your inspection and examination by a professional inspector, you should obtain an independent appraisal to make sure you don't pay too much for the property. Your lender may select an appraiser or may provide you with a list of approved appraisers, whose fees you will probably pay. If you want your own appraisal as well, you can find a professional appraiser through one of these organizations:

National Association of Master Appraisers
P.O. Box 12617
303 W. Cypress St.
San Antonio, TX 78212-0617
Telephone: 800-229-NAMA
http://www.masterappraisers.org

Appraisal Institute
875 N. Michigan Ave., Suite 2400
Chicago, IL 60611-1980
Telephone: 312-335-4100
http://www.appraisalinstitute.org

If the appraisal indicates a lower amount than the seller is asking, you may be able to use it as a bargaining chip to get a better price. The bank will use the appraisal to determine how large a mortgage you may receive (banks lend only a certain percentage of a home's appraised value).

Setting Sail

Buying Your Home—At Last!

▶ Preparing to Depart: What to Expect

In Maine they pass papers; in California they close escrow. It's closing, settlement, transfer of title—the moment when the seller gets the money and you get legal ownership and the front-door keys. In few real estate matters does local custom vary so widely.

In your area, closing may be conducted by attorneys, title companies, an escrow service, a lending institution, even by real estate brokers. It may take place at the county courthouse, a bank, an attorney's office, or another location. Sometimes everyone sits around a big table; sometimes buyer and seller never meet.

Whatever it's called and wherever it's held, the last step in buying your dream home is the closing, where the many players involved in the transaction come together and checks for thousands of dollars are distributed. You should enter the final leg of this house-buying marathon knowing who will be present, what legal documents you must bring, and how much money you must hand over to finish the deal. Generally, the cast of characters attending a closing includes the buyer, the seller, a real estate attorney for both parties, a representative of the bank making the mortgage, an escrow agent from the bank holding your down payment and earnest money, a representative of the title insurance company, and the real estate broker for both parties.

Your purchase contract provides a blueprint for the final transfer. The seller's main responsibility is to prove title, to show that you are receiving clear and trouble-free ownership. Depending on the mortgagee's requirements and local custom, the seller may prove title by furnishing an abstract and lawyer's opinion, title insurance, or, in some states, a Torrens certificate.

There are two types of title insurance. A fee policy, which may be required by your lender, protects the mortgagee—the lender—against loss if other parties challenge your ownership. If you need the policy for your mortgage loan, you may be asked to pay for it. The premium is a single payment; good for the whole time you own the property. For a relatively small additional fee, you can purchase it at the same time as an owner's policy, which protects you personally.

An abstract is a history of all transactions affecting the property, researched from the public records. Typically, the seller must furnish an up-to-date abstract and forward it to you (better yet, to your attorney) for inspection before the closing, just to make sure no problems exist. Where escrow or title companies handle closings, many of the same procedures are followed within the company.

A third method of proving title, the Torrens system, is used in some states and provides a central, permanent registration of title to real property.

Traveling Alone or with a Partner: Forms of Joint Ownership

If two persons are buying together, the wording of the deed determines their respective shares of ownership, their legal rights and the disposition of the property on the death of one of them. Depending on state law, types of joint ownership include:

► Tenancy in common. Each owner has the right to leave their share to chosen heirs.

► Joint tenancy with right of survivorship. The survivor automatically becomes complete owner.

► Tenancy by the entirety. This is a special form of joint tenancy for married couples.

If the owners have unequal shares, tenancy in common is the usual form. Except with tenancy by the entirety, any owner would have the right to force a division or sale of the property (partition). When there is more than one owner, it is important to check with an attorney or the title company and to make sure that the deed clearly states the desired form of ownership.

Travel Document: The Deed

The deed, the bill of sale for real estate, is drawn up ahead of time so that it can be examined and approved. A full warranty deed contains legal guarantees; that the seller really owns the property, for example, and that no one will ever challenge your right to it. In some areas, the standard is a bargain and sale deed with covenant, or special warranty deed, which contains some guarantees but not as many. If you buy from an estate, you receive an executor's deed. A quitclaim deed completely transfers whatever ownership the grantor (person signing the deed) may have had, but makes no claim of ownership in the first place.

The deed's sole purpose is to transfer ownership. You become owner at the exact moment when the deed is handed to you and accepted by you —physical transfer.

▶ Before You Go: What to Do Before Closing

You'll be alerted a few days before closing as to the exact amount of money needed. A cashier's check or wire transfer is usually required; no one wants to turn over so valuable an asset on a personal check. Except where you won't be in attendance (escrow closing), it's simplest to have a cashier's check made out to yourself or your attorney; you can always endorse it, and matters are simpler if anything goes wrong. Bring a supply of your personal checks as well. A photo ID, such as a driver's license, is also required in some states.

You may be asked to bring proof that you are placing insurance on the property (see Roadmap 7.1). Real estate in a flood prone area may be required to carry flood insurance. (A survey proving that the building is located above the 100-year flood mark may allow you to drop a flood insurance requirement.) You should have been told about the requirement for flood insurance long before this, however.

The Final Walk-Through. As closing approaches, make a last-minute walk-through of the property. If you see a window that was broken since you first

Before-Closing Checklist

_____ Homeowner's insurance	_____ Flood insurance (if required)
_____ Water meter reading	_____ Electric and gas service
_____ Fuel supplier	_____ Newspaper delivery
_____ Telephone, cable	_____ Packing
_____ Garage sale	_____ Moving companies
_____ Change-of-address cards	_____ Walk-through

inspected the house or a junked car in the backyard, don't talk directly with the seller. Instead, contact the agent and your lawyer immediately. If you see damage possibly caused by the move, point that out also.

New Home Orientation. Unless waived by the buyer, new homebuilders usually require buyers to attend a new home orientation, a fancy term for walk-through, as a stipulation of the sale. The building superintendent or customer service representative will accompany you on the inspection of both the exterior and interior of the house.

This is a golden opportunity to bring a list of questions and discuss how to maintain your home, picking your builder's brain as you go. You may even want to bring your video camera along so that you don't miss a thing being said. The builder can give you advice on how to take care of the various systems in your new home, such as heating and air conditioning (and explain thermostat setbacks for more energy efficiency). If you have a new security system, installed fancy structured wiring for home office use, need advice on what to do if one of the newer low-flow toilets clog, or want to know how to protect shiny new surfaces and seal tile grout—you name it, the builder's representative should know (or be able to get) the answers.

Before the orientation, builders generally inspect the new house and make notes (a punch list) of things that need to be fine-tuned, such as uneven paint or drywall, some sloppy trim here and there, or a missing knob on an appliance. If you are video-taping the process and the builder agrees that other things need attention, you've got proof.

▶ Getting Ready to Board: The Closing

The closing can be like a zoo, with paper after paper being put in front of you —and with check after check being written by you. Don't panic! You'll be fine if you're prepared. If you're a first-time buyer you don't know what you should sign and what you shouldn't. You don't have time to pick through and read each clause in every document.

So, don't go to the closing by yourself. Take your agent along, or even better, take your attorney. You want someone who's experienced, knowledgeable, and competent to check every document with you. If you go to the closing alone and don't know what you're doing, it can be frightening and it can be expensive, much more expensive than the cost of an attorney to represent you. Don't try to wing it. Spend a few bucks to take someone along who knows what's going on. Most real estate attorneys will include this in their overall fees for handling the sale. (Many agents do not want to accompany you to a closing because they are afraid that if anything turns out wrong later on, you will blame them. That's not acceptable. Your agent should be there to assist you or should send a counsel instead.)

Don't assume that all the documents have been prepared correctly. They may not have been. Don't assume that the escrow officer is on your side. Probably isn't. The agent just wants to get this deal signed and finished so that they can get on to the next one. And don't assume that the sellers have done everything they were supposed to do. They may not have.

The closing is the last opportunity to correct any mistakes, but as a first-time buyer, you might not recognize a mistake the size of a watermelon. With the help of your agent or attorney, be sure all the figures are right, and don't pay anything you aren't supposed to. (Normally, the escrow holder will ask for a few dollars more than necessary in order to meet any unexpected expenses, so if you notice this, don't worry about it. If there are no additional expenses, this money will be sent back to you later.)

Reviewing the Travel Documents: Passing Papers

You'll find yourself signing two papers for the mortgage. One is the bond, or note, the personal promise to repay the loan. The other is the mortgage itself, the financial lien (claim) against the property, which gives the lender the right to foreclose if you default. Then the mortgagee gives you a check, probably the largest you'll ever see. You get to hold it just long enough to endorse it and turn it over to the seller, although often the cashier's check is to be made payable to the title company.

At closing, the seller gives you a deed to the property in return for the purchase money. But you can't give the seller the cash until the lender gives you the loan. You can't get the check for the loan until you sign the mortgage (or trust deed). And you can't sign a mortgage until you own the property.

You can see why it must all take place at once and in the right order. In some areas, the buyer and seller sign all the documents ahead of time, and when everything is in order, an escrow agent, who holds all the papers, declares that the transfer has taken place.

If you are assuming a mortgage, you will receive a reduction certificate, the lender's statement that the principal has been paid down to a certain amount. You should receive proof that payments are current and property taxes paid up to date. A last-minute title search will reassure you that the seller did not borrow money against the property earlier that morning.

Holding Proceeds in Escrow. It's extremely important to have problems cleared up before you hand over your check or the lender's. Once the transfer of title has taken place, many matters are merged into the closing—you have bought the problems along with the property. Don't rely, then, on promises that something will be taken care of "in the next few days." If it is impractical to solve the problem immediately, ask that part of the purchase price be held in escrow, to be turned over to the seller only after the matter is attended to.

In new home purchases, an escrow holdback of mortgage funds can occur if there is work to be done after the close. In other cases, there may have been work that was not permitted on the builder's land before the property became yours. A swimming pool is one such example, because a homebuilder may not have wanted to permit a huge hole to be dug in the back yard until after the property was passed to you.

If the seller is to remain in occupancy after closing, be sure that there is plenty of financial motivation to move out as promised; otherwise, you could find yourself stuck with a lengthy and expensive eviction. Daily rental should be set at a high figure, with the provision that it will be deducted from that part of the purchase price held in escrow until the seller leaves as agreed.

Adjustments and Prorations. Many small items must be adjusted fairly between you and the seller. Your state will assume that the owner on the day of closing is seller or buyer. Items adjusted as of the date of closing might include property taxes, interest in a mortgage being assumed, or unpaid water bills.

If the tenants in the attic apartment have paid rent for the present month, part of that rent may belong to you. You should receive the entire security deposit they paid, because some day you will need to return it. When all items are listed on a balance sheet, you'll receive full credit for the earnest money deposit you placed with the real estate agent. If the lender requires a trust account, you'll be asked to place in escrow several months' property taxes and insurance costs, mortgage insurance, or other items.

Closing Costs. Various sums charged to either buyer or seller may include recording fees (for the new deed and mortgage), attorney's fees, transfer tax (revenue stamps), notary fees, charges for document preparation, mortgage tax, and closing agent's fee.

The entire settlement procedure is covered by a federal law called the Real Estate Settlement Procedures Act (RESPA) that helps you anticipate the costs of closing. Settlement services often arrange the details of a closing, and if you use such a service, you should shop around to get the best price on a closing cost package. Your real estate agent may have a suggestion. RESPA requires that a uniform statement be furnished to you. In addition, your attorney or escrow company handling the closing should furnish you with a simpler account of your expenses and credits.

Recording the Deed. The home isn't yours until the transfer of the deed from the seller to you is officially recorded. Before the deed can be recorded, however, your cashier's check has to clear and the lender has to fund the mortgage. The mortgage money is in the form of a lender's check delivered to the title insurance company for your mortgage amount.

To avoid any potential problems, the escrow usually will not close until at least 24 hours after all monies have been deposited. At that time, the escrow will be declared complete or "perfect," and the deed can be recorded. The title insuring company will record the deed either last thing at night or first thing in the morning at the county hall of records. (The reason it's done first or last thing in the day is to ensure a sneaky seller doesn't first dash down there and sell the property a second time to someone else! Of course

Tollbooth 7.1

Closing Costs

Depending on the price of your home and the price you get for all
these items, your closing costs may amount to between 2 percent and 4
percent of the cost of your home. These are the most common closing costs:

- ▶ First mortgage payment
- ▶ Mortgage application fees
- ▶ Loan origination fees (fees the bank charges to process your loan)
- ▶ Points, or prepaid interest, charged by the lender. (One point equals 1
  percent of the loan amount. You may have to pay between 1 and 3 points.)
- ▶ Loan assumption fee (if you are assuming the seller's mortgage)
- ▶ Mortgage insurance premiums. (This insurance covers the lender's risk if
  the buyer fails to make loan payments.)
- ▶ Credit report fees
- ▶ Survey, inspection, and appraisal fees
- ▶ Recording deed fee
- ▶ Homeowner's insurance premiums for the first year
- ▶ Escrow account reserves that the lender might require to cover insurance
  or property taxes over the coming year
- ▶ Property tax payments for the first year (prorated to the closing date)
- ▶ Legal fees for your lawyer and the bank's attorney
- ▶ Settlement company's fees
- ▶ Title search fees and title insurance premiums (usually paid by the seller)
- ▶ Down payment (which should include the earnest money you have already
  set aside)

it's highly unlikely, but when lots of money and insurance are involved, all
the precautions have to be taken.)

At last, the home is yours. You may also receive those keys, the garage
door opener, and security system codes. In some areas, these will come later,
once the real recording of title has taken place. In those cases, the agent will
meet you at the house, which has now been fully cleared out, and will present
you with the key. (In special cases possession can be given earlier by arrangement between buyer and seller, but that's unusual.) Regardless, you'll walk
out with a mass of papers and head for the nearest glass of champagne.

Congratulations! The journey may have seemed long and complicated, but you'll no doubt feel it was well worth it when you wake up in your new home for the first time.

Off the Beaten Path: Nontraditional Closings

Online Closings. Online, paperless closings are now possible. With the federal government approving the use of electronic signatures, everything that once required hard-copy attention can now be done in a secure, online environment. As this grows in popularity, agents, principals, and various companies, such as inspection services, escrow services, lenders, and appraisers (just use your imagination), will be arranged for without the benefit of phone calls, overnight messenger services, or bulky mail. This will change how real estate transactions are done all over the world.

Long Distance Closings. If you are in Massachusetts and about to close on a house in Oregon, closing long distance can be arranged in a variety of ways. In some cases, when title companies are involved and have offices in both states, you may merely go to the nearest branch and sign paperwork there. Documents are now routinely being transferred electronically and printed in remote locations, or overnight courier services can be arranged. Agents on both ends must prepare themselves well ahead of time, helping to smooth the process and avoid any last-minute hitches.

▶ Packing for Your Trip: The Move

At last, you can start packing. Yes, start throwing stuff away that won't make the move. Call the moving company you selected a month or so ago and let them know your timeframe. Start getting boxes and putting things into them. You also will need to buy bubble wrap for fragile items, several rolls of carton sealing tape, a couple of marking pens, and lots of labels to slap on the outside of boxes so you know what's inside them. (If you're really organized, you can color code them according to room.) The last boxes to be packed will be the children's toys and the kitchen and bathroom stuff. (They'll also be the first to be unpacked.)

"The Move" is the exclamation point on your real estate transaction—and it is all downside. One of two things can happen: Either it goes the way it is supposed to go and you later describe it in passionless tones like, "Yeah,

Mom,

I just couldn't deal with it, so I hired the movers and told them to do everything—all the packing, the moving, and the unpacking. I'd just ~~meet~~ them on the other end to show them where things went.
So they did. When we got to the new house, I watched them unpack garbage cans that still had garbage in them. They even unpacked ashtrays that still had cigarette butts in them. I don't even want to think about what it cost me to have my trash shipped cross-country.

John

it went OK," or it's a complete disaster that you will, for years, describe in terms so lively that they cannot be printed in this book.

Moving is not something that should be left to amateurs. Long before you had any idea of exactly where you were moving, you should have contacted and interviewed at least a couple of moving companies and had estimators give you an idea of how much all your stuff weighed and what additional charges there might be. They explained that the primary expense in moving was weight multiplied by distance, factoring in destination.

Moves between urban areas tend to be less costly than moves from urban areas to far rural areas. It's a matter of efficiency. A truck going from Boston to Chicago has a good chance of securing a load in Chicago to bring back to Boston. A truck going from Boston to Mattoon, Illinois, alternatively, has little chance of bringing a load back. Someone—you, of course—will have to pay for that truck to return empty.

Also, since the day your purchase offer was accepted, you have been throwing away or giving away everything that you knew would not be making the move. You've been packing boxes and more boxes and more boxes (and you've been really wondering how you accumulated all this stuff).

One of the most important things about working with movers is to be sure to work with the movers. You need to be there to supervise how your goods get on the truck and you have to be at the other end when they are taken off. You'll want to identify the crew chief, probably the driver. Any problems or special concerns should be worked out with before they start loading the truck. There is a charge for everything concerning a move—expect it. If you need to change something—your living room won't be painted for another couple of days so all that furniture will have to be taken to storage—you can, but it's going to cost you money.

Be nice to your movers and they will be nice to you. Buy them donuts and coffee. Offer to pick up lunch at McDonald's. If it's hot, provide water or Gatorade. The trappings of your entire life are literally in their hands; be nice to them.

At the destination, be ready to make payment for everything. You will need cash or cashier's check or a money order. They may take credit cards but be sure to work it out in advance. They will want to be paid before they open the doors of the moving van at your new home. Just be aware of it. Also, you might consider tipping the driver and crew if they do a good job. It's up to you.

Embarkation: Moving Day

Here's a list of things to do that will make your moving day run smoothly:

1. Before the movers arrive, be packed. Throw away flammable materials and cleaning supplies. A lot of those things are illegal to move. The movers have probably supplied you with a list. Also, get rid of the trash.
2. Before the movers arrive, make sure they know where they can park their truck. It would be helpful if they can park it as close to the front door as possible. (The same thing goes for the destination. They need to be able to park close to your house.)
3. Have boxes labeled, including a brief description of contents. Set aside in one place anything and everything that will not be going on the truck —including jewelry and legal papers. This includes the documentation regarding the move itself. Keep the bill of lading with you.
4. Make sure the movers know which boxes go on the truck last—kitchen utensils, sheets and blankets, critical boxes of children's toys—because those will be the boxes that come off first on the other end.
5. Clear out obstacles. Do not make the movers dig their way through your house to get to the boxes that need to be loaded first. Nice wide paths are good.
6. Unspring the springs on screen doors and leave them open. Remove anything overhead (like wind chimes) that could be a constant obstacle.

7. Let the driver know which bathroom you'd prefer that the crew used. It will be one of the last rooms you clean before you leave.
8. Finally, before the truck rolls away, go through the house again (and again) to make sure that everything that should be on the truck is on the truck and there are no forgotten boxes in the basement.

Also, make sure you have the bill of lading (your move order) in your hands and that you and the driver again discuss payment, any special circumstances, and the delivery time and date. You will want to exchange cell phone numbers, e-mail addresses, and every other conceivable contact information you can think of.

Things can and do go wrong in moves. Delays can happen all along the way on both sides. Trucks can break down or closings can be delayed for hours or days. All you can do is make sure everyone is in communication with everyone else.

Bumps in the Road: Problems with the Move

Everyone does their best to make sure a move goes well but things do go wrong. Things will get broken in shipment. There will be delays caused by mismanagement. If a problem arises with the movers, the first thing you (and maybe your lawyer) should do is review the bill of lading. The bill of lading is your contract, and by law it must accompany every shipment of household goods. It outlines your rights. The bill of lading requires the mover to do what was promised and requires that you pay them for doing it.

The kind of insurance you have is listed in the bill of lading. If you need to make a claim, you should do it as soon as possible but no later than nine months after the date your shipment arrived. Although the Federal Highway Administration has jurisdiction over interstate movers, it is not allowed to adjudicate claims. You will have to go to court—either small claims court or a superior court—if you cannot work out the problem with the moving company.

Under federal law, if your claim is less than $5,000, you likely will be required to submit it to binding arbitration where you promise to abide by whatever the arbitrator rules. For more information about claims and settlements, go the Web site operated by the American Moving and Storage Association: http://www.moving.org.

Traveling with Kids

Child psychologists believe moving is one of the most stressful things parents can do to their children. Part of what makes it so bad, they say, is that the child has no real control over the situation. The move may be the result of a relocation, a divorce, a death in the family, or a change for the worse (or even for the better) in the family's economic status. All these are factors children tend not to create, but are required to live with. The children will likely resist the move. The only real question is whether to make it difficult on Mom and Dad or make it very difficult on Mom and Dad. There are some things, however, that can smooth what invariably will be a bumpy ride.

Once the decision is made, tell the children right away. You don't want your kids to hear from someone else that they're moving. They need to hear it from you first. If you have maps of the new city or pictures of attractions, have them ready so you can put a positive spin on things from the outset. It's not what they have to do but what they get to do. Even before you tell the children, do a little groundwork on the things important to them. If they take ballet lessons now, will they be able to continue at your destination? If soccer is important, make contact with the league in the destination city. Normally, it is easy enough to track down such information, either on the Internet or by simply asking a local authority for a referral to the destination. Scout leaders know how to get in touch with other scout leaders. Sometimes real estate agents can help find Little League or softball officials, and often recreation departments have directories of services and contacts.

Future Travel Plans

When is it time to sell? As you have probably already guessed, the answer to that question: "It depends." No hard-and-fast rule declares the ideal moment to sell. The right time varies according to the economy, the needs and desires of owners, and the wishes of potential buyers.

Many variables influence timing. You may soon be getting married and need more room than that provided by your one-bedroom flat. Your employer might have just informed you of a new opportunity opening up across the country, and you realize the benefits of a quick move. You could just be tired of your present location. You might even see the wisdom of investing your money in property as opposed to monthly rent payments. Perhaps you've been reading the financial and real estate pages and have realized that your property has appreciated to the point where you should consider cashing in on your investment. Approximately one in five Americans move in any given year; that means 20 percent of the population is in motion and looking for a place to live. One of those places could very well be yours.

When You're Ready to Move On

When the time comes to sell your home, you must do just as much homework as you did when you bought the property. The first step in getting the highest price possible for your home is to obtain a realistic appraisal of its current value. If you have paid little attention to the market for the past several years, you may have an outdated sense of what your home is worth. You should get a feel for the market by scanning newspaper ads for similar properties and by visiting nearby open houses. Real estate agents will be glad to give you a free assessment of your home's strengths, weaknesses, and fair price range. For a fee, you can also obtain a professional appraiser's opinion.

As with buying a home, we believe it's best to work with a real estate professional—this time a listing or seller's agent—who can guide you through this tricky area. They will put together a comparative market analysis (CMA) for you based on the ups and downs of your local market during the past six months. This information is invaluable in setting your price and in knowing an approximate timeframe in which you can expect to make a sale.

A CMA allows you to compare apples to apples and develop a realistic picture of what you can expect when selling your home. Not only will you get a useful guide on pricing, but you'll also get a useful idea of how long the sale might take. If homes in your area are moving quickly, you can expect the same results—provided your pricing is within market norms. A CMA should be provided by your broker at no charge; the information shouldn't vary from one agent to another because all of them share the same information on which your report is based.

It's difficult to put together your own CMA. The Internet is a great source of all kinds of information, but the agents in any given area generally have more, better, more current, and more accurate information. They have access to local multiple listing services, which provide a staggering amount of current information. Even with access to the Internet, it's hard to compete on your own.

An agent should also be able to tell you if there are any likely buyers for your home. The market time (MT) on the CMA also tells you how many days or weeks it takes to sell homes like yours—again, invaluable information for making your plans. Of course, local economies, location, amenities, and other factors have an effect on the price and timing of your sale, but a CMA still provides a sound set of guidelines. It's a solid base of real-world information essential to ensuring that you get the best deal possible for your property.

If you want to avoid the real estate broker's fee, you can try to sell your home yourself with newspaper ads and a "For Sale" sign on your front lawn. Although you will have to deal with browsers and people unqualified to buy your property, you may be lucky enough to find someone who falls in love with your home and places a bid on it.

In either case, before you let anyone past the front door, make sure your home is in tip-top shape. Add a fresh coat of paint. Locate plants and flowers strategically. Mow the lawn. Spruce up the exterior. Clean every room thoroughly. Remove excess clutter and furniture to maximize the appearance of living space. Distribute a one-page fact sheet listing your home's selling points and illustrating the layout. If you're located in an active real estate market, you might be able to sell within a few weeks. It is always best, however, to sell your home before you buy another property. You don't want to owe two mortgage payments if your home sells more slowly than you had anticipated.

As you know from our discussion of disclosure (to review the details, see Chapter 6), more and more states require that you disclose all of your home's problems in writing to prospective buyers. The document covers a property's structure, utilities (such as plumbing, air-conditioning, and water system), and municipal status (such as building permits, zoning restrictions, certificate of occupancy, and property tax rates). If the buyer signs this sales disclosure form acknowledging that they have been informed of the home's problems, the buyer has little right to sue you later if any problems crop up for any of the items listed.

If you cannot sell your home on your own, bring in several real estate agents to compete for your listing. Unless you deal with a flat-fee or discount broker, you must pay the agent you choose a commission of 6 percent to 7 percent of your home's selling price, but if they can find a buyer when you can't, the fee is worthwhile.

When you sell your home, either on your own or through an agent, you must deduct all selling and closing costs from the gross sales price to arrive at your net proceeds. The worksheet in Roadmap 7.2 lists some of the costs you might incur and helps you determine your profit.

Roadmap 7.2

Roadmap: Net Proceeds Worksheet

	$ Amount	Total
Gross equity		
Sale price of property	_____	
Minus remaining mortgage balance	(_____)	
Minus other home-related debts	(_____)	
Total gross equity		$ _____
Selling and closing costs		
Escrow or other fees	$ _____	
Legal and document preparation fees	_____	
Title search and insurance fees	_____	
Transfer taxes	_____	
FHA, VA, or lender discounts	_____	
Mortgage prepayment penalties	_____	
Real estate taxes owed	_____	
Appraisal fees	_____	
Survey fees	_____	
Termite and other pest inspection fees	_____	
Fees for repair work required by sales contract	_____	
Home protection or warranty plan fees	_____	
Unpaid assessments	_____	
Real estate commissions	_____	
Other selling or closing costs	_____	
Total selling and closing costs		$ _____
Total gross equity minus		$ _____
Total selling and closing costs equals		(_____)
Net proceeds		$ _____

The Price Should Be Right. Pricing your property to sell is a critical task. Note the phrase *to sell;* just as when you were buying your home, you must recognize market realities when setting the price for selling it. You may have hundreds of warm memories of people and events associated with that property, but you can't set a price on them. As wonderful as those memories may be, they are irrelevant to buyers. They don't have that connection, so you must factor that reality into your price. Pricing a property too high or too low can cost you a lot of money, so do your homework.

Whatever course you set out on, it's best that you have a well-considered plan. You want your property to sell quickly and at the right price so that you can get on with your life and move on and up to your next property. You don't want to be saddled with a piece of property that's holding you back. The real factor in any sale is what's right for you. Some people can afford to wait for top dollar, whereas others have to make a move right away and may have to settle for less. Keep in mind that settling for less than top dollar could be the wisest move for some people.

The key to pricing is the realization that the time to sell and the price of the sale are personal decisions with no across-the-board rules as guides. Think about all the factors that are important to you and your family. Whatever they may be, they will have as much effect on the time and price of your sale as market forces, although ultimately the market rules.

You can't allow yourself to become overly emotional when selling. The value of the upgrades and improvements you've made are still governed by market realities. Those improvements might not increase your price as much as you'd like, but they should make the sale a little bit easier and faster and assure a little better price. Of course, this depends on how much the new buyer likes and wants what you've done. The buyer won't be looking at the unit with your eyes. The buyer will be seeing it for the first time as it is, not as it was before you made the upgrades and changes made to enhance your lifestyle and not necessarily important to someone else. Again, market realities determine the final price and timeframe for selling your unit.

A Virtual Vacation: Using Your Computer to Buy and Sell Real Estate

The real estate market has always been considered local. But the advent of the computer and the Internet is quickly transforming real estate into a national marketplace, making it easier for you to buy and sell your home and get financing from lenders anywhere in the country. As we noted, it can't replace the agent yet, but it is fast becoming a bigger and bigger part of the industry.

All of the major institutions involved in the homebuying and selling business now have a significant presence on the Web. Mortgage lenders, Realtors, builders, relocation firms, home-oriented magazines, housing-related government agencies, and many others now have Web sites (some are listed in the Appendix) that can educate you about real estate and help you go through much of the homebuying process online; for example:

1. You can use various buy-vs.-rent calculators to evaluate whether it makes sense for you to be buying in the first place. Other calculators help you determine how large a mortgage you can afford based on your income and assets.

2. You can shop for homes online through the many Realtor-sponsored Web sites. These sites offer information about various communities you may be interested in, as well as pictures and details about houses for sale. Just type in the name of your Realtor's company to browse these sites. Here are some of them:

   ▶ Century 21: http://www.c21realty.com
   ▶ Coldwell Banker: http://www.coldwellbanker.com
   ▶ RE/MAX: http://www.remax.com

3. You can shop for the most competitive mortgage rate online. As we've discussed, you do not have to be limited to what your local lender is offering. These sites are constantly updated with the latest rates on fixed and adjustable loans, points, fees, closing costs, and even online applications. A few sample sites to help you tap into this market include:

   ▶ American Mortgage Online: http://www.amo-mortgage.com
   ▶ HSH Mortgage Information: http://www.hsh.com
   ▶ Mortgage Mart: http://www.mortgage-mart.com
   ▶ Mortgage-Net: http://www.mortgage-net.com
   ▶ Mortgage Rate Shopper Service of the United Homeowners Association, reachable through keyword UHA on America Online

As in many other areas, the computer is making the real estate market much more efficient. If you take advantage of the power of the computer, you can save thousands of dollars on financing and end up with the home of your dreams that you might never have found the old-fashioned way.

Home ownership is a fantastic adventure—one that will always hold great appeal for Americans. More people in this country have amassed fortunes in real estate than in any other asset. By buying a home, you not only acquire pride of ownership, you also get real value out of your property by using it every day, even if its market value falls, and the added bonus of appreciation if the market rises.

Have a great trip ...

Learn the Language

Key Terms to Know When Buying a Home

Certificate of title The certificate issued by a title examiner stating the condition of a title.

Clear title Ownership of property free of liens, title defects, encumbrances, or claims.

Closing (settlement) The act of transferring a property from the seller to the buyer according to the terms of a sales contract; also used to refer to the actual meeting at which the transfer takes place.

Closing costs Fees and charges related to the closing that are paid by the seller and the buyer, including broker's fees, lender's discount fees, title insurance premium, application fees, title examination, abstract of title, title insurance, deed recording fees, loan prepayment penalty, inspection/appraisal fees, attorney fees, credit report fees, and notary fees.

Commitment (binder) The document issued by a title insurance company that states the conditions under which a title insurance policy will be issued.

Comparative market analysis (CMA) The document prepared by a sales associate to show sellers what other homes—either similar in size or neighborhood—have sold for over a recent period of time to help sellers establish the asking price for their homes.

Conveyance The transfer of title to property from one person to another.

Deed The document through which a conveyance of property is effected; *deed restriction:* covenant contained in a deed imposing limits on the use or occupancy of the real estate or the type, size, purpose, or location of improvements to be constructed on it.

Deed of trust (trust deed) The document used to secure the collateral in financing the property; title is transferred to the trustee, with payments made to the beneficiary by the trustor (grantor in some states).

Disclosures The items that, by law, must be revealed by buyers, sellers, real estate agents, lenders, and others.

Easement The right of someone to have access to land for a specific purpose, such as a municipality's right to come onto a privately owned land to maintain sewers or utility lines, or an individual's negotiated right to cross a piece of property to gain access to his own property.

Encumbrance An interest, right, or lien legally recorded on a property, such as unpaid taxes, that could represent a burden on the property that would have to be resolved before sale.

Equity The difference between what is owed and what the property could be sold for.

Execute To sign a legal instrument.

Fee simple deed Absolute ownership of a parcel of land; the highest degree of ownership that a person can have in real estate.

General warranty deed The deed with a covenant that says the seller agrees to protect the buyer against being dispossessed because of any adverse claim against the land.

Guaranty policy A title insurance policy that insures only against defects of title appearing in the public records; other policies insure against defects whether or not they appear in public records.

Home appreciation The amount the value of your home goes up based on market conditions or improvements.

Interest and tax proration The interest accrued between the time the mortgage is funded and the time your first month's interest begins. (Interest on mortgages is paid at the end of the month, unlike rent, which is paid in advance.)

Joint tenants Persons who are co-owners of interests in the same land. In most states, upon the death of a joint tenant, interest automatically passes to the surviving joint tenant. The survivorship feature is the principal distinction between a joint tenancy and a tenancy in common.

Lien A monetary charge imposed on a property, usually arising from a debt owed by the seller.

Lien waiver (waiver of liens) The waiver of a mechanic's lien rights, signed by contractors or subcontractors.

Lis pendens A legal notice that there is litigation pending against a property, usually because of an unpaid debt such as amounts owed to home repair people or roofers, etc.; warns that there could be a problem with the title.

Mechanic's lien A recorded claim with government agency that secures payment to those who perform labor or services or furnish materials to the construction of buildings and improvements on the real estate.

Mediation A nonbinding method of settling after-the-fact disputes between sellers and buyers; between consumers and their real estate agents; and between real estate agents themselves.

Metes and bounds A land description used in some states in which boundaries are described by courses, directions, distances, and monuments.

Quieting title The removal of a cloud on title by property action in a court.

Online lending Accessing mortgage programs and lenders via the World Wide Web.

Power of attorney (attorney in fact) A legal power given to a person to act on behalf of another; can be either specific (for special circumstances) or general (in all activities).

Quitclaim deed This deed transfers whatever interest the maker of the deed may have in the particular parcel of land; contains no covenants or warranties.

Recording Placement in the public record of a legal document, like a deed or mortgage, affecting the title to real estate.

Restrictions The limitations on the use of property imposed by deeds or other documents in the chain of title.

Settlement (closing) The meeting of all parties or their representatives in the final transfer of property to a new owner.

Special warranty deed The deed containing a covenant whereby the seller agrees to protect the buyer against being dispossessed because of any adverse claims to the land by the seller or anyone claiming through the seller.

Tax deed The deed given to a purchaser at a public sale of land for nonpayment of taxes, which conveys to the purchaser only such title as the defaulting taxpayer had.

Tenancy by the entirety (entireties) A form of ownership in some states where husband and wife together are treated as one entity.

Title search Review of all recorded documents in the land records relating to a particular piece of real property.

Total closing costs Total upfront costs to close your loan; the sum of the loan origination fee, amount paid for points, and other closing costs.

Warranty deed A deed in which the grantor warrants or guarantees that good title is being conveyed.

Appendix A

An Itinerary

Here's a quick review of what to do, as you set out on the road to home ownership.

Stop #1. Decide if you want to buy, and, if so, work out the pros and cons of home ownership in your situation. This will help you determine if you can afford to buy now.

- ▶ Why do you want to buy a home? Is it a desire to retreat from the pressures of an increasingly crowded society, as a hedge against inflation and the tax incentives that come with owning a home, the need for self-expression or privacy, a desire to "have it now," and/or the potential for profit?
- ▶ Take stock of your present financial situation—this is the first step toward determining if you can afford to buy a home. List your income and present expenses, and calculate the additional costs you'll incur with home ownership.
- ▶ Calculate the tax savings that come with home ownership. For each dollar that you spend toward your mortgage interest and property taxes, you are entitled to subtract a dollar from your adjusted gross income. If you pay state income taxes, you should have savings on them, and you can perform the same calculation.
- ▶ Determine interest rates. The higher the interest rate, the smaller the mortgage you can afford; the lower the interest rate, the larger the mortgage.
- ▶ Using the figures you've gathered, do the math to determine what mortgage you can comfortably afford.
- ▶ If you can't afford to buy now, but know you want to buy, determine where you can cut costs and begin to save for a down payment. If you've decided to buy, educate yourself about the homebuying process.

Stop #2. What type of home do you want to buy? It's time to assess your needs. It's about more than the house itself.

- ▶ Single family, detached house; condo/townhome; co-op: Price, maintenance, and location are among the factors that go into this decision. Determine what is important to you.

- ▶ If you decide to go the condo or co-op route, educate yourself on the legal, tax, and social ramifications of these types of ownership.

- ▶ No matter what form of ownership you choose, create a "wants" list, not a "dreams" list. Start by listing things you want to avoid and then convert them into "positives."

- ▶ Establish priorities. What's most important to you; for example, location, schools, lot or house size, transportation, proximity to friends, family, employment, and so on.

- ▶ Create a "personal profile" of things that are absolute musts, nice to have, and that you can live without.

- ▶ Decide what type of home you want: new construction, an older home, mobile home, or a fixer-upper. There are pros and cons to each in terms of time, money, amenities, stress, etc.

- ▶ Whatever choice you make, you'll probably sell this house one day, so consider saleability—even when you buy.

Stop #3. You now know, more or less, how much you can afford and the type of home you'd like to own; now it's time to determine how you are really going to finance the purchase.

- ▶ Before you begin, it's time to do the math again to determine how much you can spend on your home. The amount of mortgage you can get will depend on monthly income from all sources (a rule of thumb: 24 percent for mortgage payments and 4% for taxes and insurance), current interest rates, and amount you have for a down payment.

- ▶ The down payment: Do you have the cash? If not, what other sources are available to you?

- ▶ Investigate types of mortgages available to you and where to get them. The entire process of uncovering and qualifying for a mortgage is crucial to making the most of your real estate dollar, so do your homework. Which kind of lender is right for you; what are their fees? Not all lenders are alike, so shop around.

- ▶ Preapproval (which involves applying for a mortgage before you've even found a house) is the next step—it will give you peace of mind, give you leverage with the seller, expedite the purchase when you do find your dream home, and, in a period of rising interest rates, you may be able to "lock in" your mortgage at a favorable rate. (And, if a credit problem or error on your credit report is discovered, it will give you time to correct it.)

Stop #4. The hunt is on; it's time to go out and find your dream home.

▶ Once again, you need to make a decision: Should you use the services of a broker or go it alone? If you decide to use a broker, how do you find one and what type of broker do you need?

▶ If you decide to go the broker route, you should conduct a careful search and thoroughly interview several prospective candidates. Different types of brokers assume different fiduciary responsibilities. Understand the differences and work with them accordingly.

▶ After hiring the agent, remember a broker is someone who is going to help you accomplish a specific task, and only succeeds when you succeed. Be straightforward and expect the same in return.

▶ You are ready to look at houses now; the better prepared you are and the more feedback you give the agent the easier the search will be. Take notes, ask questions, don't be swayed by emotion, and keep your focus —house hunting is fun, but it's not easy.

Stop #5. You've found the home you want to buy, but it's not over yet. You still have to negotiate the price, protect your investment, and finalize the financing.

▶ The home-buying process differs from state to state, but whoever handles it, the steps are similar (you may want to hire a lawyer even in places where they are not required). Whatever the process, there will be documents and money to be held in escrow, title to be searched, and sales contract to be negotiated.

▶ By closing, you will need homeowner's insurance, so now's the time to investigate the various options.

▶ Negotiating the contract is a process of give-and-take. Local customs vary, but once the process begins it can feel as if you're in the middle of a whirlwind. You'll need to decide on the initial offer, bargain for extras, negotiate contingencies (if any), and, in all probability, be faced with a counteroffer to which you'll respond with yet another offer. Ideally, this will be the end of it—at least for this round.

Stop #6. You are nearly there. The seller will disclose (if they haven't already) anything you need to know about the property and the home you are buying that could adversely affect its value or cause you problems (it's the law), and you will want to have the home professionally inspected.

▶ Disclosure statements can be tricky; read it carefully. Prepare yourself by knowing what to look for (both what's said and what isn't said is important); learn how to read between the lines.

▶ Hire a professional inspector; no matter how much you know or think you know, you need the protection of a competent licensed inspector.

▶ Always go on the home inspection; bring the disclosure statement with you and investigate anything that you have questions about; discuss them with the inspector.

▶ Study the written inspection report carefully and question the inspector about anything you don't understand.

▶ In all probability, you'll be back at the bargaining table once again—but only if there are "real" issues; don't ask the seller to repair or reduce the selling price because of normal wear and tear on a house, but if there's something significant that wasn't factored into your initial offer, now's the time to correct it.

Stop #7. You're now ready to conclude the purchase of your home. All that's left is the paperwork and the writing of checks—the closing.

▶ Right before the closing, make a final walk-through to make certain nothing has happened to affect the condition of the home.

▶ Again, this varies from place to place, but the essentials are the same. The seller proves title, and title insurance is purchased; you may be required to bring proof of insurance, the deed is examined and approved, and ownership—at last!—is transferred to you. Many checks will be exchanged.

▶ Bring your agent and your lawyer, if you have one, and check all documents carefully.

▶ Deed is recorded—you are a home owner! You are now ready to move.

▶ Some years pass, you may now be ready to sell this home and move into another or purchase that second home away from home.

Bon voyage!

Appendix B

The Best of *Buying a Home*: A Resource Guide

▶ Bibliography

The following books were used as resources for this book. In addition, we have provided lists of other books and Web sites that offer more detailed information on some of the topics covered in this book. We hope you find all these resources useful.

Cook, Frank. *You're Not Buying That House, Are You? Everything You May Forget to Do, Ask, or Think About Before Signing on the Dotted Line.* Chicago: Dearborn Trade Publishing, 2004.

Garrett, Sheryl. *Just Give Me the Answers: Expert Advisors Address Your Most Pressing Financial Questions.* Chicago: Dearborn Trade Publishing, 2004.

Garton-Good, Julie. *All About Mortgages: Insider Tips to Finance or Refinance Your Home.* Chicago: Dearborn Trade Publishing, 2004.

Goodman, Jordan E. *Everyone's Money Book,* 3rd ed. Chicago: Dearborn Trade Publishing, 2001.

Irwin, Robert. *Buy Your FIRST Home!* 2nd ed. Chicago: Dearborn Trade Publishing, 2000.

Irwin, Robert. *The Home Inspection Troubleshooter.* Chicago: Dearborn Trade Publishing, 1995.

Lank, Edith with Dena Amoruso. *The Homebuyer's Kit,* 5th ed. Chicago: Dearborn Trade Publishing, 2001.

Steinmetz, Thomas C. *The Mortgage Kit,* 5th ed. Chicago: Dearborn Trade Publishing, 2002.

Stone, Barry. *Consumer Advocate's Guide to Home Inspection.* Chicago: Dearborn Trade Publishing, 2003.

Weiss, Mark. *Condos, Co-Ops, & Townhomes: A Complete Guide to Finding, Buying, Maintaining, and Enjoying Your New Home.* Chicago: Dearborn Trade Publishing, 2003.

▶ Recommended Books and Web Sites

For Chapter 1: Plan Your Trip

Books

Home Buying for Dummies by Eric Tyson and Ray Brown. IDG Books, 919 E. Hillsdale Blvd., Suite 400, Foster City, CA 94404. Telephone: 650-653-7000; 800-434-3422 (http://www.idg.com, http://www.dummies. com). Shows how buying a home fits into your financial picture, from saving for the down payment to selecting the best loan and determining the after-tax cost of ownership.

Starting Out: The Complete Home Buyer's Guide by Dian Davis Hymer. Chronicle Books. Telephone: 800-722-6657 (http://www.chroniclebooks. com). Helps you find the home to fit your needs and budget. Includes charts, checklists, and sample contracts.

The Unofficial Guide to Buying a Home by Alan Perlis (IDG Books, 919 E. Hillsdale Blvd., Suite 400, Foster City, CA 94404. Telephone: 650-653-7000; 800-434-3422 (http://www. idg.com, http://www.dummies.com). Provides guidance on such topics as how much loan you can afford, how to find a Realtor, where to buy, mortgages and fees.

Web sites

▶ *Real Estate ABC.com.* Lists the 100 most-visited real estate Web sites. http://www.realestate.com

▶ *Realtor.com.* National Association of Realtors site offers homebuying, selling, moving, and borrowing information. http://www.realtor.com

For Chapter 3: Financing Your Trip

Books

The Common-Sense Mortgage: How to Cut the Cost of Home Ownership by $50,000 or More by Peter G. Miller. Contemporary Books, 4255 W. Touhy Ave., Lincolnwood, IL 60712-1975. Telephone: 800-621-1918 (http://www. contemporarybooks.com).

How to Get the Best Home Loan by W. Frazier Bell. John Wiley & Sons, 1 Wiley Dr., Somerset, NJ 08875. Telephone: 212-850-6000 (http://www.wiley.com). Describes different types of home loans and how to choose the best one for you.

How to Save Thousands of Dollars on Your Home Mortgage by Randy Johnson. John Wiley & Sons, 1 Wiley Dr., Somerset, NJ 08875. Telephone: 212-850-6000; 800-225-5945 (http://www.wiley.com). Describes the different types of mortgages available to homeowners.

Tips and Traps When Mortgage Hunting by Robert Irwin. McGraw-Hill, P.O. Box 543, Blacklick, OH 43004. Telephone: 800-634-3961 (http://www.mcgraw-hill.com). Explains the pros and cons of different kinds of mortgages and helps you determine which is best for you.

The following booklets are available free of charge:

A Consumer's Glossary of Mortgage Terms; Self Test. Will help you determine how much house you can afford and what documentation the lender may require; and *What Happens after You Apply for a Mortgage.* The Mortgage Bankers' Association, 1125 15th Street, NW, Washington, DC 20005 (http://www.mbaa.org).

The Mortgage Money Guide. Gives detailed comparisons of costs borrowers can expect to pay for various types of loans. Good for loan comparison shopping. Federal Trade Commission Bureau of Consumer Protection, Pennsylvania Avenue and 6th Street, NW, Washington, DC 20580 (http://www.ftc.gov).

Unraveling the Mortgage Loan Mystery. Who makes loans, the types of loans available, and how to choose the best loan. Federal National Mortgage Association, Drawer MM, 3900 Wisconsin Avenue, NW, Washington, DC, 20006 (http://www.fanniemae.com).

Web sites

▶ *American Mortgage Online.* Offers deals by state, prequalification online. http://www. amortgage.com

▶ *AppOnline.com.* Full-service online mortgage bank. http://www. apponline. com

▶ *Bankrate.com.* Compares mortgage interest rates by lending company. Also compares different mortgage features as offered by different mortgage companies. http://www.bankrate.com

▶ *Consumer Mortgage Information Network.* Links to many Realtors and lenders around the country. http://www.mortgagemag.com

▶ *Countrywide.* Online home mortgage site. Calculate and select a home loan, apply for and get your home mortgage loan online. http://www.countrywide.com

▶ *E-Loan.* Online broker for consumer loans, including home mortgages, using about 70 loan companies. Online application, current interest rates, and online loan tracking. http://www.eloan.com

▶ *Fannie Mae's Homepath.com.* Lists and links to all Fannie Mae-approved lenders by state and other criteria. Lists properties for sale and includes mortgage calculators. http://www.homepath.com

▶ *Finet.com.* Online supplier of home mortgage loans. Site includes mortgage home loan calculator, interest rate tracker, and advisors. http://www.finet.com

▶ *Iown.com.* Online home mortgage broker site. Apply and complete your loan online. http://www.iown.com

▶ *LoansDirect.com.* Offers online mortgages. http://www.loansdirect.com

▶ *Microsurf, Inc.* Online site for mortgage quotations. Obtain home mortgage quotes from up to 1,000 lenders. http://www.mortgagequotes.com

▶ *Mortgage.com.* Home mortgage site; calculate and apply your loan. http://www.mortgage.com

▶ *MortgageBot.com.* Online mortgage broker offers a sophisticated set of online calculators. http://www.mortgagebot.com

▶ *MortgageInterest.com.* A good general mortgage loan site. http://www.interest.com

▶ *MortgageIT.com.* Online mortgage broker offers online mortgage advisors, instantaneous rate quotes, online tracking of your loan, and online loan applications. http://www.mortgageit.com

▶ *Mortgage Mart.* Offers online loan applications, mortgage calculators, and details about government lending programs. http://www.mortgagemart.com

▶ *Mortgage.com.* Links to online mortgage lenders and brokers. http://www.mortgages.com

▶ *National Average Mortgage Rates.* A complete listing of national mortgage rates. http://www.interest.com/ave.htm

▶ *Quicken.com.* Full-service online mortgage broker. http://www.quicken.
com

▶ *Realtor.com.* The site of the National Association of Realtors. You can
locate homes, home mortgage lenders, home insurers, home moving
companies, and many other home-related entities on this site. http://
www.realtor.com

For Chapter 4: Self-Directed or Guided Tour
Books

Buying More House for Less Money by Ceil R. Lohmar. McGraw-Hill, P.O.
Box 543, Blacklick, OH 43004. Telephone: 800-634-3961 (http://www.
mcgraw-hill.com). Techniques for house hunting and bargaining to get
the best value for your housing dollar.

Find It, Buy It, Fix It: The Insider's Guide to Fixer-Uppers by Robert Irwin.
Dearborn Trade, 155 N. Wacker Dr., Chicago, IL 60606. Telephone.
312-836-4400; 800-245-2665 (http://www.dearborntrade.com). Buying
and renovating a handyman's special; shows how to find the real bargains
and how to avoid the money pits.

How to Buy the Home You Want, for the Best Price, in Any Market by Terry
Eilers. Hyperion, 77 W. 66th, 11th Floor, New York, NY 10023. Telephone:
212-456-0100 (http://www.hyperionbooks.go.com).

How to Sell Your Home Without a Broker by Bill Carey. John Wiley &
Sons, 1 Wiley Dr., Somerset, NJ 08875-1272. Telephone: 212-850-6000;
800-225-5945 (http://www.wiley.com). Explains how to prepare your
property for sale and how to find buyers so you can avoid paying the real
estate broker's commission.

Web sites

▶ *America's HomeNet.* Links to databases of home listings in most areas
of the country. Also includes data about local schools, businesses, and
lenders. http://netprop.com

▶ *Cyberhomes.* Listings of homes for sale over the Internet, including pictures, the listing agent's name and phone number, and e-mail addresses.
http://www.cyberhomes.com

▶ *eRealty.com.* Online real estate brokerage. http://www.erealty.com

▶ *HomeAdvisor.com.* A comprehensive site with home listings, mortgages,
insurance, and other tools. http://www.homeadvisor.com

► *Homebid.com.* Gives agents and their clients the power to accomplish key steps of the homebuying and selling process via the Internet. http://www.homebid.com

► *Homebytes.com.* Home sale service that charges a flat fee instead of traditional commission. http://www.homebytes.com

► *HomeFair.com.* Offers reports on cities, schools, crime, and home prices and comparisons of telephone, Internet, cable, and satellite services. http://www.homefair.com

► *Homeseekers.com.* Provides a database of homes and other properties for sale throughout the country. Includes MLS listings in every state. http://www.homeseekers.com

► *Homestore.com.* An all-purpose site with home listings, mortgages, insurance, and other tools. http://www.homestore.com

► *Realty.com.* Advice on buying and selling, with home listings. http://www.realty.com

Sites for locating new homes
► HomeBuilder.com
► NewHomeNetwork.com
► NewHomes.com
► BuilderOnline.com
► mHousing.com
► manufacturedhousing.org

For Sale By Owner and Discount Broker Sites
► Help-u-sell.com
► Owners.com
► Americas-real-estate.com
► iOwn.com
► eBay.com

For Chapter 5: Navigating the Waters
Books

How to Negotiate Real Estate Contracts: For Buyers and Sellers: With Forms by Mark Warda. Sourcebooks, Inc., P.O. Box 4410, Naperville, IL 60567. Telephone: 630-961-3900; 800-432-7444 (http://www.sourcebooks.com). Explains the pros and cons of each clause in the real estate contract.

Tips and Traps When Buying a Home by Robert Irwin. McGraw-Hill, P.O. Box
543, Blacklick, OH 43004. Telephone: 800-634-3961 (http://www.mcgraw-
hill.com). Discusses how to inspect the home and negotiate.

For Chapter 6: Know Before You Go
Books

Bob Vila's Guide to Buying Your Dream House by Bob Vila. Time Warner, 3
Center Plaza, Boston, MA 02108. Telephone: 800-343-9204. A practical
guide to inspecting and buying a high-quality house.

The Home Buyer's Inspection Guide by Warren Boroson. John Wiley & Sons,
1 Wiley Dr., Somerset, NJ 08875. Telephone: 212-850-6000; 800-225-5945
(http://www.wiley.com). Explains how to find and work with a home inspector and what to look for in a home.

Web sites

▶ *PestWeb.com.* Information on pest control. http://www.pestweb.com
▶ *Quality Builders Warranty Corporation.* Online insurer of new homes.
http://www.qbwc.com
▶ *Residential Warranty Corporation.* Online insurer for new homes. http://
www.rwcwarranty.com

For Chapter 7: Setting Sail
Books

*All about Escrow and Real Estate Closings: Or How to Buy the Brooklyn Bridge
and Have the Last Laugh* by Sandy Gadow and Dave Patton. Escrow
Publishing Company, P.O. Box 2165, Palm Beach, FL 33480. Telephone:
561-659-1474 (http://www.escrowhelp.com).

Buying Your Vacation Home for Fun and Profit by Ruth Rejnis and Claire Wal-
ter. Dearborn Trade, 155 N. Wacker Dr., Chicago, IL 60606. Telephone:
312-836-4400; 800-245-2665 (http://www.dearborntrade.com).

Finding and Buying Your Place in the Country by Les and Carol Scher.
Dearborn Trade, 155 N. Wacker Dr., Chicago, IL 60606. Telephone:
312-836-4400; 800-245-2665 (http://www.dearborntrade.com). Explains
what the reader needs to know about on rural land.

The Homeseller's Kit by Edith Lank. Dearborn Trade, 155 N. Wacker Dr.,
Chicago, IL 60606. Telephone: 312-836-4400; 800-245-2665 (http://www.
dearborntrade.com). How to list and price your house.

The Homeseller's Survival Guide by Kenneth W. Edwards. Dearborn Trade, 155 N.Wacker Dr., Chicago, IL 60606. Telephone: 312-836-4400; 800-245-2665 (http://www.dearborntrade.com). Identifies hazards associated with selling a home and provides guidance to avoid them or deal with them.

How to Sell Your Home Fast, for the Highest Price, in Any Market by Terry Eilers. Hyperion, 77 W. 66th, 11th Floor, New York, NY 10023. Telephone: 212-456-0100 (www.hyperionbooks.go.com). Reviews every step of the process, from finding a qualified agent and establishing a list price, to marketing and advertising the house and managing the closing.

Seller Beware: Insider Secrets You Need to Know About Selling Your House —From Listing through Closing the Deal by Robert Irwin. Dearborn Trade, 155 N. Wacker Dr., Chicago, IL 60606. Telephone: 312-836-4400; 800-245-2665 (http://www.dearborntrade.com). Explains what defects to disclose (all), when to disclose them (upfront), and more.

Sell It Yourself by Ralph Roberts. Adams Media Corp., 260 Center St., Holbrook, MA 02343. Telephone: 781-767-8100; 800-872-5627 (http://www.adamsmedia.com).

Tips and Traps When Selling a Home by Robert Irwin. McGraw-Hill, P.O. Box 543, Blacklick, OH 43004. Telephone: 800-634-3961 (http://www.mcgraw-hill.com). Strategies for getting the highest price.

Web sites

▶ *Domania.com.* Lists prices of neighborhood properties for the past three to four years. To obtain detailed information (number of bedrooms, baths, etc.), you must register and become a member. Members can also obtain a valuation of their own home, based on neighborhood sales. http://www.domania.com

▶ *Home Gain.* Makes approximate appraisals of your home by looking up comparable, recent home sales in your area and using information you supply about your home. http://www.homegain.com

▶ *Owners.com.* Allows owners to display their homes without an agent, using virtual 360-degree photos, descriptions, and maps, and allows buyers looking for a home to peruse the site. http://www.owners.com

▶ *Virtual Relocation.com.* Lists of moving companies, storage companies, and mortgage companies, many with links to sites. Info on moving automobiles, pets, truck rentals, and storage boxes. http://www.virtualrelocation.com

Index